Test Bank

for

Tan's

Calculus for the Managerial, Life, and Social Sciences

Seventh Edition

Test Bank

for

Tan's

Calculus for the Managerial, Life, and Social Sciences

Seventh Edition

Tracy Wang
Curry College

Australia • Canada • Mexico • Singapore • Spain • United Kingdom • United States

Printed in the United States of America
1 2 3 4 5 6 7 09 08 07 06 05

Printer: Thomson/West

0-534-42006-0

For more information about our products, contact us at:
Thomson Learning Academic Resource Center
1-800-423-0563

For permission to use material from this text or product, submit a request online at
http://www.thomsonrights.com.
Any additional questions about permissions can be submitted by email to **thomsonrights@thomson.com.**

Thomson Higher Education
10 Davis Drive
Belmont, CA 94002-3098
USA

Asia (including India)
Thomson Learning
5 Shenton Way
#01-01 UIC Building
Singapore 068808

Australia/New Zealand
Thomson Learning Australia
102 Dodds Street
Southbank, Victoria 3006
Australia

Canada
Thomson Nelson
1120 Birchmount Road
Toronto, Ontario M1K 5G4
Canada

UK/Europe/Middle East/Africa
Thomson Learning
High Holborn House
50–51 Bedford Row
London WC1R 4LR
United Kingdom

Latin America
Thomson Learning
Seneca, 53
Colonia Polanco
11560 Mexico
D.F. Mexico

Spain (including Portugal)
Thomson Paraninfo
Calle Magallanes, 25
28015 Madrid, Spain

TABLE OF CONTENTS

Chapter 1 ■ Preliminaries

Section 1.1

1. Determine whether the statement $\frac{4}{5} < \frac{2}{3}$ is true or false. Answer: False

2. Determine whether the statement $-3 \le -3$ is true or false. Answer: True

3. Show the interval $(-4,3]$ on a number line.
Answer:

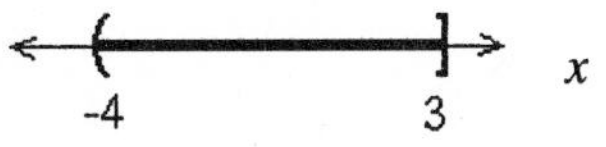

4. Show the interval $(-\infty,5]$ on a number line.
Answer:

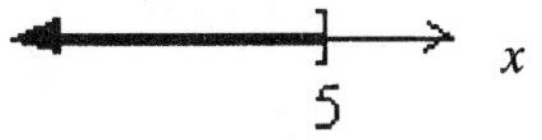

5. Find the values of x that satisfy the inequality $2x+3<11$. Answer: $x<4$

6. Find the values of x that satisfy the inequalities $2 \le x-1 \le 7$.
Answer: $3 \le x \le 8$

7. Find the values of x that satisfy the inequalities $2 \le 2-2x \le 8$.
Answer: $[-3,0]$

8. Find the values of x that satisfy the inequalities $x-2<4$ and $x+1 \ge 3$.
Answer: $2 \le x < 6$

9. Find the values of x that satisfy the inequalities $3x-2<4$ or $x+1 \ge 7$.
Answer: $(-\infty,2) \cup [6,\infty)$

10. Evaluate the expression $|-4+3|$. Answer: 1

11. Evaluate the expression $2-|2-4|$. Answer: 0

12. Evaluate the expression $|\pi-4|-3$. Answer: $1-\pi$

13. Evaluate the expression $|2-\sqrt{5}|-|6-2\sqrt{5}|$. Answer: $-8+3\sqrt{5}$

14. Suppose that a and b are positive real numbers and that $a > b$. State whether the given inequalities are true or false.
(a) $b-a<0$ Answer: True

(b) $\frac{a}{b} < 1$ Answer: False

(c) $-a > -b$ Answer: False

15. Suppose that a and b are positive real numbers and that $a > b$. State whether the given inequalities are true or false.

(a) $\frac{1}{a} < \frac{1}{b}$ Answer: True

(b) $a^2 < b^2$ Answer: False

(c) $\frac{b}{a} > 0$ Answer: True

16. Evaluate $64^{2/3}$. Answer: 16

17. Evaluate $\left[\left(\frac{1}{4}\right)^{1/2}\right]^{-1}$. Answer: 2

18. Evaluate $\left(\frac{1}{4}\right)^{-3/2}$. Answer: 8

19. Evaluate $\sqrt[3]{\frac{-1}{64}}$. Answer: $\frac{-1}{4}$

20. Evaluate $\left(\frac{3^{1.1} \cdot 3^{0.9}}{3^2}\right)^{1/2}$. Answer: 1

21. Rewrite the expression $(xy)^{-3}$ using positive exponents only.

Answer: $\frac{1}{(xy)^3}$

22. Rewrite the expression $\sqrt{x^{-3}}\sqrt{9x^4}$ using positive exponents only.

Answer: $3x^{1/2}$

23. Simplify the expression $\left(x^3y^{-2}\right)\left(x^4y^{-5}\right)$. Answer: $\dfrac{x^7}{y^7}$

24. Simplify the expression $\dfrac{x^{5/3}}{x^{-1}}$. Answer: $x^{8/3}$

25. Simplify the expression $\left(\dfrac{e^{x+1}}{e^{x-3}}\right)^{3/2}$. Answer: e^6

26. Simplify the expression $\sqrt[3]{x^{-4}}\cdot\sqrt{9x^3}$. Answer: $3x^{1/6}$

27. Simplify the expression $\sqrt{64x^2y^{-8}}$. Answer: $\dfrac{8x}{y^4}$

28. Rationalize the denominator of the expression $\dfrac{4}{3\sqrt{2x}}$. Answer: $\dfrac{2\sqrt{2x}}{3x}$

29. Rationalize the denominator of the expression $\sqrt{\dfrac{3x}{2y}}$. Answer: $\dfrac{\sqrt{6xy}}{2y}$

30. Rationalize the numerator of the expression $\dfrac{2\sqrt{x}}{3y}$. Answer: $\dfrac{2x}{3y\sqrt{x}}$

31. Rationalize the numerator of the expression $\dfrac{\sqrt[3]{xy^2 3y}}{3y}$. Answer: $\dfrac{x}{(3x)^{2/3}}$

32. Find the minimum cost C (in dollars), given that $2(C-15)\geq 1.5+1.25C$.
Answer: 42

33. Find the maximum profit P (in thousands of dollars), given that $2(P-2)\geq 3.5P-22$.

Answer: \$12 thousand

Section 1.1 Multiple Choice Questions

1. Find the values of x that satisfy the inequality $2x+4<10$.
   a. $x<3$
   b. $x>3$
   c. $x>7$
   d. $x<7$
   Answer: a.

2. Find the values of x that satisfy the inequality $-2x+6<-10$.
   a. $x<8$
   b. $x>8$
   c. $x>2$
   d. $x<-8$
   Answer: b.

3. Find the values of x that satisfy the inequality $2x-10\leq 12$.
   a. $x\leq 2$
   b. $x\leq 22$
   c. $x\geq 11$
   d. $x\leq 11$
   Answer: d.

4. Find the values of x that satisfy the inequality $-5x+10\leq -15$.
   a. $x\leq 5$
   b. $x\geq 5$
   c. $x\geq -5$
   d. $x\leq -5$
   Answer: b.

5. Evaluate the expression $|-10+2|$.
   a. -8
   b. 8
   c. 12
   d. -12
   Answer: b.

6. Evaluate the expression $\left|\sqrt{5}-20\right|+4$.
   a. $\sqrt{5}+24$
   b. $24-\sqrt{5}$
   c. $16+\sqrt{5}$
   d. $\sqrt{5}-16$
   Answer: b.

7. Evaluate the expression $\left|\sqrt{5}-2\right|+\left|4-\sqrt{5}\right|$.

a. $2\sqrt{5}+2$

b. $2\sqrt{5}-2$

c. 2

d. $2\sqrt{5}+6$

Answer: c.

8. Rewrite the expression $\left(xy^{-2}\right)^{-3}$ using positive exponents only.

a. $\dfrac{x^3}{y^9}$

b. $\dfrac{y^6}{x^3}$

c. x^3y^6

d. x^3y^9

Answer: b.

9. Rewrite the expression $\left(x^{-3}y^2\right)^{-4}$ using positive exponents only.

a. $\dfrac{x^{12}}{y^8}$

b. $\dfrac{1}{x^{12}y^8}$

c. $\dfrac{y^8}{x^{12}}$

d. $x^{12}y^8$

Answer: a.

10. Rationalize the denominator of the expression $\dfrac{5}{3\sqrt{x}}$.

a. $\dfrac{5}{3x}$

b. $\dfrac{5\sqrt{3}}{3x}$

c. $\dfrac{5\sqrt{3}}{x}$

d. $\dfrac{5\sqrt{x}}{3x}$

Answer: d.

11. Rationalize the denominator of the expression $\frac{2}{\sqrt[3]{x}}$.

a. $\frac{2\sqrt[3]{x^2}}{x}$

b. $\frac{2\sqrt[3]{x}}{x}$

c. $\frac{2\sqrt[2]{x}}{x}$

d. $\frac{\sqrt[3]{x^2}}{x}$

Answer: a.

12. Rationalize the denominator of the expression $\frac{1}{\sqrt{x}-2}$.

a. $\frac{\sqrt{x}-2}{x+4}$

b. $\frac{\sqrt{x}+2}{x+4}$

c. $\frac{\sqrt{x}-2}{x-4}$

d. $\frac{\sqrt{x}+2}{x-4}$

Answer: d.

13. Rationalize the numerator of the expression $\frac{\sqrt{2x}}{3}$.

a. $\frac{2}{3x}$

b. $\frac{2\sqrt{x}}{3x}$

c. $\frac{2x}{\sqrt{3x}}$

d. $\frac{2x}{3\sqrt{2x}}$

Answer: d.

14. Rewrite the expression $\frac{x^{-3}}{x^2}$ using positive exponents only.

a. x^5

b. $\dfrac{1}{x^5}$

c. $\dfrac{1}{x}$

d. x

Answer: b.

15. Rewrite the expression $\sqrt{x^{-3}}\sqrt{25x^{-5}}$ using positive exponents only.

a. $\dfrac{5}{x^2}$

b. $\dfrac{5}{x^4}$

c. $\dfrac{1}{5x^4}$

d. $5x^4$

Answer: b.

16. Find the maximum profit P (in dollars) given that $2(P-3) \le 274-12P$

a. 28

b. 15

c. 20

d. 14

Answer: c.

17. Simplify the expression $\left(x^{-2}y\right)\left(x^{-13}y^4\right)$.

a. $x^{26}y^4$

b. $\dfrac{x^{15}}{y^5}$

c. $\dfrac{y^5}{x^{15}}$

d. $x^{15}y^5$

Answer: c.

Section 1.2

1. Perform the indicated operations and simplify $(2x^2+5x+3)-(4x^2+x-6)$.
   Answer: $-2x^2+4x+9$

2. Perform the indicated operations and simplify $\left(\frac{1}{4}+2+e\right)+\left(-\frac{1}{4}+1-e^{-1}\right)$.
   Answer: $3+e-\frac{1}{e}$

3. Perform the indicated operations and simplify $x-\{3x-[-2x-(2-x)]\}$.
   Answer: $-3x-2$

4. Perform the indicated operations and simplify $(a-4)^2$.
   Answer: $a^2-8a+16$

5. Perform the indicated operations and simplify $(2x-5)(5+2x)$.
   Answer: $4x^2-25$

6. Perform the indicated operations and simplify $3\left(t-\sqrt{t}\right)^2-3t^2$.
   Answer: $-6t\sqrt{t}+3t$

7. Factor out the greatest common factor from $3ab^2+6ab+3a^2b$.
   Answer: $3ab(b+2+a)$

8. Factor out the greatest common factor from $7xye^{xy}+21x^2ye^{xy}$.
   Answer: $7xye^{xy}(1+3x)$

9. Factor out the greatest common factor from $3x^{-3/2}+6x^{-1/2}$.
   Answer: $3x^{-3/2}(1+2x)$

10. Factor the expression x^2+3x-4. Answer: $(x+4)(x-1)$

11. Factor the expression $x^2+13x+12$. Answer: $(x+12)(x+1)$

12. Factor the expression $(x-y)^2-1$. Answer: $(x-y+1)(x-y-1)$

13. Perform the indicated operations and simplify the algebraic expression
    $(x^2-y^2)x+2x(2y)$. Answer: x^3-xy^2+4xy

14. Perform the indicated operations and simplify the algebraic expression $4(x^2+2)^2(3x)$.
Answer: $12x^5+48x^3+48x$

15. Find the real roots of $2x^2+x-1=0$ by factoring. Answer: $x=\frac{1}{2},-1$

16. Use the quadratic formula to solve $3x^2-4x-5=0$. Answer: $x=\frac{2\pm\sqrt{19}}{3}$

17. Simplify the expression $\frac{2x-3x^2+6x^4}{4+12x^3-6x}$. Answer: $\frac{1}{2}x$

18. Simplify the expression $\frac{x^2-5x+6}{x^2-9}$. Answer: $\frac{x-2}{x+3}$

19. Simplify the expression $\frac{x^3-y^3}{x^2-y^2}$. Answer: $\frac{x^2+xy+y^2}{x+y}$

20. Simplify the expression $\frac{\frac{2}{x}-1}{1-\frac{3}{x}}$. Answer: $\frac{2-x}{x-3}$

21. Simplify the expression $\frac{\frac{1}{x}-\frac{1}{y}}{\frac{1}{y^2}-\frac{1}{x^2}}$. Answer: $\frac{xy}{x+y}$

22. Simplify the expression $\frac{4}{x+3}-\frac{5}{2x+1}$. Answer: $\frac{3x-11}{(x+3)(2x+1)}$

23. Simplify the expression $\frac{x^2+6x+5}{x^2-25}$. Answer: $\frac{x+1}{x-5}$

24. Simplify the expression $\frac{5x+1}{x^2-9}-\frac{4x-2}{x^2-9}$. Answer: $\frac{1}{x-3}$

25. Rationalize the denominator of the expression $\dfrac{\sqrt{x}+\sqrt{y}}{\sqrt{x}-\sqrt{y}}$.

Answer: $\dfrac{x+2\sqrt{xy}+y}{x-y}$

26. Rationalize the denominator of the expression $\dfrac{2}{\sqrt{x}+1}$.

Answer: $\dfrac{2\sqrt{x}-2}{x-1}$

Section 1.2 Multiple Choice Questions

1. Perform the indicated operations on the expressoin $2x(3x-5)$.

a. $10x^2-6x$
b. $-9x$
c. $6x^2+15x$
d. $6x^2-10x$

Answer: d.

2. Perform the indicated operations on the expression $5x^3-\{x^2-[x-(2x-1)]+4\}$.

a. $5x^3-x^2-x-3$
b. $5x^3-x^2-x+3$
c. $5x^3-x^2-x-5$
d. $5x^3-x^2-3x-3$

Answer: a.

3. Perform the indicated operations on the expression $(x^2+1)(3x^2+10x+3)$.

a. $3x^4-10x^3+12x^2+10x+3$
b. $3x^4+10x^3+6x^2+10x+3$
c. $3x^4+10x^3+6x^2+10x-3$
d. $3x^4+10x^3+10x+3$

Answer: b.

4. Rewrite the expression $(x+y)(x^{-1}-y^{-1})$ using positive exponents only.

a. $\dfrac{y}{x}-\dfrac{x}{y}$

b. $\dfrac{y}{x}+\dfrac{x}{y}$

c. $-\frac{y}{x}-\frac{x}{y}$

d. $2+\frac{x}{y}-\frac{y}{x}$

Answer: a.

5. Factor the expression $2x^{2/3}-5x^{1/3}$.

a. $x^{1/3}(2x^{1/3}+5)$

b. $x^{1/3}(2x^{2/3}-5)$

c. $x^{1/3}(2x^{1/3}-5x)$

d. $x^{1/3}(2x^{1/3}-5)$

Answer: d.

6. Factor the expression $25-x^2$.

a. $(x-5)(x+5)$

b. $(5-x)(5+x)$

c. $(x-5)^2$

d. $(x+5)^2$

Answer: b.

7. Factor the expression x^2-3x+2.

a. $(x+1)(x-2)$

b. $(x-1)(x-2)$

c. $(x-1)(x+2)$

d. $(x+1)(x+2)$

Answer: b.

8. Factor the expression $x^2-8x+16$.

a. $(x-4)^2$

b. $(x-8)^2$

c. $(x+4)^2$

d. $(x+8)^2$

Answer: a.

9. Factor the expression $3x^2+4x-4$.

a. $(x-2)(3x+2)$

b. $(x-2)(3x-2)$

c. $(x+2)(3x+2)$

d. $(x+2)(3x-2)$

Answer: d.

10. Factor the expression $2x^2-4x-16$.

a. $2(x-4)(x+2)$

b. $2(x+4)(x+2)$

c. $2(x-4)(x-2)$

d. $(x-4)(x+2)$

Answer: a.

11. Find the solutions of the quadratic equation $4x^2-8x-32=0$.

a. 4 and 2

b. -4 and 2

c. -4 and -2

d. 4 and -2

Answer: d.

12. Find the solutions of the quadratic equation $4x^2-25=0$.

a. $\frac{2}{5}$

b. $\frac{5}{2}$

c. $\pm\frac{2}{5}$

d. $\pm\frac{5}{2}$

Answer: d.

13. Perform the indicated operation and simplify: $\frac{x^2-25}{x+2}\cdot\frac{x^2+3x+2}{x+5}$

a. $(x+5)(x+1)$

b. $(x-5)(x+1)$

c. $(x+5)(x-1)$

d. $(x-5)(x-1)$

Answer: b.

14. Perform the indicated operation and simplify: $\frac{x^2-3x}{x+4}\cdot\frac{x^2+3x-4}{x^2+5x}$

a. $\dfrac{(x-3)(x-1)}{x+5}$

b. $\dfrac{(x+3)(x-1)}{x+5}$

c. $\dfrac{(x-3)(x+1)}{x+5}$

d. $\dfrac{(x+3)(x+1)}{x+5}$

Answer: a.

15. Perform the indicated operation and simplify: $\dfrac{x^2+3x}{x+4}-\dfrac{4}{x+4}$

a. $x+1$
b. $x-4$
c. $x-1$
d. $x+4$
Answer: c.

16. Perform the indicated operation and simplify: $\dfrac{2x}{2x-1}-\dfrac{3x}{2x+5}$

a. $-\dfrac{x(2x-13)}{(2x-1)(2x+5)}$

b. $\dfrac{x(2x-13)}{(2x-1)(2x+5)}$

c. $\dfrac{2x-13}{(2x-1)(2x+5)}$

d. $-\dfrac{2x^2-2x+3}{(2x-1)(2x+5)}$

Answer: a.

Section 1.3

1. In which quadrant is the point $(-3,2)$? Answer: II

2. In which quadrant is the point $(1,-7)$? Answer: IV

3. Find the distance between the points $(3,6)$ and $(6,10)$. Answer: 5

4. Find the distance between the points $(-4,5)$ and $(8,10)$. Answer: 13

5. Find the distance between the points $(-2,1)$ and $(-2,7)$. Answer: 6

6. Find the distance between the points $(-2,5)$ and $(-1,8)$. Answer: $\sqrt{10}$

7. Find the distance between the points $(-5,-8)$ and $(-3,5)$. Answer: $\sqrt{173}$

8. Find the distance between the points $(-1,-2)$ and $(1,2)$. Answer: $2\sqrt{5}$

9. Find the distance between the points $(-2,5)$ and $(-1,8)$. Answer: $\sqrt{10}$

10. Find the distance between the points $(-9,9)$ and $(6,-7)$. Answer: $\sqrt{481}$

11. Find the distance between the points $(-1,2)$ and $(6,7)$. Answer: $\sqrt{74}$

12. Find the coordinates of any points 10 units away from the origin with an x-coordinate of 8.
Answer: $(8,6)$ and $(8,-6)$

13. Find the coordinates of any points 5 units away from the origin with an x-coordinate of 4.
Answer: $(4,3)$ and $(4,-3)$

14. Find the coordinates of any points 13 units away from the origin with a y-coordinate of 5.
Answer: $(12,5)$ and $(-12,5)$

15. Find the coordinates of any points 8 units away from the origin with a y-coordinate of 5.
Answer: $(\sqrt{39},5)$ and $(-\sqrt{39},5)$

16. Darryl's range with a water balloon is 15 meters. If John is standing 12 meters south and 10 meters west of Darryl, is Darryl able to hit him?
Answer: No

17. The captain of a sinking ocean liner sends out a distress signal. If the ship's radio has a range of 14 km and the nearest port is located 12 km south and 5 km east of the sinking ship, will the signal reach the port?
Answer: Yes

18. Find an equation of the circle centered at the origin with radius 8.
Answer: $x^2 + y^2 = 64$

19. Find an equation of the circle centered at the origin with radius $\sqrt{3}$.
Answer: $x^2 + y^2 = 3$

20. Find an equation of the circle centered at $(3,5)$ with radius 2.
Answer: $(x-3)^2 + (y-5)^2 = 4$

21. Find an equation of the circle centered at $(-2,0)$ with radius $\frac{1}{3}$.
Answer: $(x+2)^2 + y^2 = \frac{1}{9}$

22. Find an equation of the circle centered at $(1,-3)$ that passes through the point $(3, 3)$.
Answer: $(x-1)^2 + (y+3)^2 = 40$

23. Find an equation of the circle centered at $(-1,-3)$ that passes through the point $(0,3)$.
Answer: $(x+1)^2 + (y+3)^2 = 37$

Section 1.3 Multiple Choice Questions

1. If the point $(a, -c)$ lies in the third quadrant, which quadrant does the point $(-a, c)$ lie in.
   a. I
   b. II
   c. III
   d. IV
   Answer: a.

2. Find the coordinates of the points that are 10 units away from the origin and have an *y*-coordinate equal to 6.

a. $(\pm 8, -6)$
b. $(\pm 8, 6)$
c. $(8, \pm 6)$
d. $(-8, \pm 6)$
Answer: b.

3. Find the coordinates of the points that are 11 units away from the origin and have an x-coordinate equal to -2.
   a. $\left(-2, \sqrt{117}\right)$
   b. $\left(\pm\sqrt{117}, -2\right)$
   c. $\left(2, \pm\sqrt{117}\right)$
   d. $\left(-2, \pm\sqrt{117}\right)$
   Answer: d.

4. Find the distance between the points $(2, -1)$ and $(0, -2)$.
   a. $\sqrt{5}$
   b. $\sqrt{13}$
   c. 5
   d. 3
   Answer: a.

5. Find the distance between the points $(-2, -1)$ and $(-1, 1)$.
   a. $\sqrt{10}$
   b. $\sqrt{13}$
   c. 1
   d. $\sqrt{5}$
   Answer: d.

6. Find the distance between the points $(-4, 3)$ and $(a, 0)$.
   a. $\sqrt{7}$
   b. $\sqrt{a^2 + 8a + 25}$
   c. $\sqrt{a^2 - 8a + 25}$
   d. $\sqrt{a^2 + 8a + 6}$
   Answer: b.

7. Find the distance between the points $(-a, b)$ and $(2, 6)$.

a. $\sqrt{(2+a)^2+(6-b)^2}$

b. $\sqrt{(2-a)^2+(6-b)^2}$

c. $\sqrt{(2-a)^2+(6+b)^2}$

d. $\sqrt{(2+a)^2+(6+b)^2}$

Answer: a.

8. Find an equation of the circle with center (0, -5) and radius 4.

a. $x^2+(y-5)^2=16$

b. $x^2+(y-4)^2=25$

c. $x^2+(y+5)^2=16$

d. $(x+5)^2+(y-5)^2=16$

Answer: c.

9. Find an equation of the circle with center (1, -5) and radius 2.

a. $(x-1)^2+(y-5)^2=4$

b. $(x+1)^2+(y+5)^2=4$

c. $(x-1)^2+(y+5)^2=4$

d. $(x+5)^2+(y-1)^2=4$

Answer: c.

10. Find an equation of the circle with radius 3 and center located at the origin.

a. $x^2+y^2=3$

b. $(x-3)^2+y^2=3$

c. $x^2+(y-3)^2=3$

d. $x^2+y^2=9$

Answer: d.

11. Find an equation of the circle that passes through (5, -1) and has center (1, 2).

a. $(x-1)^2+(y-2)^2=25$

b. $(x+1)^2+(y+2)^2=25$

c. $(x-1)^2+(y-2)^2=5$

d. $(x-5)^2+(y+1)^2=25$

Answer: a.

12. Find an equation of the circle that passes through (0, 3) and has center (2, -3).

a. $(x+2)^2+(y-3)^2=40$

b. $(x+2)^2+(y+3)^2=40$

c. $(x-2)^2+(y+3)^2=40$

d. $(x-2)^2+(y+3)^2=4$

Answer: c.

13. Find an equation of the circle that passes through (-1, 5) and has center (-1, -5).

a. $(x-1)^2+(y+5)^2=100$

b. $(x+1)^2+(y+5)^2=100$

c. $(x+1)^2+(y+5)^2=10$

d. $(x-1)^2+(y-5)^2=100$

Answer: b.

14. Find an equation of the circle with center at (-2, 0) and diameter 12.

a. $(x-2)^2+y^2=36$

b. $(x+2)^2+y^2=144$

c. $(x-2)^2+y^2=36$

d. $(x+2)^2+y^2=36$

Answer: d.

15. Find the distance between the center of the circle $(x+2)^2+y^2=36$ and the point (1, 3).

a. $3\sqrt{2}$

b. $\sqrt{10}$

c. $\sqrt{11}$

d. $\sqrt{7}$

Answer: a.

Section 1.4

1. Find the slope of the line graphed below.

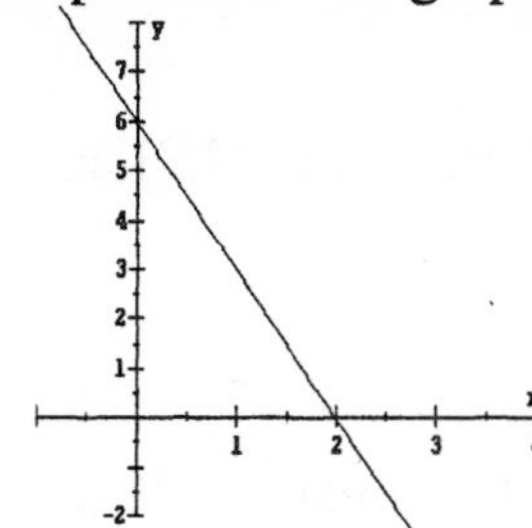

Answer: -3

2. Find the slope of the line graphed below.

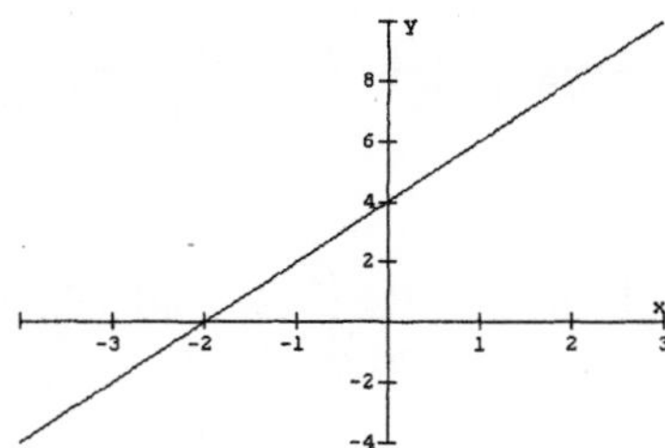

Answer: 2

3. Find the slope of the line graphed below.

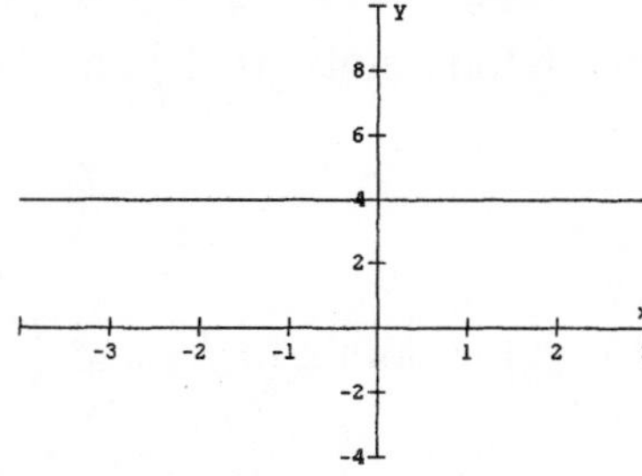

Answer: 0

4. Find the slope of the line graphed below.

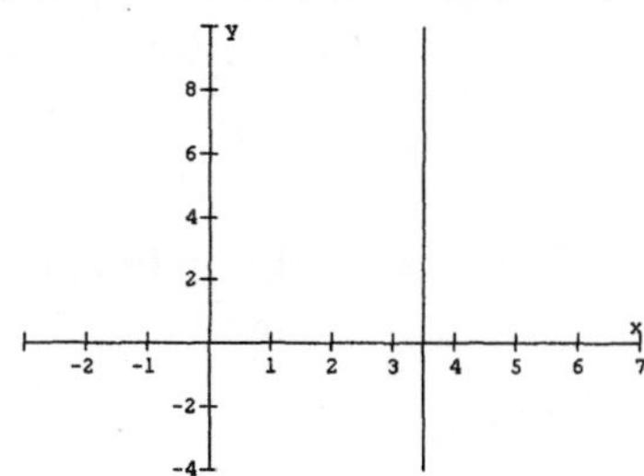

Answer: undefined

5. Find the slope of the line that passes through the points $(2,\ 3)$ and $(4,\ 9)$.
Answer: 3

6. Find the slope of the line that passes through the points $(-2,\ 5)$ and $(2,\ 3)$.
   Answer: $-\frac{1}{2}$

7. Find the slope of the line that passes through the points $(3,8)$ and $(12,-2)$.
   Answer: $-\frac{10}{9}$

8. Find the slope of the line that passes through the points $(4,2)$ and $(-3,1)$.
   Answer: $\frac{1}{7}$

9. Find the slope of the line that passes through the points $(-2,0)$ and $(-5,-3)$.
   Answer: 1

10. Find the slope of the line that passes through the points $(5,2)$ and $(9,2)$.
    Answer: 0

11. Find the slope of the line that passes through the points $(5,2)$ and $(5,-3)$.
    Answer: Undefined

12. Find the slope of the line that passes through the points $(0,-3)$ and $(4,0)$.
    Answer: $\frac{3}{4}$

13. Find the slope of the line that passes through the points (a,b) and (c,d).
    Answer: $\frac{d-b}{c-a}, c \neq a$

14. If a point moves along the line $y = 6x+1$, what would be the change in y if x were increased by 3 units?
    Answer: The y-value would increase by 18 units.

15. If a point moves along the line $4x+2y=8$, what would be the change in y if x were decreased by 1 unit?
    Answer: The y-value would increase by 2 units.

16. Determine if the lines through the given pairs of point are parallel, perpendicular, or neither: $A(2,3)$, $B(-1,2)$ and $C(4,-2)$, $D(-2,-4)$.
    Answer: parallel

17. Determine if the lines through the given pairs of point are parallel, perpendicular, or neither: $A(1,4)$, $B(-2,3)$ and $C(6,-2)$, $D(5,-5)$.
Answer: neither

18. Determine if the lines through the given pairs of point are parallel, perpendicular, or neither: $A(1,4)$, $B(3,-4)$ and $C(2,1)$, $D(6,2)$.
Answer: perpendicular

19. Express the equation $3x-y=2$ in the slope – intercept form.
Answer: $y=3x-2$

20. Find an equation of the horizontal line that passes through $(2,4)$.
Answer: $y=4$

21. Find an equation of the vertical line that passes through $(-2,3)$.
Answer: $x=-2$

22. Find an equation of the line that passes through the point $(2,-3)$ and has a slope of -2.
Answer: $2x+y-1=0$

23. Find an equation of the line that passes through the point $(-4,-6)$ and has a slope of $\frac{3}{4}$.
Answer: $3x-4y-12=0$

24. Find an equation of the line that passes through the points $(2,3)$ and $(-1,4)$.
Answer: $x+3y-11=0$

25. Find an equation of the line that passes through the points $(1,5)$ and $(9,-9)$.
Answer: $7x+4y-27=0$

26. Find an equation of the line that has a slope of 4 and a y-intercept of -7.
Answer: $y=4x-7$

27. Find an equation of the line that has a slope of $-\frac{5}{4}$ and a y-intercept of 2.

Answer: $y=-\frac{5}{4}x+2$

28. Find the slope and y-intercept of the line $3x+2y-4=0$.

Answer: $m=-\frac{3}{2};b=2$

29. Find the slope and y-intercept of the line $9x-3y+12=0$.

Answer: $m = 3; b = 4$

30. Find an equation of the line that passes through the point $(2,4)$ and is perpendicular to the line $3x - y - 4 = 0$.
Answer: $x + 3y - 14 = 0$

31. Find an equation of the line that passes through the point $(-2,3)$ and is parallel to the line $x + 2y - 12 = 0$.
Answer: $x + 2y - 4 = 0$

32. Find an equation of the line parallel to the *y*-axis with an *x*-intercept of 7.
Answer: $x = 7$

33. Find an equation of the line passing through $(6,1)$ and perpendicular to the line joining $(-2,-2)$ and $(3,8)$.
Answer: $x + 2y - 8 = 0$

34. Sketch the line given by $2x + 2y - 4 = 0$.
Answer:

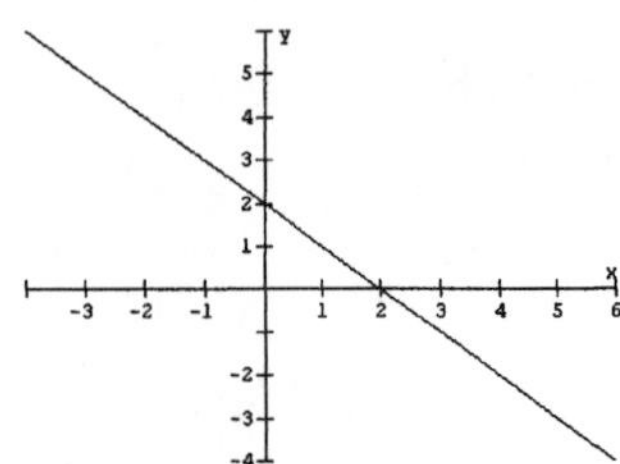

35. Sketch the line given by $3x - 5y + 15 = 0$.
Answer:

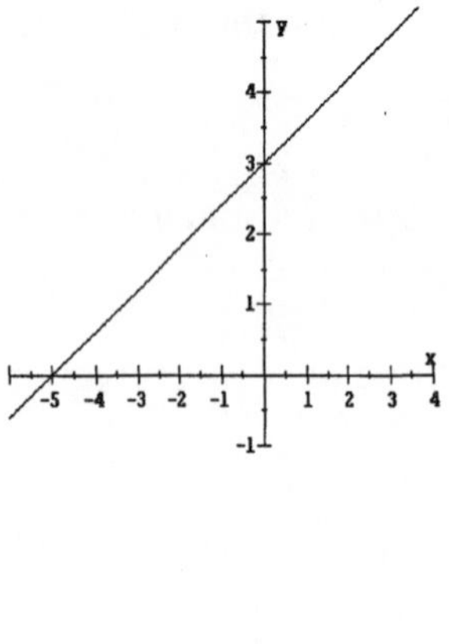

36. Sketch the line given by $x-y-4=0$.
Answer:

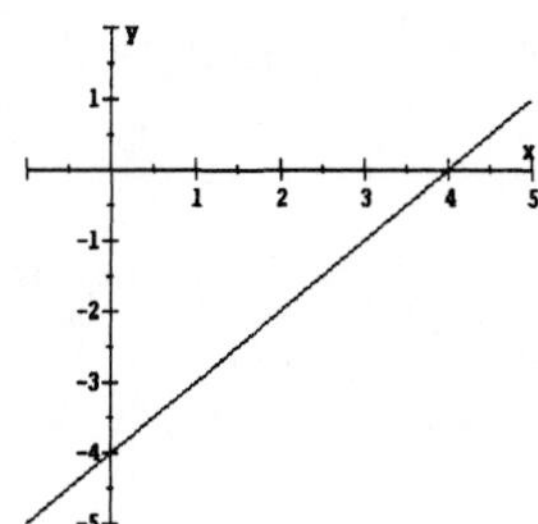

37. Sketch the line given by $3y-6=0$.
Answer:

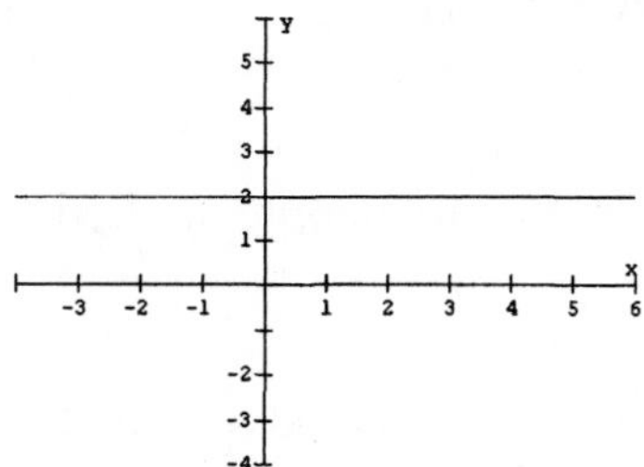

38. Sketch the line given by $\frac{1}{2}x+2=0$.

Answer:

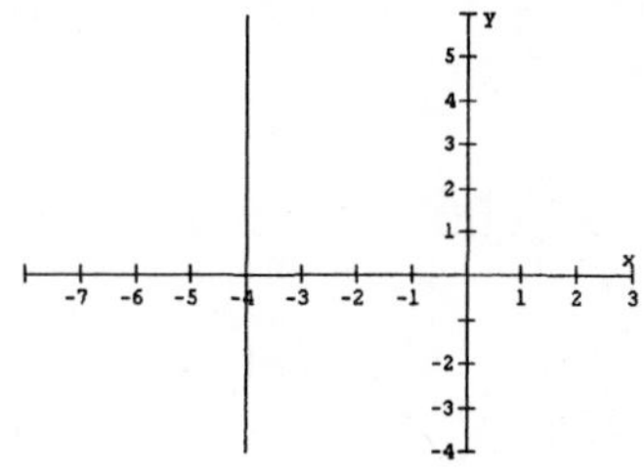

39. Sketch the line given by $2x-3y+6=0$.
Answer:

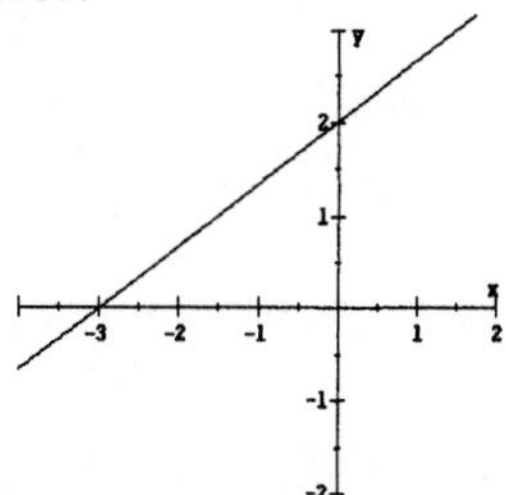

40. Find an equation of a line with an x-intercept of 6 and a y-intercept of 2.
Answer: $x+3y-6=0$

41. Find an equation of a line with an x-intercept of -4 and a y-intercept of 7.
Answer: $7x-4y+28=0$

42. The profit, P (in dollars), from sales of n souvenirs is given by $P=5.5n-220$.
Find the profit from the sale of 90 souvenirs.
Answer: $275

43. 68 percent of the people who apply for admission to a certain university are admitted.
(a) Find an equation that expresses the relationship between the number of applicants (x) and the number of admissions (y).
Answer: $y=0.68x$

(b) If 374 people are accepted this year, how many people applied?
Answer: 550

44. Scientists from the Canadian Wrestling Conglomerate developed the following equation in order to estimate the weight of unfamiliar wrestlers.
$W=7.15H-154$ where W is weight in pounds and H is height in inches.
(a) Invincible Robert is 78 inches tall. What is his expected weight?
Answer: 403.7 pounds
(b) The Muncher weighs 386 pounds. What is his expected height?
Answer: 75.5 inches

45. The price of a car is given by $y=-4000t+32{,}000$, where t is time in years after the car was purchased.
a. Find the original price of the car.
Answer: $32,000

b. Find the price of the car three years after it was purchased.
Answer: $20,000

c. Find the price of the car 8 years after it was purchased.
Answer: $0.

d. Find the slope of the line and interpret your answer in the context of the problem.
Answer: -4000. The price of the car depreciates $4000 per year.

46. The price for an antique clock was given by $y = 60t + 300$.
(a) Find the original price of the antique clock.
Answer: $300

(b) Find what the clock will be worth after 7 years.
Answer: $720

(c) Find the slope of the line and interpret the slope in the context of the problem.
Answer: 60. The price of the antique clock goes up $60 per year.

47. There is a relationship between the vocabulary a child uses and the child's age. The equation $60A - V = 900$ describes this relationship, where *A* is the age of the child, in months, and *V* is the number of words that the child uses. Suppose that a child uses 1500 words. Determine the child's age, in months.
Answer: 40 months.

48. The percentage, *P*, of adults in the United States who read the daily newspaper can be modeled by the formula $P = -0.7x + 80$, where *x* is the number of years after 1965. In what year will 52% of U.S. adults read the daily newspaper?
Answer: 2005, 40 years from 1965.

Section 1.4 Multiple Choice Questions

1. Find the slope of the line that passes through $(2, \text{-}1)$ and $(0, \text{-}2)$.

a. $\frac{2}{3}$

b. $-\frac{2}{3}$

c. 2

d. $\frac{1}{2}$

Answer: d.

2. Find the slope of the line that passes through $(-2, \text{-}1)$ and $(-1, -1)$.

a. $-\frac{1}{2}$

b. $\frac{3}{2}$

c. Undefined

d. 0

Answer: d.

3. Find the slope of the line that passes through $(-4, 3)$ and $(-4, 0)$.

   a. $-\frac{3}{8}$
   b. Undefined.
   c. 0
   d. $\frac{8}{3}$

   Answer: b.

4. Find an equation of the line that has slope 3 and y-intercept -5.

   a. $y = 3x - 5$
   b. $y = 3x + 5$
   c. $y = 5x - 3$
   d. $y = 5x + 3$

   Answer: a.

5. Find an equation of the line that has slope 0 and y-intercept 10.

   a. $x = 10$
   b. $y = 10$
   c. $y = x + 10$
   d. $x + y = 10$

   Answer: b.

6. Find an equation of the line that passes through (1, -5) and (0, 0).

   a. $y = 5x$
   b. $x = 5y$
   c. $y = -5x$
   d. $x = -5y$

   Answer: c.

7. Find an equation of the line that passes through the point (0, -2) and is parallel to the line $y = 5x + 7$.

   a. $y = \frac{x}{5} + 2$
   b. $y = \frac{x}{5} - 2$
   c. $y = 5x + 2$
   d. $y = 5x - 2$

   Answer: d.

8. Find an equation of the line that passes through the point (-3, 0) and is perpendicular to the line $y = 5x + 7$.

   a. $y = -\frac{x}{5} + \frac{3}{5}$

   b. $y = \frac{x}{5} + \frac{3}{5}$

   c. $y = -\frac{x}{5} - \frac{3}{5}$

   d. $y = -5x + 15$

   Answer: c.

9. Find an equation of the line that passes through (3, -3) and is parallel to the line $2x - 3y = 0$.

   a. $y = -\frac{3}{2}x - 5$

   b. $y = \frac{3}{2}x - 5$

   c. $y = \frac{2}{3}x - 5$

   d. $y = -\frac{2}{3}x - 5$

   Answer: c.

10. Find an equation of the line parallel to the *x*-axis and 3 units below it.

    a. $x = 3$

    b. $x = -3$

    c. $y = 3$

    d. $y = -3$

    Answer: d.

11. Find an equation of the line parallel to the *y*-axis that passes through (23, 7).

    a. $y = 23$

    b. $x = 7$

    c. $x = 23$

    d. $y = 7$

    Answer: c.

12. Find the slope of the line that passes through the centers of the two circles $x^2 + (y+5)^2 = 36$ and $(x-2)^2 + y^2 = 12$.

    a. $\frac{5}{2}$

b. $-\frac{5}{2}$

c. $\frac{2}{5}$

d. $-\frac{2}{5}$

Answer: a.

13. Find the equation of the line passes through (-1, 3) and the center of the circle $(x+2)^2 + y^2 = 36$.

a. $y = -\frac{2}{3}x + 1$

b. $y = 3x - 6$

c. $y = 3x + 6$

d. $y = -3x$

Answer: c.

14. If the line passing through the points (1, a) and (4, 0) is parallel to the line passing through the points (2, 4) and (9, -3), what is the value of a?

a. $a = -3$

b. $a = 1$

c. $a = 21$

d. $a = 3$

Answer: d.

15. Find an equation of the line with the x-intercept 3 and y-intercept -2.

a. $y = -\frac{3}{2}x + 2$

b. $y = -\frac{2}{3}x - 2$

c. $y = \frac{2}{3}x - 2$

d. $y = \frac{3}{2}x + 2$

Answer: c.

Exam 1A

Name:
Instructor:
Section:

Write your work as neatly as possible.

1. Find the values of x that satisfy the inequality $5x+1>16$.

2. Evaluate the expression $4-|5-11|$.

3. Find the distance between the points $(6,3)$ and $(1,-1)$.

4. Suppose that a and b are real numbers other than zero and that $a > b$. State whether the given inequalities are true or false.
(a) $b-a<0$
(b) $\frac{a}{b}<1$
(c) $-a>-b$

5. Evaluate $25^{-3/2}$.

6. Simplify the expression $\sqrt[4]{x^{-3}}\sqrt{16x^5}$.

7. Rationalize the denominator of the expression $\sqrt{\frac{5}{7x}}$.

8. Perform the indicated operations and simplify $\frac{4}{x+1}-\frac{3}{x-5}$.

9. Factor out the greatest common factor from $2ab^2+4ab+6a^2b$.

10. Factor the expression $x^2+4x-12$.

11. Perform the indicated operation and simplify the algebraic expression $(x^2 - 2y^2)x + 3x(2y)$.

12. Find the real roots of $3x^2 - 27x = 0$.

13. Find the coordinates of any points 1 unit away from the origin with an x-coordinate of 1.

14. Find the equation of the circle centered at $(2, -5)$ with a radius of 6.

15. Find the slope of the line that passes through the points $(0,0)$ and $(-2,4)$.

16. Determine if the lines through the given pairs of points are parallel, perpendicular, or neither: $A(1,1)$, $B(-3,1)$ and $C(2,-2)$, $D(2,5)$.

17. Find the slope of the line graphed below.

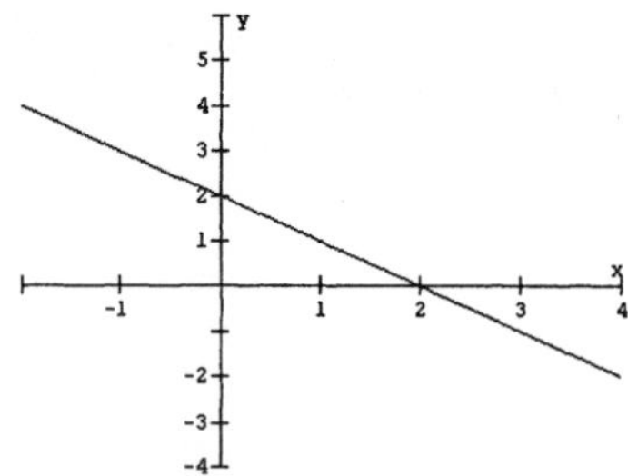

18. Find an equation of the line that passes through the points $(1,5)$ and $(2,8)$.

19. Find an equation of the line parallel to the x-axis with a y-intercept of 3.

20. Find the slope and y-intercept of the line $x - 5y = 3$.

21. Sketch the line given by $3x - 4y = 6$.

Exam 1B

Name:
Instructor:
Section:

Write your work as neatly as possible.

1. Find the values of x that satisfy the inequality $2 \le x+1 \le 9$.

2. Simplify the expression $|\pi - 3| - 2$.

3. Evaluate $81^{3/4}$.

4. Rewrite the expression $\left(x^3 y^{-1}\right)^{-2}$ using positive exponents.

5. Rationalize the denominator of the expression $\dfrac{2\sqrt{xy}}{3\sqrt{2x}}$.

6. Perform the indicated operations and simplify $\left(\frac{1}{5}+1+2e\right)+\left(-\frac{1}{5}+2-e^{-1}\right)$.

7. Factor out the greatest common factor from $3x^2y+9xy^4$.

8. Factor the expression $3x^2+10x+8$.

9. Perform the indicated operation and simplify the algebraic expression $\left(2x^2-y^2\right)y+2x(2y)$.

10. Simplify the expression $\dfrac{3x^2+10x+8}{6x^2+11x+4}$.

11. Find the distance between the points $(2,8)$ and $(-1,5)$.

12. Find the coordinates of any points 5 units away from the origin with an x-coordinate of -3.

13. Find the equation of the circle centered at $(0,8)$ that passes through the point $(5,0)$.

14. Find the slope of the line that passes through the points $(2,5)$ and $(-1,6)$.

15. Determine if the lines through the given pairs of points are parallel, perpendicular, or neither: $A(2,2)$, $B(-2,3)$ and $C(6,-1)$, $D(2,0)$.

16. Find an equation of the line that passes through the points $(0,5)$ and $(2,-3)$.

17. Find an equation of the line with x-intercept 2 and y-intercept 1.

18. Find an equation of the line perpendicular to the x-axis passing through the point $(2,3)$.

19. Find the slope and y-intercept of the line $x-3y+2=0$.

20. Find the slope of the line graphed below.

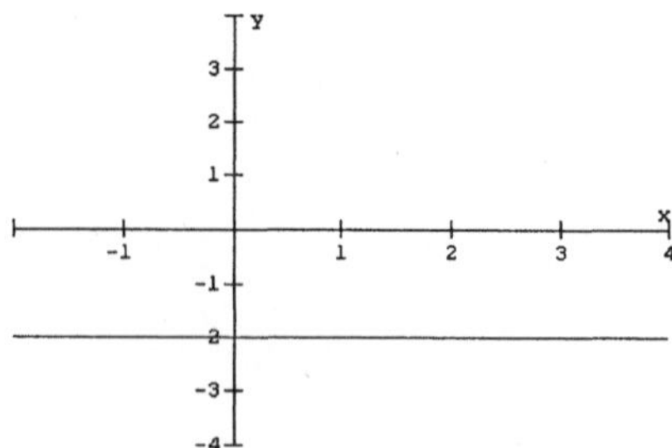

21. Sketch the line $y=-x+1$.

Exam 1C

Name:
Instructor:
Section:

Write your work as neatly as possible.

1. Find the values of x that satisfy the inequality $x-7<3$ and $x+6\geq 5$.

2. Evaluate the expression $|5-2\sqrt{2}|-|3-3\sqrt{2}|$.

3. Evaluate $(2^{1.1}\cdot 2^{2.9})^{\frac{2}{3}}$.

4. Rewrite the expression $\left(3x^2y^{-1}\right)^{-3}$ using positive exponents.

5. Rationalize the denominator of the expression $\dfrac{2}{3\sqrt{3x}}$.

6. Perform the indicated operations and simplify $\left(9x^2+5x+3\right)-\left(x^2+2x-3\right)$.

7. Factor out the greatest common factor from $2xy^3-8x^3y$.

8. Perform the indicated operation and simplify the algebraic expression $\left[\left(x^2-1\right)^2-1\right](2x)$.

9. Use the quadratic formula to solve $x^2+7x+1=0$.

10. Simplify the expression $\dfrac{4x^2+8x+3}{8x^2+12x}$.

11. Find the distance between the points $(2,3)$ and $(2,-3)$.

12. Find the coordinates of any points 7 units away from the origin with a y-coordinate of 1.

13. Find the equation of the circle centered at $(3,2)$ that has radius 6.

14. Find the slope of the line that passes through the points $(5,4)$ and $(-1,6)$.

15. Determine the slope of the line graphed below.

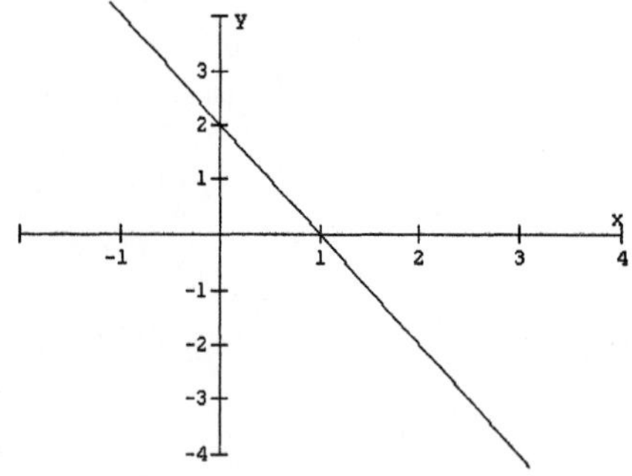

16. Find an equation of the line that passes through the points $(0,1)$ and $(1,3)$.

17. Find an equation of the line with x-intercept 2 that passes through the point $(1,-3)$.

18. Find an equation of the line perpendicular to the x-axis passing through the point $(4,-4)$.

19. Find the slope and y-intercept of the line $2y = \frac{5}{2}x + 1$.

20. If the cost, C (in dollars) to rent a car for m miles is given by $C = 0.25m + 25$, find the cost to rent the car for 130 miles.

21. Sketch the line $3x - 3 = 0$.

Exam 1D

Name:
Instructor:
Section:

Write your work as neatly as possible.

1. Find the values of x that satisfy the inequality $0 \le x+7 \le 12$.

2. Evaluate the expression $|1-\sqrt{3}|-|3-3\sqrt{3}|$.

3. Evaluate $16^{3/2}$.

4. Rewrite the expression $(x^2y^{-1})(x^{-2}y^2)$ using positive exponents.

5. Rationalize the denominator of the expression $\sqrt{\dfrac{5x}{3y}}$.

6. Find the minimum cost C (in dollars), given that $3(C-10) \ge 1.75+2.75C$.

7. Perform the indicated operations and simplify $(x+2)^3$.

8. Factor out the greatest common factor from $2a^2b^2+4ab^2+8a^3b$.

9. Factor the expression x^2-5x-6.

10. Perform the indicated operation and simplify the algebraic expression $(x^2+y)x+2x(2y^2)$.

11. Find the real roots of $2x^2-3x-9=0$ by factoring.

12. Use the quadratic formula to solve $2x^2-5x-4=0$.

13. Simplify the expression $\frac{4x^2+16x+15}{6x^2+9x}$.

14. Find the distance between the points $(0,2)$ and $(-3,5)$.

15. Find the coordinates of any points 6 units away from the origin with a y-coordinate of 3.

16. Find the equation of the circle centered at the origin that has radius 5 .

17. Find the slope of the line that passes through the points $(8,1)$ and $(7,-1)$.

18. Determine if the lines through the given pairs of points are parallel, perpendicular, or neither: $A(2,-2)$, $B(-1,3)$ and $C(6,5)$, $D(3,2)$.

19. Find an equation of the line that passes through the points $(4,-1)$ and $(-2,4)$.

20. Find an equation of the line graphed below.

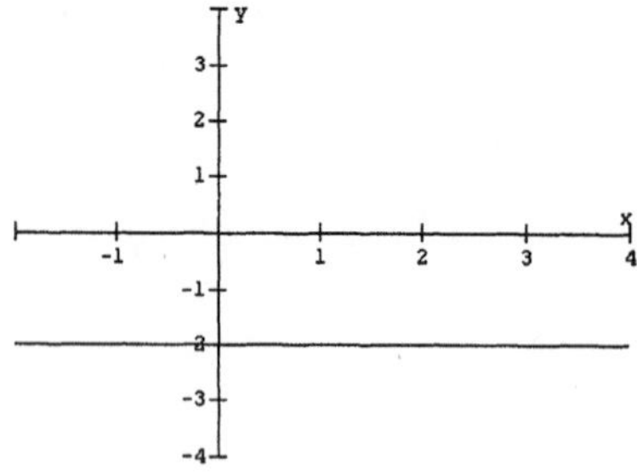

21. Sketch the line $2y=-4x+4$.

Answers to Chapter 1 Exams

Exam 1A

1. $(3,\infty)$
2. -2
3. $\sqrt{41}$
4. (a) True

   (b) False

   (c) False
5. 1/125
6. $4x^{7/4}$
7. $\dfrac{\sqrt{35x}}{7x}$
8. $\dfrac{x-23}{(x+1)(x-5)}$
9. $2ab(b+2+3a)$
10. $(x-2)(x+6)$
11. x^3-2xy^2+6xy
12. $x=0,9$
13. (1,0)
14. $(x-2)^2+(y+5)^2=36$
15. -2
16. Perpendicular
17. $m=-1$
18. $3x-y+2=0$
19. $y=3$
20. $m=\dfrac{1}{5}; b=-\dfrac{3}{5}$
21.

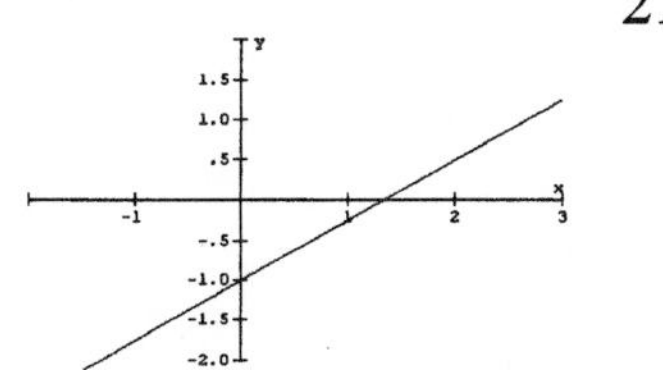

Exam 1B

1. $[1,8]$
2. $\pi-5$
3. 27
4. $\dfrac{y^2}{x^6}$
5. $\dfrac{\sqrt{2y}}{3}$
6. $3+2e-\dfrac{1}{e}$
7. $3xy(x+3y^3)$
8. $(3x+4)(x+2)$
9. $2x^2y-y^3+4xy$
10. $\dfrac{x+2}{2x+1}$
11. $3\sqrt{2}$
12. $(-3,4),(-3,-4)$
13. $x^2+(y-8)^2=89$
14. $-\dfrac{1}{3}$
15. Parallel
16. $4x+y=5$
17. $x+2y=2$
18. $x=2$
19. $m=\dfrac{1}{3}; b=\dfrac{2}{3}$
20. $m=0$
21.

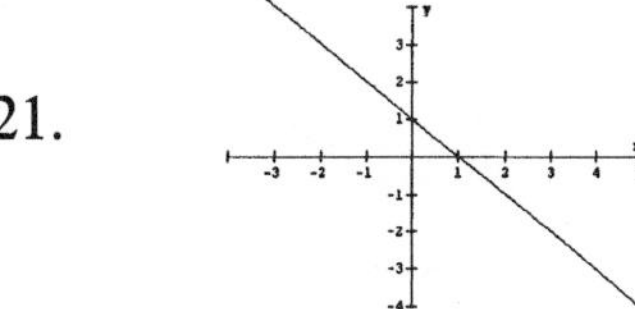

Exam 1C

1. $[-1,10)$
2. $8-5\sqrt{2}$
3. 4
4. $\dfrac{y^3}{27x^6}$
5. $\dfrac{2\sqrt{3x}}{9x}$
6. $8x^2+3x+6$
7. $2xy(y-2x)(y+2x)$
8. $2x^5-4x^3$
9. $x=\dfrac{-7\pm 3\sqrt{5}}{2}$
10. $\dfrac{2x+1}{4x}$
11. 6
12. $(4\sqrt{3},1),(-4\sqrt{3},1)$
13. $(x-3)^2+(y-2)^2=36$
14. $-\dfrac{1}{3}$
15. –2
16. $2x-y+1=0$
17. $3x-y-6=0$
18. $x=4$
19. $m=\dfrac{5}{4};\ b=\dfrac{1}{2}$
20. \$57.50
21.

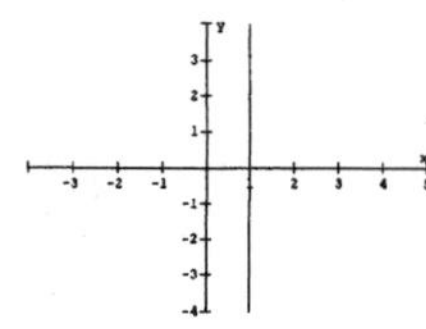

Exam 1D

1. $[-7,5]$
2. $2-2\sqrt{3}$
3. 64
4. y
5. $\dfrac{\sqrt{15xy}}{3y}$
6. 127
7. $x^3+6x^2+12x+8$
8. $2ab\left(ab+2b+4a^2\right)$
9. $(x-6)(x+1)$
10. $x^3+xy+4xy^2$
11. $x=3,-3/2$
12. $x=\dfrac{5\pm\sqrt{57}}{4}$
13. $\dfrac{2x+5}{3x}$
14. $3\sqrt{2}$
15. $(3\sqrt{3},3),\ (-3\sqrt{3},3)$
16. $x^2+y^2=25$
17. $m=2$
18. Neither
19. $5x+6y-14=0$
20. $y=-2$
21.

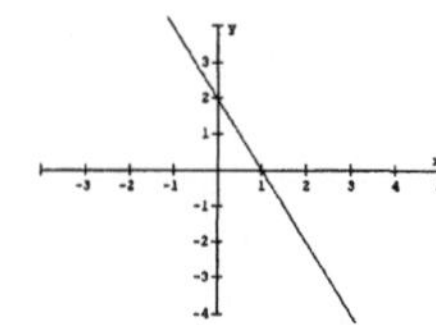

Chapter 2 ■ Functions, Limits, and the Derivative

Section 2.1

1. Let *f* be the function defined by $f(x) = 2x^2 + 3x - 4$. Find $f(0), f(2), f(a), f(-a)$, and $f(a+1)$.
   Answer: $-4,\ 10,\ 2a^2 + 3a - 4,\ 2a^2 - 3a - 4,\ 2a^2 + 7a + 1$

2. Let *g* be the function defined by $g(x) = x^3 + 2x^2 - 3$. Find $g(0),\ g(3),\ g(a),\ g(-x)$, and $g(h+1)$.
   Answer: $-3,\ 42,\ a^3 + 2a^2 - 3,\ -x^3 + 2x^2 - 3,\ h^3 + 5h^2 + 7h$

3. Let *h* be the function defined by $h(x) = \begin{cases} x^2 + 3 \text{ if } x \le 2 \\ \sqrt{2x} \ \ \text{if x} > 2 \end{cases}$. Find $h(0),\ h(2)$, and $h(3)$.
   Answer: $3, 7, \sqrt{6}$

4. Let *f* be the function defined by $f(x) = \dfrac{3}{4t+2}$ Find $f(1), f(-2)$, and $f(a+1)$.
   Answer: $\dfrac{1}{2},\ -\dfrac{1}{2},\ \dfrac{3}{4a+6}$

5. Find the domain of the function $g(x) = 3x^2 + 2x + 1$. Answer: $(-\infty, \infty)$

6. Find the domain of the function $F(x) = 1 - \sqrt{x}$. Answer: $[0, \infty)$

7. Find the domain of the function $f(x) = \dfrac{x+2}{x^2 - 1}$. Answer: $\{x \mid x \ne \pm 1\}$

8. Find the domain of the function $f(x) = \dfrac{x^4}{x^2 + x - 6}$.
   Answer: $\{x \mid x \ne -3, 2\}$

9. Find the domain of the function $g(x) = \sqrt[4]{x^2 - 6x}$.
   Answer: $(-\infty, 0] \cup [6, \infty)$

10. Sketch a graph of $f(x) = x^2 + 2$

Answer:

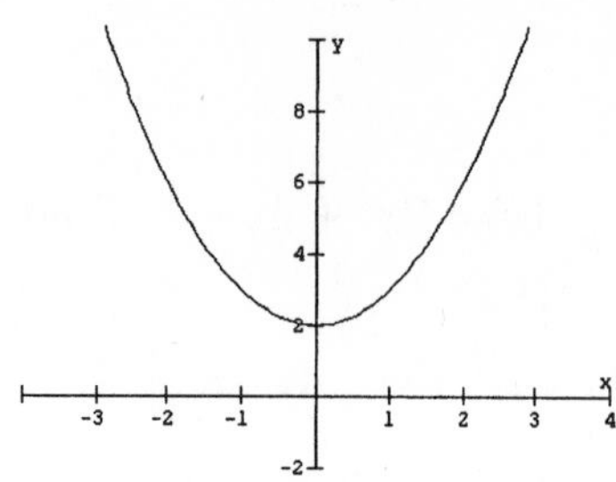

11. Sketch a graph of $h(x) = \sqrt{x} + 3$.

Answer:

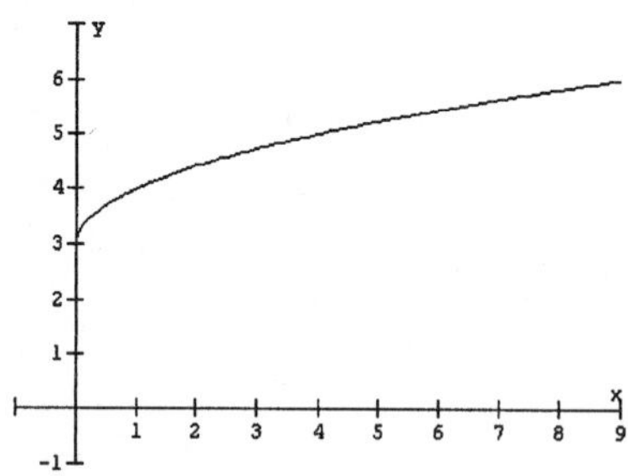

12. Sketch a graph of $g(x) = |x| - 2$.

Answer:

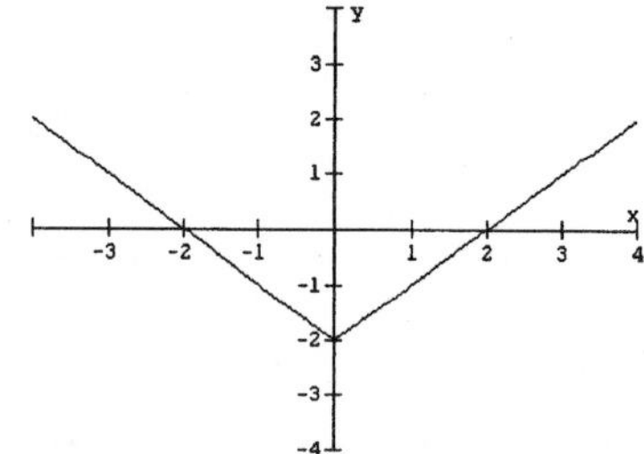

13. Sketch a graph of $h(x) = \begin{cases} 2 - x & \text{if } x \le 0 \\ x^2 + 2 & \text{if } x > 0 \end{cases}$.

Answer:

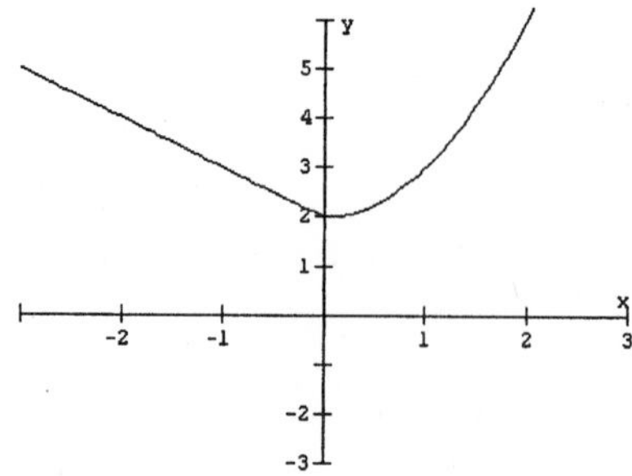

14. Refer the graph of $y = f(x)$ in the following figure.

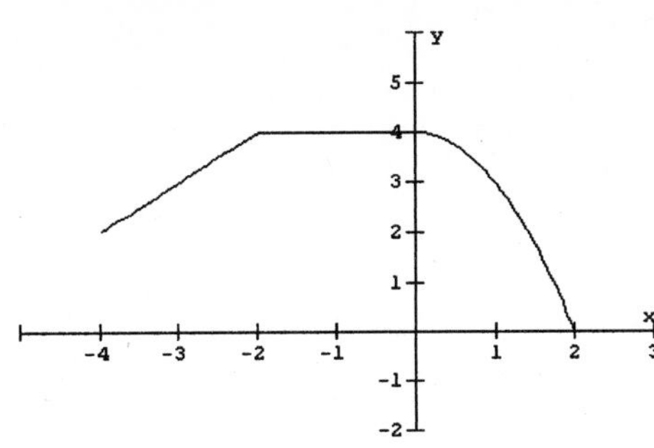

(a) Find the value of $f(-4)$. Answer: 2

(b) Find the value of x for which $f(x) = 0$. Answer: 2

(c) Find the domain of f. Answer: $[-4,2]$

(d) Find the range of f. Answer: $[0,4]$

15. Refer the graph of $y = f(x)$ in the following figure.

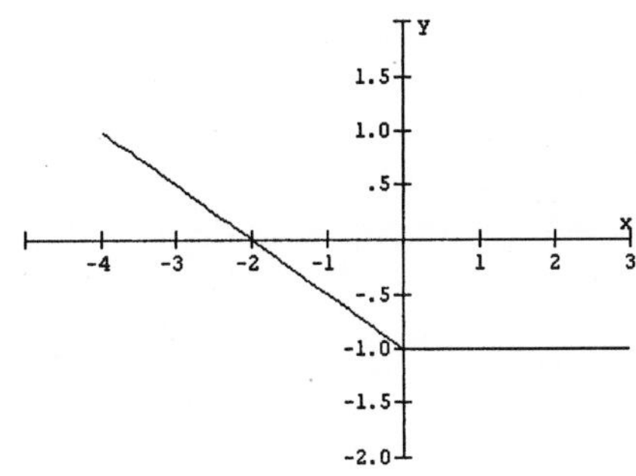

(a) Find the value of $f(-4)$. Answer: 1

(b) Find the value of x for which $f(x) = 0$ Answer: –2

(c) Find the domain of f. Answer: $[-4,\infty)$

(d) Find the range of f. Answer: $[-1,1]$

16. Determine whether the graph represents y as a function of x.

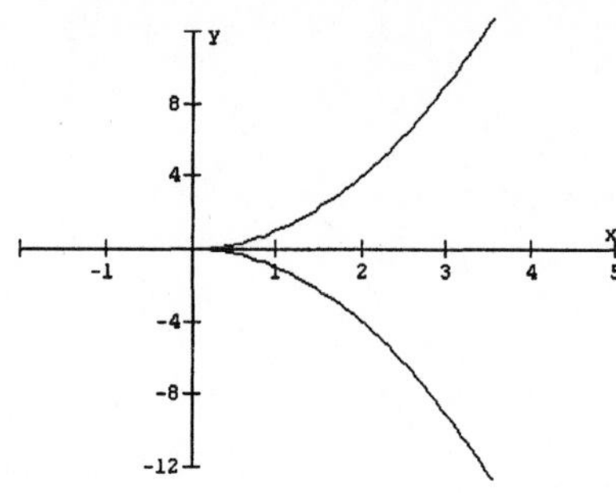

Answer: No

17. Determine whether the graph represents y as a function of x.

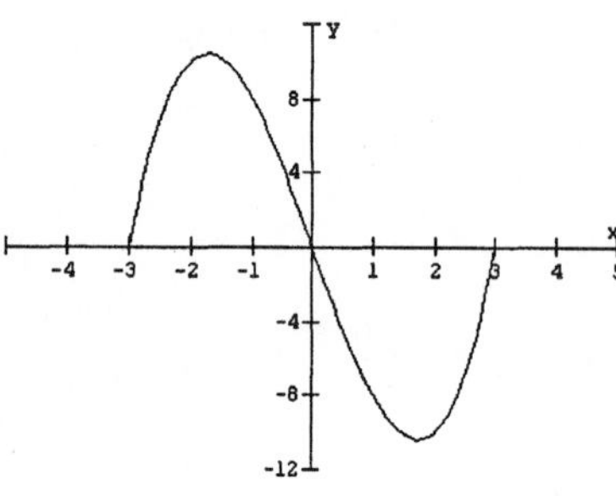

Answer: Yes

18. A company purchases a copier for \$8000. The copier is depreciated linearly over 5 years and has a scrap value of \$1200.
(a) Express the book value of the copier (V) as a function of the age, in years, of the copier (n).
Answer: $V = -1360n + 8000$

(b) Find the copier's value at the end of three years.
Answer: \$3920

Section 2.1 Multiple Choice Questions

1. Let f be the function defined by $f(x)=2x-10$. Find $f(-1)$.
   a. 12
   b. -12
   c. 8
   d. -13
   Answer: b.

2. Let f be the function defined by $f(x)=\begin{cases} 3x-4 & \text{if } x\leq 0 \\ x^2-12x+5 & \text{if } x>0 \end{cases}$. Find $f(-1)$.

   a. 18
   b. -7
   c. -1
   d. -6
   Answer: b.

3. Given $g(x)=-2x+3$, find $g(x-h)$.
   a. $-2x-2h+3$
   b. $-2x+2h+3$
   c. $-2x-h+3$
   d. None of these

   Answer: b

4. Find the domain of the function $f(x)=x^2-25$.
   a. $x>5$ or $x<-5$
   b. All real numbers
   c. $-5<x<5$
   d. $-5\leq x\leq 5$
   Answer: b.

5. Find the domain the function $f(x)=\dfrac{3}{\sqrt{x^2-49}}$.

   a. $x>7$ or $x<-7$
   b. $x>7$
   c. $x<-7$
   d. $-7<x<7$
   Answer: a.

6. Find the domain of the function $f(x)=\dfrac{2x+1}{3-x}$.

   a. $x>3$
   b. $x<-3$

c. $x \neq 3$

d. $x \neq -\frac{1}{2}$

Answer: c.

7. Find the domain of the function $f(x) = \sqrt{x+6}$.

a. $x > 6$

b. $x > -6$

c. $x < -6$

d. $x \geq -6$

Answer: d.

8. Find the domain of the function $f(x) = \frac{2x}{x^2 - 4}$.

a. $x \neq -2$

b. $x \neq 2$

c. $x \neq \pm 2$

d. $x \neq 0$

Answer: c.

9. Evaluate the function $f(x) = \frac{2x}{x^2 - 4}$ when $x = 3$.

a. $\frac{5}{6}$

b. $\frac{2}{3}$

c. $\frac{2}{9}$

d. $\frac{6}{5}$

Answer: d.

10. Let f be the function defined by $f(x) = \begin{cases} 3x - 4 & \text{if } x \leq 0 \\ x^2 - 12x + 5 & \text{if } x > 0 \end{cases}$. Find $f(0)$.

a. -4

b. 5

c. 4

d. Undefined

Answer: a.

11. Find the range of the function $f(x) = \begin{cases} -3x & \text{if } x \leq 0 \\ x^2 + 5 & \text{if } x > 0 \end{cases}$.

a. $x \geq 0$

b. $0 < y < 5$
c. All real numbers
d. $y \geq 0$
Answer: d.

12. Find the range of the function $f(x) = \sqrt{x-7} + 3$.
a. $x > 7$
b. $y \geq 3$
c. $y > 10$
d. $x \geq 7$
Answer: b.

13. The circumference of a circle is given by $C(r) = 2\pi r$, where r is the radius of the circle. What is the circumference of a circle with a 4-in radius?
a. 8π
b. 4π
c. 16π
d. $8\pi C$
Answer: a.

14. If the total revenue at a barbershop is given by $R(p) = -\frac{5}{2}p^2 + 70p$, where p is the price per haircut, determine the daily revenue when haircuts cost \$10.
a. \$950
b. \$675
c. \$750
d. \$450
Answer: d.

Section 2.2

1. Let $f(x) = x^2 - 4$ and $g(x) = 2x - 3$. Find the rule for the function $f + g$.
   Answer: $x^2 + 2x - 7$

2. Let $f(x) = x^2 - 4$ and $g(x) = 2x - 3$. Find the rule for the function fg.
   Answer: $2x^3 - 3x^2 - 8x + 12$

3. Let $f(x) = 2x^2 - 1$ and $g(x) = 3x + 2$. Find the rule for the function $f - g$.
   Answer: $2x^2 - 3x - 3$

4. Let $f(x) = 2x^2 - 1$ and $g(x) = 3x + 2$. Find the rule for the function $\dfrac{f}{g}$.
   Answer: $\dfrac{2x^2 - 1}{3x + 2}$

5. Let $f(x) = x + 2$ and $g(x) = \sqrt{x - 1}$. Find the rule for the function fg.
   Answer: $(x + 2)\sqrt{x - 1}$

6. Let $f(x) = x + 2$ and $g(x) = \sqrt{x - 1}$. Find the rule for the function $\dfrac{f}{g}$.
   Answer: $\dfrac{x + 2}{\sqrt{x - 1}}$

7. Let $f(x) = x + 2$, $g(x) = \sqrt{x + 2}$ and $h(x) = 3x^3 - 2$. Find the rule for the function $\dfrac{fg}{h}$.
   Answer: $\dfrac{(x + 2)^{3/2}}{3x^3 - 2}$

8. Let $f(x) = x + 2$, $g(x) = \sqrt{x + 2}$ and $h(x) = 3x^3 - 2$. Find the rule for the function $\dfrac{gh}{g - f}$.
   Answer: $\dfrac{\sqrt{x + 2}(3x^3 - 2)}{\sqrt{x + 2} - x - 2}$

9. Let $f(x) = x^2 - x - 1$ and $g(x) = 4x$. Find the rule for the composite function $f \circ g$.
   Answer: $16x^2 - 4x - 1$

10. Let $f(x) = x^2 - x - 1$ and $g(x) = 4x$. Find the rule for the composite function $g \circ f$.
Answer: $4x^2 - 4x - 4$

11. Let $f(x) = 4x + 5$. Find the rule for the composite function $f \circ f$.
Answer: $16x + 25$

12. Let $f(x) = \frac{2}{x}$. Find the rule for the composite function $f \circ f \circ f$.
Answer: $\frac{2}{x}$

13. Let $f(x) = 3\sqrt{x} + 4$ and $g(x) = x^2 - 1$. Find the rule for the composite function $f \circ g$.
Answer: $3\sqrt{x^2 - 1} + 4$

14. Let $f(x) = 3\sqrt{x} + 4$ and $g(x) = x^2 - 1$. Find the rule for the composite function $g \circ f$.
Answer: $9x + 24\sqrt{x} + 15$

15. Evaluate $h(3)$ where $h = g \circ f$, $f(x) = 3x + 2$ and $g(x) = x^2 + 5$.
Answer: 126

16. Evaluate $h(4)$ where $h = g \circ f$, $f(x) = 3\sqrt{x} + 4$ and $g(x) = x^2 - 1$
Answer: 99

17. If $h(x) = \sqrt{x^2 - 4}$, find functions f and g such that $h = g \circ f$ (the answer is not unique).
Answer: $g(x) = \sqrt{x}, f(x) = x^2 - 4$

18. If $h(x) = \frac{1}{\sqrt{2x - 1}} - 3\sqrt{2x - 1}$, find functions f and g such that $h = g \circ f$ (the answer is not unique).
Answer: $g(x) = \frac{1}{x} - 3x,\ f(x) = \sqrt{2x - 1}$

19. If $h(x) = (2x - 5)^{5/2}$, find functions f and g such that $h = g \circ f$ (the answer is not unique).
Answer: $g(x) = x^{5/2}, f(x) = 2x - 5$

20. If $f(x)=5x+7$, find and simplify $f(a+h)-f(a)$. Answer: $5h$

21. If $f(x)=x^2-1$, find and simplify $f(a+h)-f(a)$. Answer: $2ah+h^2$

22. If $f(x)=x^2-2$, find and simplify $\dfrac{f(a+h)-f(a)}{h}$, $(h\neq 0)$.
Answer: $2a+h$

23. If $f(x)=\dfrac{2}{x}$, find and simplify $\dfrac{f(a+h)-f(a)}{h}$, $(h\neq 0)$.
Answer: $-\dfrac{2}{a(a+h)}$

24. Determine whether the equation $15x-5=5y$ defines y as a linear function of x. If so, write it in the form $y=mx+b$.
Answer: $y=3x-1$

25. Determine whether the equation $x+y=3$ defines y as a linear function of x. If so, write it in the form $y=mx+b$.
Answer: $y=-x+3$

26. Determine whether the equation $\sqrt[3]{x}+4y=1$ defines y as a linear function of x. If so, write it in the form $y=mx+b$.
Answer: No

27. Determine whether the equation $x^2+y^2=3$ defines y as a linear function of x. If so, write it in the form $y=mx+b$.
Answer: No

28. Determine whether the equation $x^2=y^2$ defines y as a linear function of x. If so, write it in the form $y=mx+b$.
Answer: No

29. Find m and b in $f(x)=mx+b$ such that $f(0)=4$ and $f(4)=0$.
Answer: $m=-1, b=4$

30. Find m and b in $f(x)=mx+b$ such that $f(1)=-3$ and $f(2)=2$.
Answer: $m=5, b=-8$

31. Determine whether the given function is a polynomial function, a rational function, or some other function. State the degree of each polynomial function.
(a) $f(x)=\sqrt[5]{x}$ Answer: Other

(b) $g(x)=\sqrt{1-x^2}$ Answer: Other

(c) $h(x)=x^9+x^4$ Answer: Polynomial, degree 9

(d) $w(x)=\dfrac{x+5}{x-1}$ Answer: Rational function

(e) $w(x)=x^{-5}+x-10$ Answer: Rational function

32. Determine whether the given function is a polynomial function, a rational function, or some other function. State the degree of each polynomial function.

(a) $r(x)=\dfrac{x^2+1}{x^3+x}$ Answer: Rational Function

(b) $f(t)=2t^6+t^4-\pi$ Answer: Polynomial degree 6

(c) $h(\theta)=\cos\theta+\sin\theta$ Answer: Other

Section 2.2 Multiple Choice Questions

1. Let $f(x)=2x-10$ and $g(x)=x^2-10$. Find $f+g$.

a. x^2+2x-0

b. $x^2+2x-20$

c. x^2-20

d. $x^2+2x+20$

Answer: b.

2. Let $f(x)=2x-10$ and $g(x)=x^2-10$. Find $f-2g$.

a. $2x^2+2x+10$

b. $-2x^2+2x+10$

c. $-2x^2+2x-30$

d. $-2x^2+2x-20$

Answer: b.

3. Let $f(x)=\dfrac{x}{x-5}$ and $g(x)=\dfrac{x}{x^2-4x-5}$. Find $\dfrac{f}{g}$.

a. $\dfrac{x^2}{x+1}$

b. $\dfrac{1}{x+1}$

c. $x+1$

d. $\dfrac{x+1}{x}$

Answer: c.

4. Let $f(x)=\dfrac{x-2}{x+5}$ and $g(x)=\dfrac{x^2-25}{x^2-2x}$. Find fg.

a. $\dfrac{x-5}{x}$

b. $x(x-2)$

c. $x(x-5)$

d. $(x-2)(x-5)$

Answer: a.

5. Let $f(x)=2x-10$ and $g(x)=x^2-10$. Find $f \circ g$.

a. x^2-30

b. $2x^2+30$

c. $2x^2-30$

d. $2x^2-10$

Answer: c.

6. Let $f(x)=2x-10$ and $g(x)=x^2-10$. Evaluate $h(0)$, where $h(x)=f \circ g$.

a. -20

b. 100

c. 30

d. -30

Answer: d.

7. Let $f(x)=\sqrt{x+6}$ and $g(x)=x^2-36$. Find $g \circ f$.

a. $\sqrt{x-30}$

b. $x-30$

c. $x+42$

d. $\sqrt{x^2-30}$

Answer: b.

8. Let $g(x)=x^2-36$. Find $g(x+h)-g(x)$.

a. $2xh+h^2$

b. $2x^2+2xh+h^2$

c. $-2xh+h^2$

d. h^2

Answer: a.

9. Let $f(x) = -3x - 4$. Find $\dfrac{f(x+h) - f(x)}{h}$, $(h \neq 0)$.

a. -6
b. 4
c. 3
d. -3
Answer: d.

10. Let $f(x) = x^2 - 4x + 10$. Find $\dfrac{f(x+h) - f(x)}{h}$, $(h \neq 0)$.

a. $2x - 2h - 4$
b. $2x + 2h + 4$
c. $2x - 4$
d. $2x + h - 4$
Answer: d.

11. Suppose Puritron, a manufacturer of water filters, has a monthly fixed cost of \$20,000 and a variable cost of $-0.0005x^2 + 13x$ $(0 \le x \le 40{,}000)$ dollars, where x denotes the number of filters manufactured per month. Find a function C that gives the total cost incurred by Puritron in the manufacture of x filters.

a. $20{,}000 - 0.0005x^2 - 13x$
b. $-0.0005x^2 + 13x - 20{,}000$
c. $-0.0005x^2 - 13x + 20{,}000$
d. $-0.0005x^2 + 13x + 20{,}000$
Answer: d.

12. Find the profit function when the cost function is given by $C(x) = 2x - 56$ and the revenue function is given by $R(x) = x^2 + 45$, where x is the number of the items to be produced and sold.

a. $x^2 + 2x - 101$
b. $x^2 + 2x + 101$
c. $x^2 - 2x + 11$
d. $x^2 - 2x + 101$
Answer: d.

Section 2.3

1. A manufacturer has a monthly fixed cost of \$65,000 and a production cost of \$23 for each unit produced. The product sells for \$30 per unit.
   (a) What is the cost function? Answer: $C(x) = 65{,}000 + 23x$

   (b) What is the revenue function? Answer: $R(x) = 30x$

   (c) What is the profit function? Answer: $P(x) = 7x - 65{,}000$

   (d) Compute the profit or loss corresponding to a production level of 12,000 units.
   Answer: \$19,000 profit

2. A manufacturer has a monthly fixed cost of \$3500 and a production cost of \$7.50 for each unit produced. The product sells for \$16.75 per unit.
   (a) What is the cost function? Answer: $C(x) = 3500 + 7.5x$

   (b) What is the revenue function? Answer: $R(x) = 16.75x$

   (c) What is the profit function? Answer: $P(x) = 9.25x - 3500$

3. For the following pair of supply and demand equations, where x represents the quantity demanded in units of a thousand and p the unit price in dollars, find the equilibrium price and quantity: $5x + 2p - 33 = 0,\ 7x - 4p + 32 = 0$.

   Answer: $x = 2,\ p = \frac{23}{2}$

4. For the following pair of supply and demand equations, where x represents the quantity demanded in units of a thousand and p the unit price in dollars, find the equilibrium price and quantity: $3x + 12p - 69 = 0,\ 3x - 4p + 15 = 0$.

   Answer: $x = 2,\ p = \frac{21}{4}$

5. Thomas Young has suggested that following rule for calculating the dosage of medicine for children from ages 1 to 12 yr. If a denotes the adult dosage (in milligrams) and t is the age of the child (in years), then the child's dosage is given by $D(t) = \frac{at}{t+12}$. If the adult dose of a substance is 400 mg, how much should a 4-yr-old child receive?

   Answer: 100 mg.

Section 2.3 Multiple Choice Questions

1. Which function defines y as a linear function of x?
   a. $y = x^2 + 2x - 20$
   b. $2x + 3y = 10$
   c. $x + y^2 = 19$
   d. $y = \dfrac{1}{x^2 + 2x - 1}$

   Answer: b.

2. Given the following table of values for a linear function, find the missing number.

x	-1	0	1
y	-7		-3

   a. 5.5
   b. −4
   c. −5
   d. −6

   Answer: c.

3. Let f be the function that defined by $f(x) = \dfrac{x}{x-5}$. Which statement is true?
   a. It is a polynomial function.
   b. It is a linear function.
   c. It is a rational function.
   d. It is a power function.

   Answer: c.

4. Find the constants m and b in the linear function $y = mx + b$ so that $f(0) = 2$ and $f(1) = 5$.
   a. $y = 3x + 2$
   b. $y = 3x - 3$
   c. $y = 3x - 2$
   d. $y = 2x - 3$

   Answer: a.

5. A nursery can sell 1,200 red oak seedlings per season when they are priced at \$9.00, and 1000 seedlings when they are priced at \$11.00. Assuming a linear relationship, find the demand function for red oak seedlings.
   a. $q(p) = -0.01p + 200$
   b. $q(p) = 100p + 300$
   c. $q(p) = -100p + 2100$

d. $q(p) = -100p - 2100$

Answer: c.

6. During the summer, a group of students builds canoes in a neighbor's garage. The rent for the garage for the summer is \$500, and the materials needed to build a single canoe cost \$75. A canoe can be sold for \$250. Assuming a linear relationship, find the number of canoes that students must sell to make a profit of \$1,600?

   a. 6
   b. 9
   c. 14
   d. 12

   Answer: d.

7. The supply and demand functions for a new sweeper are given by $S(p) = p - 8$ and $D(p) = 90 - 3p$, respectively, where *p* is measured in dollars. Find the equilibrium price.

   a. \$22.00
   b. \$24.50
   c. \$49.00
   d. \$41.00

   Answer: b.

8. In the Fahrenheit temperature scale, water freezes at 32 degrees and boils at 212 degrees. In the Celsius temperature scale, water freezes at 0 degrees and boils at 100 degrees. Find a linear equation that represents the relationship between the Fahrenheit temperature scale and the Celsius temperature scale.

   a. $C = \frac{5}{9}(F - 32)$
   b. $C = \frac{5}{9}F - 32$
   c. $C = \frac{9}{5}(F - 32)$
   d. $C = \frac{5}{9}F + 32$

   Answer: a.

9. The Home-helper Company sells hummingbird feeders for \$6 per unit. Fixed costs are \$37,500 and the variable costs are \$2 per unit. How many feeders must be sold to realize a profit of 15% of sales?

   a. 9,375
   b. 9,740
   c. 11,209
   d. 12,097

Answer: d.

10. A manufacturer has a monthly fixed cost of \$20,000 and a production cost of \$6 for each unit produced. The product sells for \$12/unit. What is the profit function?
    a. $6x + 20,000$
    b. $6x - 20,000$
    c. $-6x - 20,000$
    d. $-6x + 20,000$

    Answer: b.

11. The production cost of the *Sweet Tooth Candy Co.* for producing x pounds of candy is given by $C(x) = 1.05x + 330$ dollars. If each pound of candy sells for \$2.00, what is the profit (loss) from selling 50 pounds of candy?
    a. Loss of \$124.30
    b. Profit of \$200.00
    c. Profit of \$282.50
    d. Loss of \$282.50

    Answer: d.

12. The supply and demand functions for a new sweeper are given by $S(p) = p^2 - 10$ and $D(p) = 20 - 7p$, respectively, where p is measured in dollars. Find the equilibrium price.
    a. \$10.00
    b. \$3.00
    c. \$2.00
    d. \$15.00

    Answer: b.

Section 2.4

1. Use the graph of the function *f* below to determine $\lim_{x \to -1} f(x)$, if it exists.

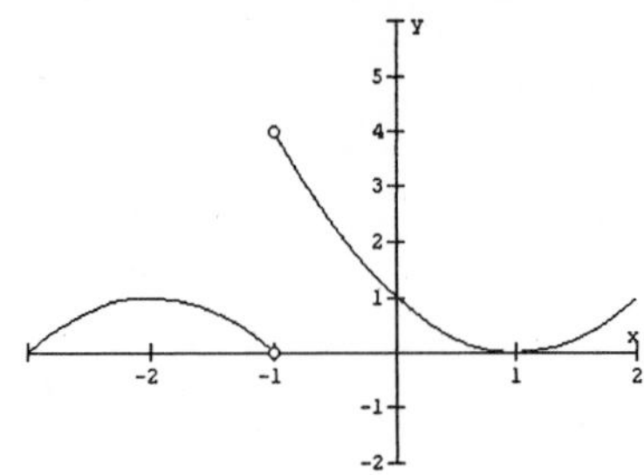

Answer: Does not exist.

2. Use the graph of the function *f* below to determine $\lim_{x \to 1} f(x)$ if it exists.

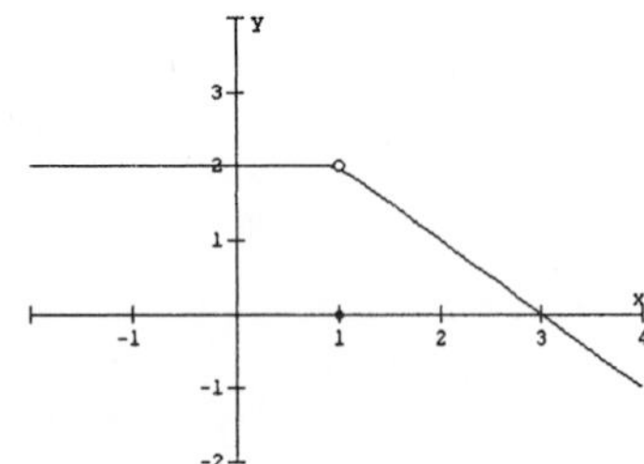

Answer: 2

3. Use the graph of the function *f* below to determine $\lim_{x \to 1} f(x)$ if it exists.

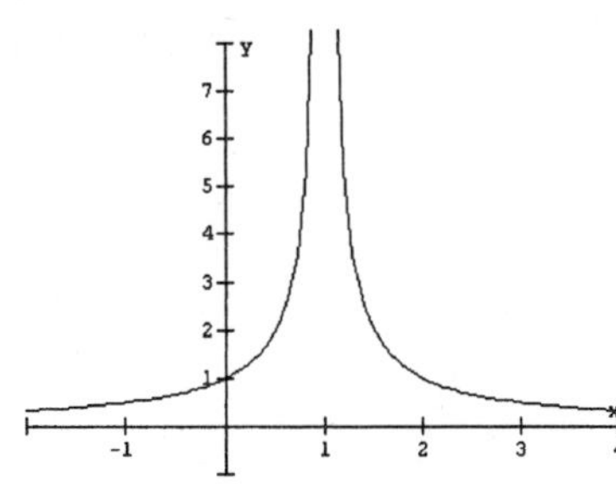

Answer: Does not exist. $(+\infty)$

4. Use the graph of the function *f* below to determine $\lim_{x \to 2} f(x)$.

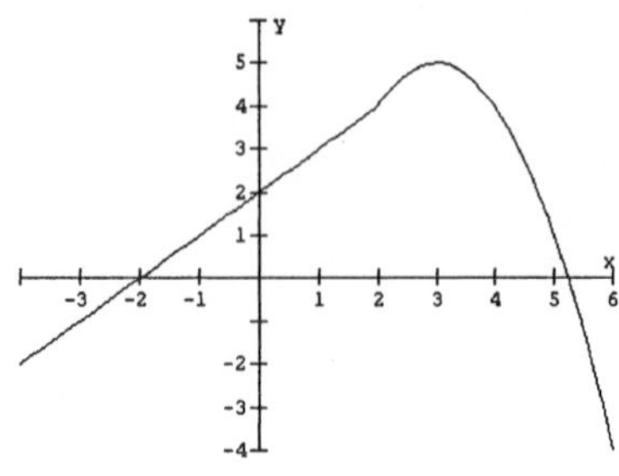

Answer: 4

5. Use the graph of the function *f* below to determine $\lim_{x\to 3} f(x)$.

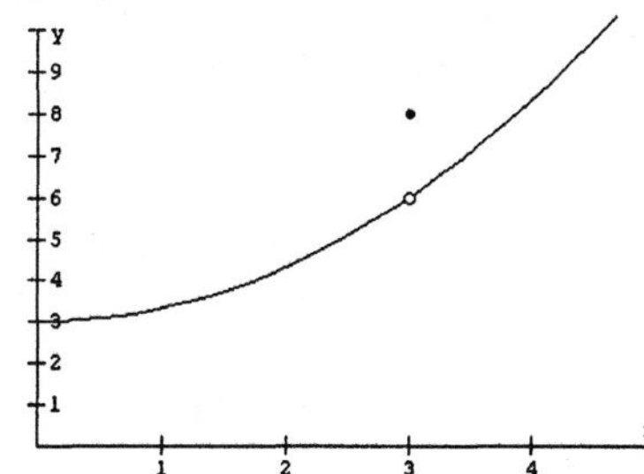

Answer: 6

6. Use the graph of the function *f* below to determine $\lim_{x\to 2} f(x)$.

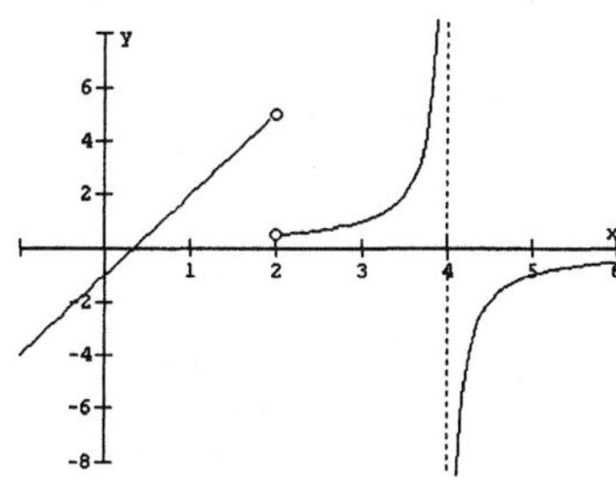

Answer: Does not exist.

7. Consider the function $f(x)=\dfrac{x^2-1}{x-1}$.

(a) Construct a table listing the x-values of 0.9, 0.99, 0.999, 1.001, 1.01, and 1.1 along with the computed values of $f(x)$ (to the nearest thousandth) associated with these x-values.

Answer:

x	0.9	0.99	0.999	1.001	1.01	1.1
$f(x)$	1.9	1.99	1.999	2.001	2.01	2.1

(b) Use the table found in part (a) to determine $\lim_{x\to 1} f(x)$.

Answer: 2

8. Consider the function $f(x)=\dfrac{x-1}{x^2+2x-3}$.

(a) Construct a table listing the x-values of 0.9, 0.99, 0.999, 1.001, 1.01, and 1.1 along with the computed values of $f(x)$ (to the nearest thousandth) associated with these x-values.

Answer:

x	0.9	0.99	0.999	1.001	1.01	1.1
$f(x)$	0.256	0.251	0.250	0.250	0.249	0.244

(b) Use the table found in part (a) to determine $\lim_{x \to 1} f(x)$.

Answer: 0.250

9. Find the value of $\lim_{x \to 2} -4$. Answer: -4

10. Find the value of $\lim_{x \to 1} \pi$. Answer: π

11. Find the value of $\lim_{x \to -1} -5x$. Answer: 5

12. Find the value of $\lim_{t \to 3} \left(t^2 + 3t - 1\right)$. Answer: 17

13. Find the value of $\lim_{w \to -2} \dfrac{3-w}{3+w}$. Answer: 5

14. Find the value of $\lim_{x \to 4} \dfrac{x^2 - 16}{x - 4}$, if it exists. Answer: 8

15. Find the value of $\lim_{x \to 16} \dfrac{\sqrt{x} - 4}{x - 16}$, if it exists. Answer: $\dfrac{1}{8}$

16. Find the value of $\lim_{x \to 0} \dfrac{x^2 + 2x}{x}$. Answer: 2

17. Find the value of $\lim_{x \to -2} \dfrac{x}{x+2}$, if it exists. Answer: Does not exist.

18. Find the value of $\lim_{x \to \infty} \dfrac{2}{x+1}$, if it exists. Answer: 0

19. Find the value of $\lim_{x \to \infty} \dfrac{3x^4 + 5x + 2}{x^7 - 2x + 12}$, if it exists. Answer: 0

20. Find the value of $\lim_{x \to \infty} \dfrac{3x - 1}{x + 2}$, if it exists. Answer: 3

21. Find the value of $\lim_{x \to -\infty} \dfrac{x^2}{3x - 1}$, if it exists. Answer: $-\infty$

22. Find the value of $\lim_{x \to -\infty} \dfrac{4x^3 + 2x^2 - 3x + 3}{2x^3 - 3x^2 - 7x - 6}$, if it exists Answer: 2

23. The number of fish in a certain lake is given by the function $N(t)=\dfrac{2000t^2+100}{t^2+1}$, where t is measured in months. Determine the limit of this function as $t\to\infty$, which represents the upper limit of the fish population.
Answer: 2000

Section 2.4 Multiple Choice Questions

1. Find the value of $\lim\limits_{x\to 10}\pi$.

   a. π
   b. 10π
   c. $10+\pi$
   d. $\pi-10$

   Answer: a.

2. Find the value of $\lim\limits_{t\to 3}\left(t^2+3t-10\right)$.

   a. -1
   b. 5
   c. 8
   d. 28

   Answer: c.

3. Find the value of $\lim\limits_{w\to -2}\dfrac{2-w}{3+w}$.

   a. 0
   b. -4
   c. 4
   d. 1

   Answer: c.

4. Find the value of $\lim\limits_{x\to 16}\dfrac{\sqrt{x}-4}{x-16}$.

   a. $\dfrac{1}{8}$
   b. Undefined
   c. 8
   d. $\dfrac{1}{4}$

   Answer: a.

5. Find the value of $\lim\limits_{x\to 0}\dfrac{x^2+5x}{x}$

   a. 3

b. 6
c. 5
d. Undefined
Answer: c.

6. Find the value of $\lim_{x \to -2} \frac{x}{x+2}$, if it exists.

a. $\frac{1}{2}$
b. $-\frac{1}{2}$
c. 0
d. Undefined
Answer: d.

7. Find the value of $\lim_{x \to \infty} \frac{6x^4 + 3x + 2}{x^7 - 2x + 12}$, if it exists.

a. 6
b. 0
c. Undefined
d. 5
Answer: b.

8. Find the value of $\lim_{x \to -\infty} \frac{4x^3 + 2x^2 - 3x + 3}{2x^3 - 3x^2 - 7x - 6}$, if it exists.

a. 2
b. 4
c. −2
d. 0
Answer: a.

9. Find the value of $\lim_{x \to \infty} \frac{10}{x+5}$, if it exists.

a. 4
b. 2
c. Undefined
d. 0
Answer: d.

10. Find the value of $\lim_{x \to \infty} \frac{20x - 1}{4x + 2}$, if it exists.

a. 0
b. 5
c. 10

d. Undefined
Answer: b.

11. Find the value of $\lim_{x \to 1} \frac{20x-1}{4x+2}$.

a. $\frac{6}{19}$
b. $\frac{19}{2}$
c. 4
d. $\frac{19}{6}$
Answer: d.

12. Find the value of $\lim_{x \to 2} \frac{x^2-4}{x-2}$.

a. 0
b. 4
c. 2
d. Undefined
Answer: b.

Section 2.5

1. Consider the function f whose graph is shown below. Find the value of each limit if it exists.

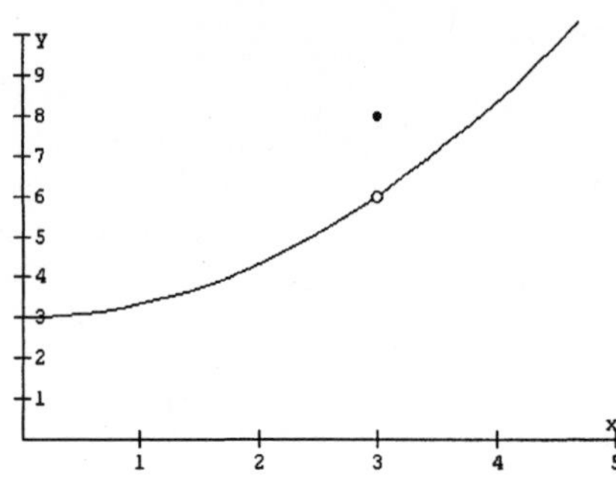

(a) $\lim_{x\to 3^+} f(x)$ Answer: 6

(b) $\lim_{x\to 3^-} f(x)$ Answer: 6

(c) $\lim_{x\to 1} f(x)$ Answer: 6

2. Consider the function f whose graph is shown below. Find the value of each limit if it exists.

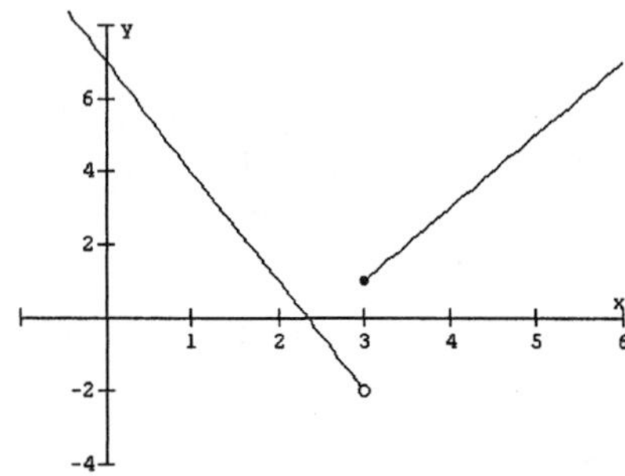

(a) $\lim_{x\to 3^+} f(x)$ Answer: 1

(b) $\lim_{x\to 3^-} f(x)$ Answer: -2

(c) $\lim_{x\to 3} f(x)$ Answer: Does not exist

3. Find the value of the one-sided limit $\lim_{x\to 1^-} \dfrac{x+2}{x-1}$. Answer: $-\infty$

4. Find the value of the one-sided limit $\lim_{x\to 3^-} \sqrt{3-x}$. Answer: 0

5. Find the value of the one-sided limit $\lim_{x\to 6^-} \sqrt{6-x}+3$. Answer: 3

6. Find the value of the one-sided limit $\lim_{x\to 1^+} f(x)$ where $f(x)=\begin{cases} 3x & \text{if } x>1 \\ 4x+2 & \text{if } x\le 1 \end{cases}$.

   Answer: 3

7. Find the value of the one-sided limit $\lim_{x\to 1^-} f(x)$ where $f(x)=\begin{cases} 3x & \text{if } x>1 \\ 4x+2 & \text{if } x\le 1 \end{cases}$.

   Answer: 6

8. Find the value of the one-sided limit $\lim_{x\to 4^+} \dfrac{x-1}{x-4}$. Answer: ∞

9. Determine the values of x, if any, at which the function $f(x)=\begin{cases} x+3 & \text{if } x<2 \\ -x+7 & \text{if } x\ge 2 \end{cases}$ is discontinuous.
   Answer: There is no such value of x.

10. Determine the values of x, if any, at which the function $f(x)=\begin{cases} -x & \text{if } x\le 0 \\ x+2 & \text{if } x>0 \end{cases}$ is discontinuous.
    Answer: $x=0$.

11. Find the values of x, if any, at which the function $f(x)=x^2+2$ is discontinuous.

    Answer: There is no such value of x.

12. Determine the values of x, if any, at which the function $f(x)=\dfrac{2}{x^2-1}$ is discontinuous.
    Answer: $x=1,\ -1$

13. Find the values of x, if any, at which the function $f(x)=\begin{cases} x^2 & \text{if } x\le 0 \\ x & \text{if } x>0 \end{cases}$ is discontinuous.
    Answer: There is no such value of x.

14. Find the values of x, if any, at which the function $f(x)=\dfrac{3}{x^2+4}$ is discontinuous.

    Answer: There is no such value of x.

15. Find the values of x, if any, at which the function $f(x)=\dfrac{x+3}{|x+3|}$ is discontinuous.

    Answer: $x=-3$

16. Find the values of x, if any, at which the function graphed below, is discontinuous.

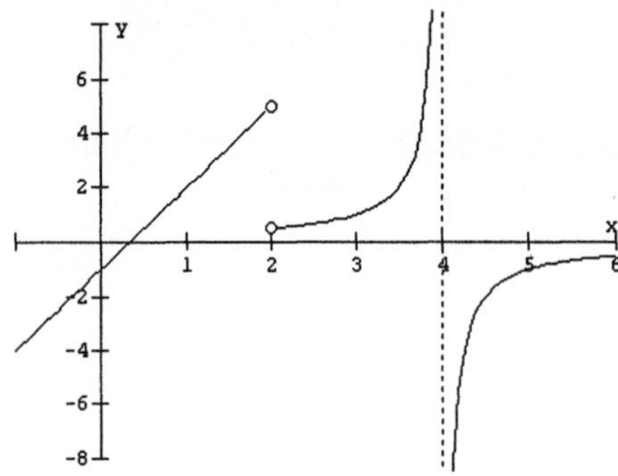

Answer: $x = 2$ and $x = 4$

17. Find the values of x, if any, at which the function graphed below, is discontinuous.

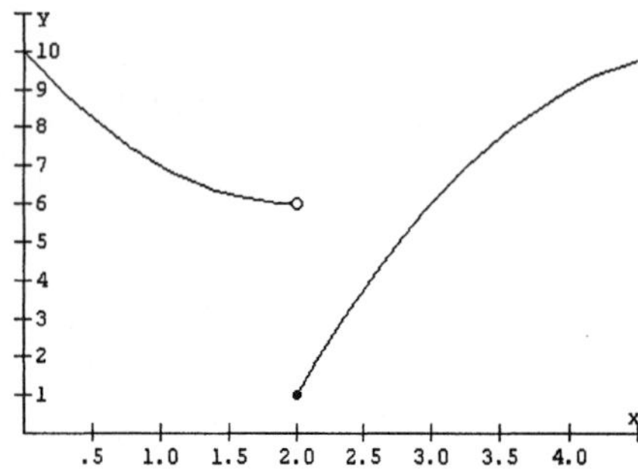

Answer: $x = 2$

18. Use the Intermediate Value Theorem to find c such that $f(c) = 3$ where $f(x) = x^2 + 2x$ on [0, 2].
Answer: $c = 1$.

19. Use the Intermediate Value Theorem to find c such that $f(c) = 3$ where $f(x) = \dfrac{4}{x+1}$ on [0, 1].

Answer: $c = \dfrac{1}{3}$.

Section 2.5 Multiple Choice Questions

1. Find the value of the one-sided limit $\lim_{x \to 10^-} (\pi + 10x)$.

   a. 100π
   b. $10 + \pi$
   c. $100 + \pi$
   d. $\pi - 10$

   Answer: c.

2. Find the value of the one-sided limit $\lim_{t \to 3^+} \left(t^2 + 3t - 10\right)$.

   a. -1
   b. 5
   c. 8
   d. 28

   Answer: c.

3. Find the value of the one-sided limit $\lim_{w \to -2^-} \dfrac{2-w}{3+w}$, if it exists.

   a. 0
   b. -4
   c. 4
   d. 1

   Answer: c.

4. Find the value of one-sided limit $\lim_{x \to 16^-} \dfrac{\sqrt{x}-4}{x-16}$, if it exists.

   a. $\dfrac{1}{8}$
   b. Undefined
   c. 8
   d. $\dfrac{1}{4}$

   Answer: a.

5. Find the value of the one-sided limit $\lim_{x \to 0^+} \dfrac{x^2 + 5x}{x}$, if it exists.

   a. 3
   b. 6
   c. 5
   d. Undefined

   Answer: c.

6. Find the value of the one-sided limit $\lim_{x\to -2^-} \frac{|x+2|}{x+2}$, if it exists.

a. -1
b. 2
c. 0
d. 1
Answer: d.

7. Find the value of the one-sided limit $\lim_{x\to 2^+} \frac{|2-x|}{2-x}$, if it exists.

a. 1
b. -1
c. Undefined
d. 2
Answer: b.

8. Find the value of the one-sided limit $\lim_{x\to 4^-} \frac{x-4}{x^2-16}$, if it exists.

a. $\frac{1}{8}$
b. 4
c. $-\frac{1}{8}$
d. 0
Answer: a.

9. Find the value of the one-sided limit $\lim_{x\to -5^-} \frac{10}{x+5}$, if it exists.

a. 10
b. 2
c. Undefined
d. 0
Answer: c.

10. Find the value of the one-sided limit $\lim_{x\to 3^-} \frac{20x-1}{4x+2}$, if it exists.

a. $\frac{59}{14}$
b. $-\frac{59}{10}$
c. 5
d. Undefined
Answer: a.

11. Find the value of k such that the function $f(x)=\begin{cases} x^2-5 & x\le 1 \\ x+k & x>1 \end{cases}$ is continuous at $x=1$.

a. -4
b. 5
c. 4
d. -5
Answer: d.

12. Find the value of k such that the function $f(x)=\begin{cases} 2x-5 & x\le 1 \\ k & x>1 \end{cases}$ is continuous at $x=1$.

a. 7
b. -3
c. 3
d. -7
Answer: b.

13. Find the value(s) of x for which the function $f(x)=\begin{cases} x+1 & x\le 2 \\ x^2-1 & x>2 \end{cases}$ is continuous.

a. $(-\infty, 2)\cup(2, \infty)$
b. $(-\infty, \infty)$
c. $(-\infty, 2)$
d. $(2, \infty)$
Answer: b.

14. Find the value(s) of x for which the function $f(x)=\begin{cases} \dfrac{1}{x-4} & x\le 2 \\ x^2+3 & x>2 \end{cases}$ is continuous.

a. $(-\infty, 2)\cup(2, \infty)$
b. $(-\infty, 2)\cup(2, 4)\cup(4, \infty)$
c. $(-\infty, 4)$
d. $(4, \infty)$
Answer: a.

Section 2.6

1. Find the slope of the tangent line to the graph of $f(x) = 7x + 8$ at any point x.
   Answer: 7

2. Find the slope of the tangent line to the graph of $f(x) = 3$ at any point x.
   Answer: 0

3. Find the slope of the tangent line to the graph of $f(x) = 3x^2 + 6$ at any point x.
   Answer: $6x$

4. Let $f(x) = 4x + 5$.
   (a) Find the slope of the tangent line to f at the point $(-1,1)$. Answer: 4

   (b) Find the equation of the tangent line to f at the point $(-1,1)$.
   Answer: $y = 4x + 5$

5. Let $f(x) = 2x^2$.
   (a) Find the slope of the tangent line to f at the point $(1,2)$. Answer: 4

   (b) Find the equation of the tangent line to f at the point $(1,2)$.
   Answer: $y = 4x - 2$

6. Let $f(x) = x^2 + 3x$.
   (a) Find the slope of the tangent line to f at the point $(1,4)$. Answer: 5

   (b) Find the equation of the tangent line to f at the point $(1,4)$.
   Answer: $y = 5x - 1$

7. Let $f(x) = \frac{2}{x}$.
   (a) Find the slope of the tangent line to f at the point $(1,2)$. Answer: -2

   (b) Find the equation of the tangent line to f at the point $(1,2)$.
   Answer: $y = -2x + 4$

8. A ball is thrown straight up into the air with an initial velocity of 64 feet per second, so that its height (in feet) after t seconds is given by $s(t) = -16t^2 + 64t$.
   (a) Calculate the average velocity of the ball over the intervals
   [1, 1.5], [1, 1.1], and [1, 1.05].

Answer: 24 ft/sec, 30.4 ft/sec, 31.2 ft/sec

(b) Calculate the instantaneous velocity of the ball at time $t = 1$.
Answer: 32 ft/sec

(c) Calculate the time when the ball will hit the ground.
Answer: 4 seconds

Section 2.6 Multiple Choice Questions

1. Compute the average rate of change of the function $f(t) = 2t + 7$ from $t = 1$ to $t = 4$.
   a. 6
   b. 3
   c. 2
   d. 1
   Answer: c.

2. Find the slope of the tangent line to the graph of $f(x) = 3x - 7$ at any point.
   a. -7
   b. -4
   c. 3
   d. 6
   Answer: c.

3. Find the slope of the tangent line to the graph of $f(x) = 3x^2 + 2$ at any point.
   a. $6x + 2$
   b. $4x + 2$
   c. $6x$
   d. 6
   Answer: c.

4. Find the slope of the tangent line to the graph of $f(x) = x^2 - 2x$ at (0, 0).
   a. -2
   b. 0
   c. 4
   d. $\frac{1}{4}$
   Answer: a.

5. Find the slope of the tangent line to the graph of $f(x) = \frac{1}{x}$ at (1, 1).

a. 1
b. 2
c. -1
d. Undefined
Answer: c.

6. Find the slope of the tangent line to the graph of $f(x)=\sqrt{x}$ at (4, 2).

a. $-\frac{1}{4}$
b. $-\frac{1}{2}$
c. $\frac{1}{2}$
d. $\frac{1}{4}$
Answer: d.

7. Find the derivative of the function $f(x)=x^3$.

a. x^2
b. $3x^2$
c. $6x$
d. $3x^2+h$
Answer: b.

8. Find the derivative of the function $f(x)=\frac{2}{x}$.

a. $-\frac{2}{x^2}$
b. $\frac{2}{x^2}$
c. $-\frac{1}{x^2}$
d. $-\frac{2}{x^3}$
Answer: a.

9. Find the derivative of the function $g(x)=\frac{1}{2}x^2+7x$.

a. $x+7$
b. $2x$
c. $2x+7$
d. $4x+7$
Answer: a.

10. Find the derivative of the function $C(x) = -10x^2 + 23x$.

a. $20x + 23$
b. $-20x - 23$
c. $-20x + 23$
d. $20x + 13$
Answer: c.

11. Find the derivative of the function $P(x) = -5x^2 + 2x - \frac{1}{10}$.

a. $-10x + \frac{19}{10}$
b. $-8x$
c. $-10x + \frac{21}{10}$
d. $-10x + 2$
Answer: d.

12. Find the equation of the tangent line to the graph of the function $h(x) = -x^2 + 2x$ at (0, 0).

a. $y = -4x$
b. $y = 2x$
c. $y = -2x$
d. $y = 4x$
Answer: b.

Exam 2A

Name:
Instructor:
Section:

Write your work as neatly as possible.

1. Let *f* be the function defined by $f(x) = 2x^2 - 3x + 4$. Find $f(0), f(2), f(a), f(-a)$, and $f(a+1)$.

2. Find the domain of the function $f(x) = \sqrt{3x+9}$.

3. Refer to the graph of the function *f*

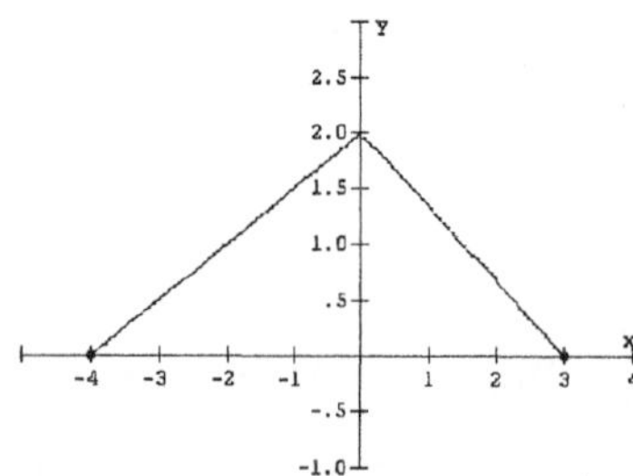

(a) Find the value of $f(0)$.

(b) Find the value(s) of *x* for which $f(x) = 0$.

(c) Find the domain of *f*.

(d) Find the range of *f*.

4. Let $f(x) = x^2 - 3x + 1$ and $g(x) = 4x + 3$. Find the rule for the function $f + g$.

5. Let $f(x) = x^2 - 2x - 1$ and $g(x) = 3x$. Find the rule for the composite function $f \circ g$.

6. If $h(x) = \left(7x^2 - 2x\right)^3$, find functions *f* and *g* such that $h = g \circ f$ (the answer is not unique).

7. If $f(x) = x^2 + 2x$, find and simplify $\dfrac{f(a+h) - f(a)}{h}$ $(h \neq 0)$.

8. Determine m and b so that $f(x) = mx + b$ defines a linear function of x with $f(1) = 2$ and $f(0) = -3$.

9. Determine whether the given function is a polynomial function, a rational function, or some other function. State the degree of each polynomial function.

(a) $f(x) = \sqrt[6]{x - x^3}$

(b) $g(x) = \dfrac{\sqrt{5}}{x}$

10. For the following pair of supply and demand equations, where x represents the quantity demanded in units of a thousand and p the unit price in dollars, find the equilibrium quantity and price: $3x + 3p - 17 = 0$, $5x - 3p + 9 = 0$.

11. Consider the function $f(x) = \begin{cases} x+2 & \text{if } x \leq 2 \\ 6-x & \text{if } x > 2 \end{cases}$ whose graph is shown below.

Find the value of each limit, if it exists.

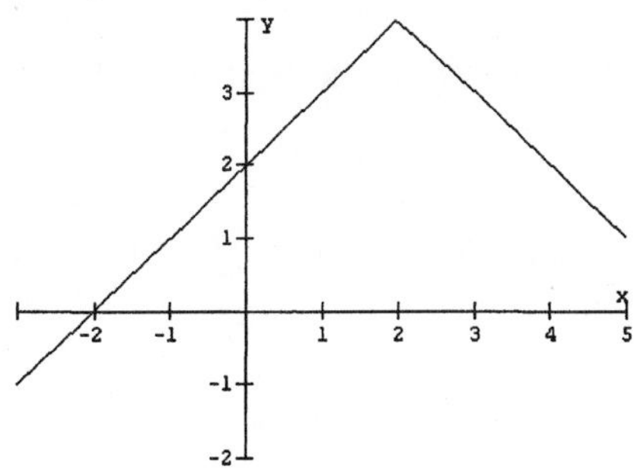

(a) $\lim_{x \to 2^+} f(x)$

(b) $\lim_{x \to 2^-} f(x)$

(c) $\lim_{x \to 2} f(x)$

12. Find the value of $\lim_{x \to 1} \frac{3x-2}{x-2}$, if it exists.

13. Find the value of $\lim_{x \to 3} \frac{x^2-9}{x-3}$, if it exists.

14. The population of a certain town is given by the function $N(t) = \frac{6000t^2+231}{2t^2+75}$, where t is measured in years. Determine the limit of this function as $t \to \infty$, which represents the upper limit of the town's population.

15. Find the value of $\lim_{x \to 2^+} \frac{\sqrt{x-2}}{x+2}$, if it exists.

16. Determine the values of x, if any at which the function $f(x) = \begin{cases} x+2 & \text{if } x \le 2 \\ 6-x & \text{if } x > 2 \end{cases}$ is discontinuous.

17. Let $f(x) = 2x^2 - 1$.
(a) Find the slope of the tangent line to the graph of $y = f(x)$ at $x = 2$.

(b) Find the equation of the tangent line to the graph of $y = f(x)$ at $x = 2$.

18. A ball is thrown straight up into the air so that its height in feet after t seconds is given by $s(t) = 128t - 16t^2$.
(a) Find the average velocity of the ball during the time interval $[2, 2.1]$.

(b) Find the instantaneous velocity of the ball at $t = 2$ seconds.

Exam 2B

Name:
Instructor:
Section:

Write your work as neatly as possible.

1. Let *f* be the function defined by $g(x) = x^2 + 2x$.
   (a) Find $g(3)$.

   (b) Find $g(t+1)$.

2. Find the domain of the function $f(x) = \dfrac{x-1}{(x-2)^2}$.

3. Refer to the graph of the function *f*

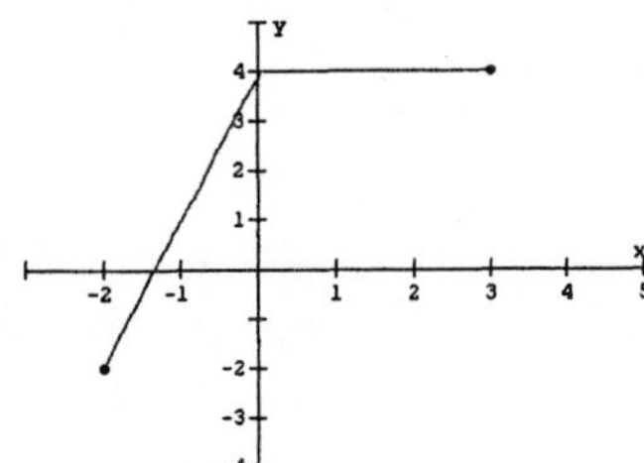

   (a) Find the value of $f(0)$.

   (b) Find the value(s) of *x* for which $f(x) = 0$.

   (c) Find the domain of *f*.

   (d) Find the range of *f*.

4. Let $f(x) = x^2 - 2x$ and $g(x) = 2x - 1$. Find the rule for the function $f \cdot g$.

5. Let $f(x) = x^2 - 2x - 1$ and $g(x) = 3x$. Find the rule for the composite function $g \circ f$.

6. If $h(x) = \frac{1}{\sqrt{2x+1}} - 3(2x+1)^3$, find functions *f* and *g* such that $h = g \circ f$ (the answer is not unique).

7. If $f(x) = x^2 - 2$, find and simplify $\frac{f(a+h) - f(a)}{h}$ $(h \neq 0)$.

8. Determine whether the equation $x^3 - \sqrt{y} = 1$ defines *y* as a linear function of *x*. If so, write in the form $y = mx + b$.

9. Determine whether the given function is a polynomial function, a rational function, or some other function. State the degree of each polynomial function.
(a) $f(x) = 4x^3 - 2x^2 + 7x$
(b) $g(x) = \frac{6 - x^2}{8x - 1}$

10. For the following pair of supply and demand equations, where *x* represents the quantity demanded in units of a thousand and *p* the unit price in dollars, find the equilibrium quantity and price: $5x + 2p - 47 = 0$, $7x - 4p + 43 = 0$.

11. Consider the function $f(x) = \begin{cases} x & \text{if } x < 3 \\ 1 & \text{if } x = 3 \\ 3 & \text{if } x > 3 \end{cases}$ whose graph is shown below. Find the value of each limit, if it exists.

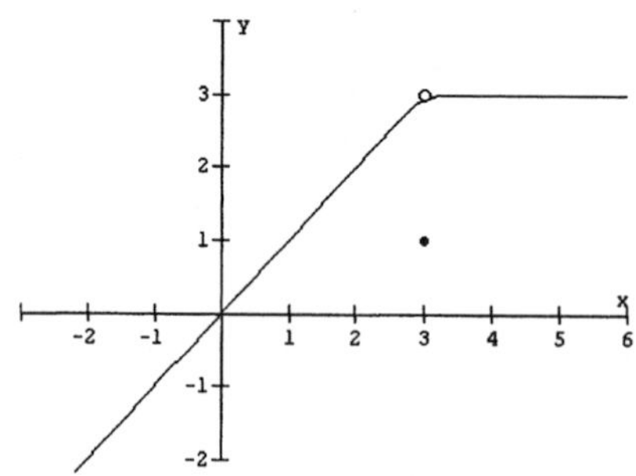

(a) $\lim_{x \to 3^+} f(x)$
(b) $\lim_{x \to 3^-} f(x)$
(c) $\lim_{x \to 3} f(x)$

12. Find the value of $\lim_{x \to 4} \frac{3x + x^2}{2x - 4}$, if it exists.

13. Find the value of $\lim_{x \to -1} \frac{x^2 + 4x + 3}{x + 1}$, if it exists.

14. The population of a certain town is given by the function $N(t) = \frac{12000t^2 + 40}{5t^2 - t}$, where t is measured in years. Determine the limit of this function as $t \to \infty$, which represents the upper limit of the town's population.

15. Find the value of $\lim_{x \to 2^+} \sqrt{2 - x}$, if it exists.

16. Determine the values of x, if any at which the function $f(x) = \begin{cases} x & \text{if } x < 3 \\ 1 & \text{if } x = 3 \\ 3 & \text{if } x > 3 \end{cases}$ is discontinuous.

17. Let $f(x) = 1 - 3x^2$.
    (a) Find the slope of the tangent line to the graph of $y = f(x)$ at $x = 1$.

    (b) Find the equation of the tangent line to the graph of $y = f(x)$ at $x = 1$.

18. A ball is thrown straight up into the air so that its height in feet after t seconds is given by $s(t) = 128t - 16t^2$.
    (a) Find the average velocity of the ball during the time interval $[2.5, 2.6]$.
    (b) Find the instantaneous velocity of the ball at $t = 2.5$ seconds.

Exam 2C

Name:
Instructor:
Section:

Write your work as neatly as possible.

1. Let g be the function defined by $g(x) = 2x^2 + x + 1$.
   (a) Find $g(-3)$

   (b) Find $g(t-1)$.

2. Find the domain of the function $f(x) = \sqrt[4]{x^2 + 2x}$.

3. Refer to the graph of the function f

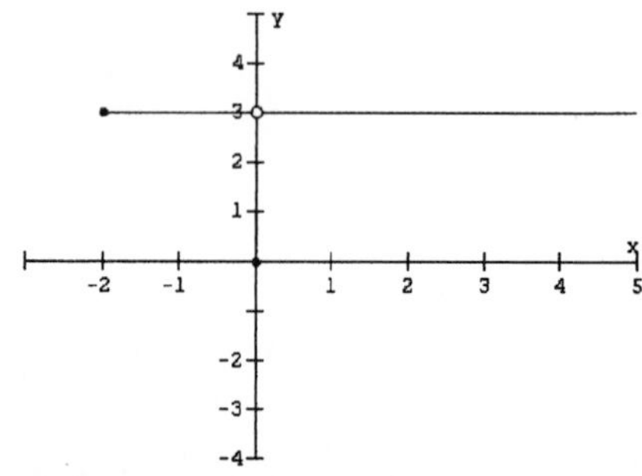

   (a) Find the value of $f(0)$.

   (b) Find the value(s) of x for which $f(x) = 0$.

   (c) Find the domain of f.

   (d) Find the range of f. Let $f(x) = 2x^2 + 3$ and $g(x) = -3x + 1$. Find the rule for the function $f - g$.

4. If $h(x) = \sqrt{3x} + 3x$, find functions f and g such that $h = g \circ f$. (The answer is not unique.)

5. Let $f(x)=3\sqrt{2x}+1$ and $g(x)=x^2-2$. Find the rule for the composite function $f\circ g$.

6. If $f(x)=\dfrac{1}{x+2}$, find and simplify $\dfrac{f(a+h)-f(a)}{h}$ $(h\neq 0)$.

7. Determine m and b so that $f(x)=mx+b$ defines a linear function of x with $f(-2)=4$ and $f(1)=3$.

8. Determine whether the given function is a polynomial function, a rational function, or some other function. State the degree of each polynomial function.

(a) $r(t)=7t^3-\pi$

(b) $f(x)=\dfrac{\sqrt{x+4}}{x-1}$

9. The demand and supply functions associated with a certain commodity are $13x - 9p + 27 = 0$ and $9x + p - 139 = 0$, respectively, where x denotes the quantity demanded in units of a thousand and p is the unit price in dollars. Find the equilibrium quantity and the equilibrium price.

10. Consider the function $f(x)=\begin{cases} x & \text{if } x<3 \\ 1 & \text{if } x=3 \\ 3 & \text{if } x>3 \end{cases}$ whose graph is shown below. Find the value of each limit, if it exists.

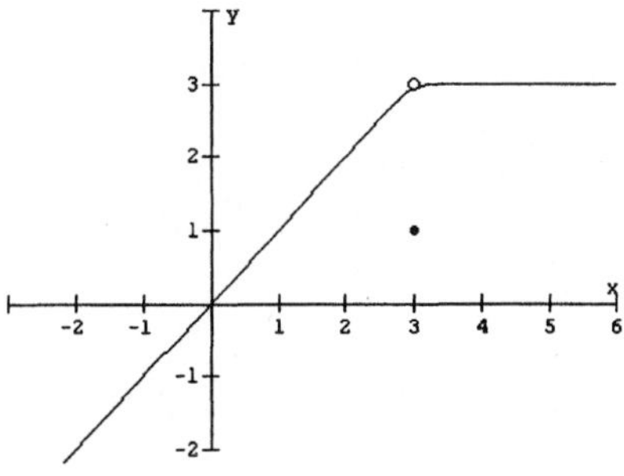

(a) $\lim\limits_{x\to 3^+} f(x)$

(b) $\lim\limits_{x\to 3^-} f(x)$

(c) $\lim_{x \to 3} f(x)$

11. Find the value of $\lim_{x \to 4} \frac{8+2x}{x}$, if it exists.

12. Find the value of $\lim_{x \to -1} \frac{x^2+4x+3}{x+1}$, if it exists.

13. The population of a certain town is given by the function $N(t) = \frac{9000t^2+100}{3t^2+10t+5}$, where t is measured in years. Determine the limit of this function as $t \to \infty$, which represents the upper limit of the town's population.

14. Find the value of $\lim_{x \to -5^+} \sqrt{5+x}$, if it exists.

15. Determine the values of x, if any at which the function $f(x) = \begin{cases} x & \text{if } x < 3 \\ 0 & \text{if } x = 3 \\ 3 & \text{if } x > 3 \end{cases}$ is discontinuous.

16. Let $f(x) = 6 + 2x^2$.
(a) Find the slope of the tangent line to the graph of $y = f(x)$ at $x = 2$.

(b) Find the equation of the tangent line to the graph of $y = f(x)$ at $x = 2$.

17. A ball is thrown straight up into the air so that its height in feet after t seconds is given by $s(t) = 128t - 16t^2$.
(a) Find the average velocity of the ball during the time interval $[2.5, 2.6]$.

(b) Find the instantaneous velocity of the ball at $t = 2.5$ seconds.

Exam 2D

Name:
Instructor:
Section:

Write your work as neatly as possible.

1. Let g be the function defined by $g(x) = x^2 + x + 5$.
   (a) Find $g(5)$.

   (b) Find $g(t-3)$.

2. Determine the domain of the function $f(x) = \dfrac{x}{3x-5}$.

3. Refer to the graph of the function f

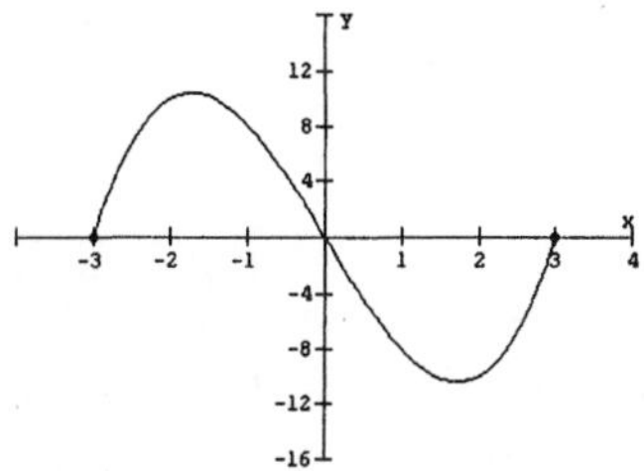

(a) Find the value of $f(0)$.

(b) Approximate the value(s) of x for which $f(x) = -2$.

(c) Find the domain of f.

(d) Find the range of f.

4. Let $f(x) = 5x^2 - 1$ and $g(x) = -5x + 2$. Find the rule for the function $\dfrac{f}{g}$.

5. Let $f(x) = 3\sqrt{2x} + 1$ and $g(x) = x^2 - 2$. Find the rule for the composite function $f \circ g$.

6. If $h(x) = \left(8x^2 - 2x\right)^{1/3}$, find functions f and g such that $h = g \circ f$ (the answer is not unique).

7. If $f(x) = \dfrac{1}{x+3}$, find and simplify $\dfrac{f(a+h) - f(a)}{h}$ $(h \neq 0)$.

8. Determine whether the equation $x + 5 = 2y^{5/2}$ defines y as a linear function of x. If so, write in the form $y = mx + b$.

9. Determine whether the given function is a polynomial function, a rational function, or some other function. State the degree of each polynomial function.

(a) $r(x) = x^{18} - 2x^{13} + 5x$

(b) $g(x) = \dfrac{\sqrt{x}}{3x^2 + 2x + 5}$

10. For the following pair of supply and demand equations, where x represents the quantity demanded in units of a thousand and p the unit price in dollars, find the equilibrium quantity and price: $5x + 3p - 117 = 0$, $7x - 3p + 69 = 0$.

11. Consider the function $f(x) = \begin{cases} -x & \text{if } x \leq 1 \\ -1 & \text{if } x > 1 \end{cases}$ whose graph is shown below. Find the value of each limit, if it exists.

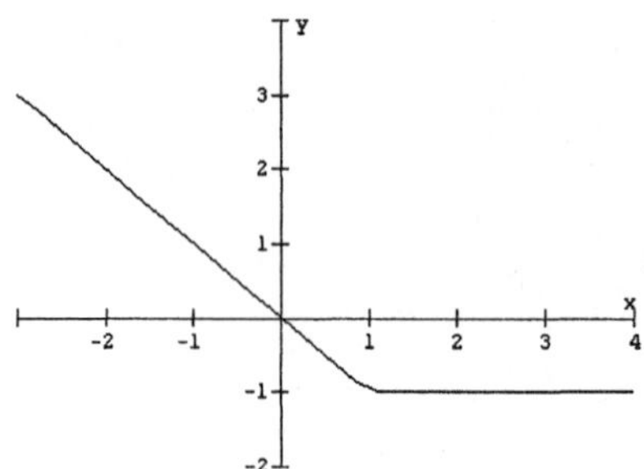

(a) $\lim\limits_{x \to 1^+} f(x)$

(b) $\lim\limits_{x \to 1^-} f(x)$

(c) $\lim\limits_{x \to 1} f(x)$

12. Find the value of $\lim\limits_{x \to -2} \dfrac{x+8}{x-1}$, if it exists.

13. Find the value of $\lim\limits_{x \to 0} \dfrac{x^2+6x}{x}$, if it exists.

14. The population of a certain town is given by the function $N(t) = \dfrac{9000t^2+150}{2t^2+t+4}$, where *t* is measured in years. Determine the limit of this function as $t \to \infty$. (This represents the upper limit of the town's population.)

15. Find the value of $\lim\limits_{x \to -3^-} \dfrac{4-x}{x+3}$, if it exists.

16. Determine the values of *x*, if any at which the function $f(x) = \begin{cases} -x & \text{if } x \le 1 \\ -1 & \text{if } x > 1 \end{cases}$ is discontinuous.

17. Let $f(x) = \dfrac{1}{2}x^2 + 3x$.
    (a) Find the slope of the tangent line to the graph of $y = f(x)$ at $x = 2$.

    (b) Find the equation of the tangent line to the graph of $y = f(x)$ at $x = 2$.

18. A ball is thrown straight up into the air so that its height in feet after *t* seconds is given by $s(t) = 128t - 16t^2$.
    (a) Find the average velocity of the ball during the time interval [3, 3.1].

    (b) Find the instantaneous velocity of the ball at $t = 3$ seconds.

Answers to Chapter 2 Exams

Exam 2A

1. $4, 6, 2a^2 - 3a + 4, 2a^2 + 3a + 4,$
   $2a^2 + a + 3$
2. $[-3, \infty)$
3. (a) 2
   (b) -4, 3
   (c) $[-4, 3]$
   (d) $[0, 2]$
4. $x^2 + x + 4$
5. $9x^2 - 6x - 1$
6. $g(x) = x^3, f(x) = 7x^2 - 2x$
7. $2a + h + 2$
8. $m = 5, b = -3$
9. (a) Other
   (b) Rational
10. $x = 1, p = \frac{14}{3}$
11. (a) 4
    (b) 4
    (c) 4
12. -1
13. 6
14. 3000
15. 0
16. There is no such value of x
17. (a) 8
    (b) $y = 8x - 9$
18. (a) 62.4 ft/s
    (b) 64 ft/s

Exam 2B

1. (a) 15
   (b) $t^2 + 4t + 3$
2. $\{x \mid x \neq -2\}$
3. (a) 4
   (b) $-\frac{4}{3}$
   (c) $[-2, 3]$
   (d) $[-2, 4]$
4. $2x^3 - 5x^2 + 2x$
5. $3x^2 - 6x - 3$
6. $g(x) = \frac{1}{\sqrt{x}} - 3x^3, f(x) = 2x + 1$
7. $2a + h$
8. No
9. (a) Polynomial (degree 3)
   (b) Rational
10. $x = 3, p = 16$
11. (a) 3
    (b) 3
    (c) 3
12. 7
13. 2
14. 2400
15. DNE
16. At $x = 3$
17. (a) -6
    (b) $y = -6x + 4$
18. (a) 46.4 ft/s
    (b) 48 ft/s

Exam 2C

1. (a) 16
   (b) $2t^2 - 3t + 2$
2. $(-\infty,-2]\cup[0,\infty)$
3. (a) 0
   (b) 0
   (c) $[-2,\infty)$
   (d) $\{0\}\cup\{3\}$
4. $g(x)=\sqrt{x}+x,\ f(x)=3x$
5. $3\sqrt{2x^2-4}+1$
6. $-\dfrac{1}{a^2+ah+4a+2h+4}$
7. $m=-\dfrac{1}{3}, b=\dfrac{10}{3}$
8. (a) Polynomial (degree 3)
   (b) Other
9. 13,021; \$21.81
10. (a) 3
    (b) 3
    (c) 3
11. 4
12. 2
13. 3000
14. 0
15. At $x=3$
16. (a) 8
    (b) $y=8x-2$
17. (a) 46.4 ft/s
    (b) 48 ft/s

Exam 2D

1. (a) 35
   (b) $t^2-5t+11$
2. $\left(-\infty,\dfrac{5}{3}\right)\cup\left(\dfrac{5}{3},\infty\right)$
3. (a) 0
   (b) 0.25
   (c) $[-3,3]$
   (d) $[-11,11]$
4. $\dfrac{5x^2-1}{-5x+2}$
5. $3\sqrt{2x^2-4}+1$
6. $g(x)=x^{1/3},\ f(x)=8x^2-2x$
7. $-\dfrac{1}{(a+3)(a+h+3)}$
8. No
9. (a) Polynomial (degree 18)
   (b) Other
10. $4,\ \dfrac{97}{3}$
11. (a) −1
    (b) −1
    (c) −1
12. −2
13. 6
14. 4500
15. $-\infty$
16. There is no such value of x
17. (a) 5
    (b) $y=5x-2$
18. (a) 30.4 ft/s
    (b) 32 ft/s

Chapter 3 ■ Differentiation

Section 3.1

1. Find the derivative of $f(x) = 22$. Answer: 0

2. Find the derivative of $f(x) = \pi^3$. Answer: 0

3. Find the derivative of $f(x) = \sqrt{5} + 3$ Answer: 0

4. Find the derivative of $f(x) = x^9$. Answer: $9x^8$

5. Find the derivative of $f(x) = -3x^4$. Answer: $-12x^3$

6. Find the derivative of $f(x) = \dfrac{3}{x^2}$. Answer: $-\dfrac{6}{x^3}$

7. Find the derivative of $f(x) = 2x^3 - 4x^2 + 3$. Answer: $6x^2 - 8x$

8. Find the derivative of $f(x) = 3x^4 - 2x^{5/3} + \sqrt{x}$. Answer: $12x^3 - \dfrac{10}{3}x^{2/3} + \dfrac{1}{2}x^{-1/2}$

9. Find the derivative of $f(x) = -0.3x^4 + 2x^2 + 4.5x$. Answer: $-1.2x^3 + 4x + 4.5$

10. Find the derivative of $f(x) = 3x^2 + \dfrac{2}{3x^2}$. Answer: $6x - \dfrac{4}{3x^3}$

11. Find the derivative of $g(t) = 5t^3 - 2t^2 + t - 3$. Answer: $15t^2 - 4t + 1$

12. Find the derivative of $s(m) = \dfrac{m^3 + 3m}{m}$. Answer: $2m$

13. Find the derivative of $f(x) = 4x^{7/3} + \dfrac{4}{\sqrt{x}}$. Answer: $\dfrac{28}{3}x^{4/3} - 2x^{-3/2}$

14. Let $f(x) = 3x^{3/2} - 2x$. Find
    (a) $f'(0)$ Answer: -2

    (b) $f'(4)$ Answer: 7

    (c) $f'(8)$ Answer: $9\sqrt{2} - 2$

15. Find the slope and an equation of the tangent line to the graph of the function $f(x) = 2x^2 + 4x + 1$ at the point $(1,7)$.
Answer: 8; $y = 8x - 1$

16. Find the slope and an equation of the tangent line to the graph of the function $f(x) = \sqrt{x} - \dfrac{2}{\sqrt{x}}$ at the point $(4,1)$.
Answer: $\dfrac{3}{8}$; $y = \dfrac{3}{8}x - \dfrac{1}{2}$

17. Let $f(x) = 2x^3 + 1$.
(a) Find the point(s) on the graph of *f* where the slope of the tangent line is equal to 6.
Answer: $(-1,-1)$, $(1,3)$
(b) Find the equation(s) of the tangent line(s) of part (a).
Answer: $y = 6x + 5$, $y = 6x - 3$

18. Let $f(x) = \dfrac{1}{3}x^3 - 4x + 5$. Find the *x*-values of the point(s) on the graph of *f* where the slope of the tangent line is equal to
(a) -2 Answer: $\pm\sqrt{2}$
(b) 0 Answer: ± 2
(c) 5 Answer: ± 3

19. A town's population is growing according to the function $P(t) = 10{,}000 + 30t + t^2$, where $P(t)$ denotes the town's population *t* months from now.
(a) How fast will the population be increasing four months from now?
Answer: 38 people per month

(b) How fast will the population be increasing twelve months from now?
Answer: 54 people per month

Section 3.1 Multiple Choice Questions

1. Find the derivative of the function $f(x)=\sqrt{5}-3$.
   - a. $\sqrt{5}$
   - b. -3
   - c. 0
   - d. $\sqrt{5}+3$

   Answer: c.

2. Find the derivative of the function $f(x)=2x^3-4x^2-100$.
   - a. $6x^2+8x-100$
   - b. $4x^2-8x$
   - c. $6x^2-8x$
   - d. $6x^2+8x$

   Answer: c.

3. Find the derivative of the function $f(x)=-2x^{5/3}+\sqrt{x}$.
   - a. $-\frac{10}{3}x^{2/3}+\frac{1}{2}x^{-1/2}$
   - b. $-\frac{10}{3}x^{2/3}+\frac{1}{2}x^{1/2}$
   - c. $\frac{10}{3}x^{2/3}+\frac{1}{2}x^{-1/2}$
   - d. $-\frac{10}{3}x^{2/3}-\frac{1}{2}x^{-1/2}$

   Answer: a.

4. Find the derivative of the function $f(x)=\frac{3}{2}x^2+\frac{1}{3x^2}$.
   - a. $3x+\frac{2}{3x^3}$
   - b. $3x+\frac{2}{3x^3}$
   - c. $6x-\frac{1}{3x^3}$
   - d. $3x-\frac{2}{3x^3}$

   Answer: d.

5. Find the derivative of the function $s(m) = \dfrac{5m^3 - 13m}{m}$.
   a. $15m$
   b. $10m$
   c. $10m - 13$
   d. $15m - 13$
   Answer: b.

6. Let $f(x) = \dfrac{1}{3}x^3 - 4x - 7$. Find the x-values of the point(s) on the graph where the slope of the tangent line is equal to 0.
   a. ± 2
   b. $\pm \dfrac{1}{2}$
   c. 0 and 2
   d. $\pm \dfrac{1}{4}$
   Answer: a.

7. Find the derivative of the function $f(x) = x^3 - 10x - 3$ at $x = 1$.
   a. 13
   b. -7
   c. 7
   d. 9
   Answer: b.

8. Let $f(x) = 2x^3 + 1$. Find the x-values of the point(s) on the graph where the slope of the tangent line is equal to 24.
   a. ± 2
   b. $\pm \dfrac{1}{2}$
   c. $\pm \sqrt{24}$
   d. $\pm \dfrac{1}{\sqrt{24}}$
   Answer: a.

9. Find the slope and an equation of the tangent line to the function $f(x) = x^2 + 4x$ at the point (1, 5).
   a. 6; $y = 6x - 1$
   b. 6; $y = 6x - 11$
   c. 6; $y = 6x + 1$
   d. 6; $y = 6x + 11$
   Answer: a.

10. Let $f(x) = 3x^2 - 4x$. Find the value of x for which $f'(x) = 2x$.

a. $\frac{1}{2}$
b. -1
c. 1
d. $-\frac{1}{2}$

Answer: c.

11. Let $P(x) = -x^2 + x - \frac{1}{10}$. Find the value of x for which $f'(x) = -x^2$.

a. ± 1
b. 1
c. -1
d. 3

Answer: b.

12. The demand function for the Luminar desk lamp is given by $p = f(x) = -0.1x^2 - 0.4x + 35$, where x is the quantity demanded (measured in thousands) and p is the unit price in dollars. Find $f'(x)$.

a. $f'(x) = -0.2x + 34.6$
b. $f'(x) = -0.2x + 0.4$
c. $f'(x) = -0.2x - 0.4$
d. $f'(x) = -0.2x + 35$

Answer: c.

13. If a function f is differentiable at $x = 7$, then $f'(7)$ is:

a. The average value of the function f over the interval [0, 7].
b. The instantaneous rate of change of f at $x = 7$.
c. The slope of the tangent line at the point $(7, f(7))$ on the graph of f.
d. Both choices b and c are correct.

Answer: d.

14. A particle moves along a straight path where the distance S, in feet, traveled after t seconds is given by $S(t) = t^2 + 3t + 1$. Find the velocity of the particle at $t = 4$ seconds.

a. 27 ft/sec
b. 11 ft/sec
c. 12 ft/sec
d. 19 ft/sec

Answer: b.

15. What is the value of k if $g(x) = x^2 + kx - 5$ and $g'(4) = 5$.

a. $-\frac{3}{4}$
b. -3
c. 3
d. $\frac{3}{2}$

Answer: b.

16. The volume of a spherical cancerous tumor is given by the function $V(r) = \frac{4}{3}\pi r^3$, where r is the radius of the tumor in centimeters. Find the rate of change in the volume of the tumor when $r = \frac{3}{2}\text{cm}$.

a. $9\pi\ \text{cm}^3/\text{cm}$
b. $\frac{9\pi}{2}\ \text{cm}^3/\text{cm}$
c. $\frac{4\pi}{9}\ \text{cm}^3/\text{cm}$
d. $\frac{9\pi}{4}\ \text{cm}^3/\text{cm}$

Answer: a.

Section 3.2

1. Find the derivative of the function $f(x) = x^2(2x-3)$. Answer: $6x^2 - 6x$

2. Find the derivative of the function $f(x) = (x^2+2)(x^2-2x+4)$.
Answer: $4x^3 - 6x^2 + 12x - 4$

3. Find the derivative of the function $f(x) = \dfrac{x+2}{x-1}$. Answer: $\dfrac{-3}{(x-1)^2}$

4. Find the derivative of the function $f(t) = \dfrac{t}{t+3}$. Answer: $\dfrac{3}{(t+3)^2}$

5. Find the derivative of the function $f(x) = \dfrac{x}{x^2+x+1}$. Answer: $\dfrac{-x^2+1}{(x^2+x+1)^2}$

6. Find the derivative of the function $f(x) = \left(x^2 + \dfrac{1}{x^2}\right)(2x+4)$.

Answer: $6x^2 + 8x - \dfrac{2}{x^2} - \dfrac{8}{x^3}$

7. Find the derivative of the function $f(x) = (x^2+1)\left(2x^2 - \dfrac{1}{x}\right)$.

Answer: $8x^3 + 4x + \dfrac{1}{x^2} - 1$

8. Find the derivative of the function $f(x) = \dfrac{x+3}{x+2}$. Answer: $\dfrac{-1}{(x+2)^2}$

9. Find the derivative of the function $f(x) = \dfrac{x+\sqrt{2}x}{4x+1}$. Answer: $\dfrac{1+\sqrt{2}}{(4x+1)^2}$

10. Find the derivative of the function $f(x) = \dfrac{x^3+2}{x^2-3}$. Answer: $\dfrac{x^4 - 9x^2 - 4x}{(x^2-3)^2}$

11. Find the derivative of the function $f(x) = \dfrac{1}{4}x^4 + (x^2-1)(x^2-2x+4) + 4$.
Answer: $5x^3 - 6x^2 + 6x + 2$

12. Find the derivative of the function $f(x) = \dfrac{u}{u^2-1}$. Answer: $-\dfrac{u^2+1}{(u^2-1)^2}$

13. Find the derivative of the function $s(t) = \dfrac{t-1}{2t^2+5}$. Answer: $\dfrac{-2t^2-4t+5}{(2t^2+5)^2}$

14. Find the derivative of the function $f(x)=(x^3+x^2-x-1)(x^2+3)$.
Answer: $5x^4+4x^3+6x^2+4x-3$

15. Let $H(x)=f(x)g(x)$, with f and g differentiable at $x=2$. Find $H'(2)$ if $f(2)=4, f'(2)=3, g(2)=-2,$ and $g'(2)=5$.
Answer: 14

16. Let $H(x)=\dfrac{f(x)}{g(x)}$, with f and g differentiable at $x=2$. Find $H'(2)$ if $f(2)=4, f'(2)=3, g(2)=-2,$ and $g'(2)=5$.
Answer: $-\dfrac{13}{2}$

17. Let $f(x)=(2x+1)(x^2-2)$. Find
(a) $f'(0)$ Answer: -4
(b) $f'(2)$ Answer: 24
(c) $f'(4)$ Answer: 100

18. Find the slope and an equation of the tangent line to the graph of the function $f(x)=(x+2)(2x^2+1)$ at the point $(-1,3)$.
Answer: -1; $y=-x+2$

19. Find the slope and an equation of the tangent line to the graph of the function $f(x)=\dfrac{2x-1}{2x+1}$ at the point $\left(2,\dfrac{3}{5}\right)$.
Answer: $\dfrac{4}{25}$; $y=\dfrac{4}{25}x+\dfrac{7}{25}$

20. Find the point(s) on the graph of $f(x)=\dfrac{x}{x^2+x+4}$ where the tangent line is horizontal.
Answer: $\left(-2,-\dfrac{1}{3}\right)$, $\left(2,\dfrac{1}{5}\right)$

21. Find the point(s) on the graph of $f(x)=3x^2-4x$ where the tangent line is horizontal.
Answer: $\left(\dfrac{2}{3},-\dfrac{4}{3}\right)$

22. Let $f(x)=\frac{1}{3}(x^2+1)(x+2)$. Find the point(s) on the graph of f where the slope of the tangent line is equal to

(a) 0 Answer: $\left(-1,\frac{2}{3}\right), \left(-\frac{1}{3},\frac{50}{81}\right)$

(b) 7 Answer: $\left(-\frac{10}{3},-\frac{436}{81}\right), \left(2,\frac{20}{3}\right)$

Section 3.2 Multiple Choice Questions

1. Find the derivative of the function $f(x)=(x-1)(x+1)$.
   a. $2x-1$
   b. $2x+2$
   c. $2x$
   d. $2x+1$
   Answer: c.

2. Find the derivative of the function $f(x)=\left(x^3+3\right)\left(x^2-x+5\right)$.
   a. $5x^4-4x^3+15x^2+6x$
   b. $5x^4-4x^3+12x^2+6x-3$
   c. $5x^4-4x^3+15x^2+6x-3$
   d. $5x^4+4x^3-5x^2+6x-3$
   Answer: c.

3. Find the derivative of the function $f(x)=(5x^2+1)(2\sqrt{x}+1)$.
   a. $\dfrac{25x^2\sqrt{x}+10x^2+\sqrt{x}}{x}$
   b. $\dfrac{25x^2\sqrt{x}+10x^2+\sqrt{x}}{\sqrt{x}}$
   c. $\dfrac{25x^2\sqrt{x}+10x^2+1}{x}$
   d. $\dfrac{25x^2+10x^2+1}{x}$
   Answer: a.

4. Find the derivative of the function $f(x) = (x^3 - 2x + 5)\left(2 + \frac{3}{x}\right)$.

   a. $\dfrac{6x^4 + 6x^3 + 4x^2 - 15}{x^2}$

   b. $\dfrac{6x^4 + 9x^3 - 4x^2 - 15}{x^2}$

   c. $\dfrac{6x^4 + 6x^3 - 8x^2 - 15}{x^2}$

   d. $\dfrac{6x^4 + 6x^3 - 4x^2 - 15}{x^2}$

   Answer: d.

5. Find the derivative of the function $s(m) = \dfrac{1}{(m+4)}$.

   a. $\dfrac{1}{(m+4)^2}$

   b. $-\dfrac{1}{(m+4)^2}$

   c. $-\dfrac{4}{(m+4)^2}$

   d. $\dfrac{4}{(m+4)^2}$

   Answer: b.

6. Find the derivative of the function $f(x) = \dfrac{x^2 - 5}{x+2}$.

   a. $\dfrac{x^2 + 4x + 5}{(x+2)^2}$

   b. $-\dfrac{x^2 + 4x + 5}{(x+2)^2}$

   c. $\dfrac{x^2 - 2x + 5}{(x+2)^2}$

   d. $\dfrac{x^2 - 4x + 3}{(x+2)^2}$

   Answer: a.

7. Find the derivative of the function $f(x)=\frac{x^2+1}{\sqrt{x}}$ at $x = 1$.

a. 2
b. 1
c. 5
d. 7

Answer: b.

8. Find the slope of the tangent line of the function $f(x)=\frac{x+1}{x^2+4}$ at $x = 0$.

a. 4
b. $-\frac{3}{4}$
c. $-\frac{1}{4}$
d. $\frac{1}{4}$

Answer: d.

9. Find the slope and an equation of the tangent line to the function $f(x)=(x^3+2)(3x^2+x+2)$ at the point (0, 4).

a. 2; $y=2x+4$
b. -2; $y=-2x+4$
c. 4; $y=4x-4$
d. -4; $y=-4x+4$

Answer: a.

10. Find the slope of the tangent line of the function $f(x)=\left(x^3+2\right)\left(x^2+1\right)$ at the point $(1,6)$.

a. 10
b. -1
c. 12
d. 24

Answer: c.

11. The concentration of a certain drug (in gm/cm^3) in a patient's blood stream t hr after injection is given by $C(t)=\frac{0.4t}{t^2+10}$. Find the rate at which the concentration of the drug is changing with respect to time.

a. $\frac{2\left(t^2-10\right)}{5\left(t^2+10\right)^2}$ $\text{gm/cm}^3\text{/hr}$

b. $\dfrac{2\left(10-t^2\right)}{5\left(t^2+10\right)^2}$ gm/cm^3/hr

c. $\dfrac{10-t^2}{5\left(t^2+10\right)^2}$ gm/cm^3/hr

d. $\dfrac{10-t^2}{\left(t^2+10\right)^2}$ gm/cm^3/hr

Answer: b.

12. A spherical balloon is being inflated. Its radius in centimeters after t minutes is given by $r(t)=3\sqrt[3]{t+6}$ where $0\leq t\leq 9$. Estimate the instantaneous rate of change of r with respect to t at $t = 3$.

a. 6.2403 cm/sec

b. 0.2311 cm/sec

c. 0.7889 cm/sec

d. 4.3267 cm/sec

Answer: b

13. Let $f(x)=\dfrac{x}{x^2+5}$. Find the x values of f where the tangent line is horizontal.

a. $\pm\sqrt{5}$

b. ± 5

c. ± 3

d. $\pm\sqrt{3}$

Answer: a.

Section 3.3

1. Find the derivative of the function $f(x) = (3x+1)^4$. Answer: $12(3x+1)^3$

2. Find the derivative of the function $f(t) = 3(t^2+1)^5$. Answer: $30t(t^2+1)^4$

3. Find the derivative of the function $f(m) = (3m^2+2)^3 + (4m-6)^5$.

   Answer: $18m(3m^2+2)^2 + 20(4m-6)^4$

4. Find the derivative of the function $f(x) = (3x+1)^{-3}$. Answer: $-9(3x+1)^{-4}$

5. Find the derivative of the function $f(x) = (4x^2+3x-1)^{3/2}$.

   Answer: $\frac{3}{2}(8x+3)\sqrt{4x^2+3x-1}$

6. Find the derivative of the function $f(x) = \sqrt[4]{1+x^2}$. Answer: $\frac{1}{2}x(1+x^2)^{-3/4}$

7. Find the derivative of the function $f(x) = \frac{3}{(x^2+1)^3}$. Answer: $-18x(1+x^2)^{-4}$

8. Find the derivative of the function $f(x) = \frac{2x}{\sqrt{3x^2+1}}$. Answer: $\frac{2}{(3x^2+1)^{3/2}}$

9. Find the derivative of the function $f(t) = \left(5+\frac{2}{t}\right)^3$. Answer: $-\frac{6}{t^2}\left(5+\frac{2}{t}\right)^2$

10. Find the derivative of the function $f(x) = \frac{2}{(3x^3+x)^{5/2}}$.

    Answer: $-5(9x^2+1)(3x^3+x)^{-7/2}$

11. Find the point(s) on the graph of $f(x) = \frac{\sqrt{x}}{x+2}$ where the tangent line is horizontal.

    Answer: $\left(2, \frac{\sqrt{2}}{4}\right)$

12. Find the derivative of the function $f(t) = \left(3t^3 + 2t^2 - 2t + 3\right)^{-2}$.

Answer: $-2\left(9t^2 + 4t - 2\right)\left(3t^3 + 2t^2 - 2t + 3\right)^{-3}$

13. Let $H(x) = \left(f(x)\right)^2$, with f differentiable at $x = 2$. Find $H'(2)$ if $f(2) = 4$ and $f'(2) = 3$.

Answer: 24

14. Let $H(x) = \sqrt{f(x)}$, with f differentiable at $x = 2$. Find $H'(2)$ if $f(2) = 4$ and $f'(2) = -8$.

Answer: -2

15. Find the derivative of the function $f(t) = \left(t^{-2} - t^{-3}\right)^4$.

Answer: $4\left(t^{-2} - t^{-3}\right)^3\left(-2t^{-3} + 3t^{-4}\right)$

16. Find the derivative of the function $f(x) = (3x - 2)^{-3/2} + \left(x^2 + 1\right)^{3/2}$.

Answer: $-\frac{9}{2}(3x - 2)^{-5/2} + 3x\sqrt{x^2 + 1}$

17. Find the derivative of the function $f(x) = (x + 1)^3(2x - 1)^5$.

Answer: $3(x + 1)^2(2x - 1)^5 + 10(x + 1)^3(2x - 1)^4$

18. Find the derivative of the function $f(x) = \left(\frac{x - 1}{x + 2}\right)^4$.

Answer: $12\left(\frac{x - 1}{x + 2}\right)^3 \frac{1}{(x + 2)^2}$

19. Find the derivative of the function $f(x) = \sqrt{\frac{x + 2}{3x - 1}}$.

Answer: $-\frac{7}{2}\left(\frac{x + 2}{3x - 1}\right)^{-1/2}(3x - 1)^{-2}$

20. Find the derivative of the function $f(x) = \frac{x}{\left(x^2 + 3\right)^4}$. Answer: $\frac{\left(-7x^2 + 3\right)}{\left(x^2 + 3\right)^5}$

21. Find $\frac{dy}{du}$, $\frac{du}{dx}$, and $\frac{dy}{dx}$ if $y = u^{-4/3}$ and $u = x^2 - 2x + 2$.

Answer:
$\frac{dy}{du} = -\frac{4}{3}u^{-7/3}$, $\frac{du}{dx} = 2x - 2$, and $\frac{dy}{dx} = -\frac{4}{3}\left(x^2 - 2x + 2\right)^{-7/3}(2x - 2)$

22. Find $\frac{dy}{dx}$ if $y = u^5$ and $u = 3x^2 + 7x$. Answer: $\frac{dy}{dx} = 5\left(3x^2 + 7x\right)^4(6x + 7)$

23. Find $\frac{dy}{dx}$ if $y = \sqrt{u}$ and $u = 13x - 3$. Answer: $\frac{dy}{dx} = \frac{13}{2\sqrt{13x - 3}}$

24. Find $\frac{dy}{dx}$ if $y = \sqrt[3]{u + 7}$ and $u = 8$. Answer: 0

Section 3.3 Multiple Choice Questions

1. Find the derivative of the function $f(x) = \sqrt{3x^2 - x}$.

a. $-\frac{6x+1}{2\sqrt{3x^2 - x}}$

b. $\frac{6x-6}{2\sqrt{3x^2 - x}}$

c. $\frac{6x-1}{\sqrt{3x^2 - x}}$

d. $\frac{6x-1}{2\sqrt{3x^2 - x}}$

Answer: d.

2. Find the derivative of the function $f(x) = \frac{5}{\left(x^2 + 2\right)^4}$.

a. $\frac{40x}{\left(x^2 + 2\right)^5}$

b. $-\frac{20x}{\left(x^2 + 2\right)^5}$

c. $-\dfrac{40x}{\left(x^2+2\right)^5}$

d. $-\dfrac{5x}{\left(x^2+2\right)^5}$

Answer: c.

3. Find the derivative of the function $f(x)=\dfrac{1}{\sqrt{5x^2-7}}$.

a. $-\dfrac{x}{\left(5x^2-7\right)^{3/2}}$

b. $\dfrac{5x}{\left(5x^2-7\right)^{3/2}}$

c. $-\dfrac{5x}{\left(5x^2-7\right)^{3/2}}$

d. $\dfrac{10x}{\left(5x^2-7\right)^{3/2}}$

Answer: c.

4. Find the derivative of the function $g(x)=\dfrac{4x}{\sqrt{x^2+1}}$.

a. $\dfrac{8}{\sqrt{(x^2+1)^3}}$

b. $\dfrac{4}{\sqrt{(x^2+1)^5}}$

c. $\dfrac{4}{\sqrt{x^2+1}}$

d. $\dfrac{4}{\sqrt{(x^2+1)^3}}$

Answer: d.

5. Find the derivative of the function $s(m)=\left(3m^2+5m-1\right)^{-4}$.

a. $-\dfrac{4(6m+5)}{\left(3m^2+5m-1\right)^6}$

b. $-\dfrac{4(6m+5)}{\left(3m^2+5m-1\right)^5}$

c. $\dfrac{4(6m+5)}{(3m^2+5m-1)^5}$

d. $-\dfrac{2(6m+5)}{(3m^2+5m-1)^5}$

Answer: b.

6. Find the derivative of the function $f(x)=\left(x^{-1}+x^{-2}\right)^3$.

a. $-\dfrac{3(x+2)(x+1)^2}{x^7}$

b. $\dfrac{3(x+2)(x+1)^2}{x^7}$

c. $\dfrac{3(x+2)(x+1)^2}{x^8}$

d. $-\dfrac{3(x+2)(x+1)^2}{x^8}$

Answer: a.

7. Find the derivative of the function $f(x)=\left(\dfrac{x}{x+1}\right)^{3/2}$ at $x = 3$.

a. $\dfrac{3\sqrt{3}}{4}$

b. $\dfrac{\sqrt{3}}{64}$

c. $\dfrac{3\sqrt{3}}{32}$

d. $\dfrac{3\sqrt{3}}{64}$

Answer: d.

8. Find the slope of the tangent line to the graph of the function $f(t)=\dfrac{\sqrt{t+1}}{\sqrt{t^4+1}}$ at $t = 0$.

a. 2

b. $-\dfrac{1}{2}$

c. $-\dfrac{1}{4}$

d. $\dfrac{1}{2}$

Answer: d.

9. Find the slope and an equation of the tangent line to the graph of the function $f(x) = (x+1)(x^2-1)^2$ at the point (0, 1).
   a. $-1;\ y = -x+1$
   b. $1;\ y = x+1$
   c. $1;\ y = x-1$
   d. $-1;\ y = -x-1$
   Answer: b.

10. Find the slope of the tangent line to the graph of the function $f(x) = x\sqrt{3x^2+6}$ at the point $(1,\ 3)$.
   a. 7
   b. –4
   c. 4
   d. $4\sqrt{3}$
   Answer: c.

11. Let $y = u^{5/3}$ and $u = 3x^2+1$. Find $\dfrac{dy}{dx}$.
   a. $5x\left(3x^2+1\right)^{2/3}$
   b. $10x\left(3x^2+1\right)^{2/3}$
   c. $\dfrac{5}{3}x\left(3x^2+1\right)^{2/3}$
   d. $10\left(3x^2+1\right)^{2/3}$
   Answer: b.

12. The population of Americans age 55 and over as a percent of the total population in a certain city is approximated by the function $f(t) = 11(0.9t+10)^{0.3}$, $0 \le t \le 20$, where t is measured in years, with $t = 0$ corresponding to the year 2000. At what rate was the percent of Americans age 55 and over changing at the beginning of 2000?
   a. 0.42365 per year
   b. 0.59259 per year
   c. 0.95127 per year
   d. 0.23562 per year
   Answer: b.

13. According to a joint study conducted by Oxnard's Environmental Management department and a state government agency, the concentration of CO in the air due to

automobile exhaust y yr from now is given by $y = C(t) = 0.01\left(0.2t^2 + 4t + 64\right)^{2/3}$ parts per million. Find the rate at which the level of CO is changing with respect to time.

a. $\frac{8}{3}\left(0.2x^2+4x+64\right)^{-\frac{1}{3}}\left(0.4x+4\right)$ or $\frac{\sqrt[3]{5}\left(x+10\right)}{375\sqrt[3]{x^2+20x+320}}$ ppm/yr

b. $\frac{2}{3}\left(0.2x^2+4x+64\right)^{-\frac{1}{3}}\left(0.4x+4\right)$ or $\frac{\sqrt[3]{5}\left(x+10\right)}{375\sqrt[3]{x^2+20x+320}}$ ppm/yr

c. $\frac{0.02}{3}\left(0.2x^2+4x+64\right)^{-\frac{1}{3}}\left(0.4x+4\right)$ or $\frac{\sqrt[3]{5}\left(x+10\right)}{375\sqrt[3]{x^2+20x+320}}$ ppm/yr

d. $\frac{\sqrt{5}\left(x+10\right)}{\sqrt[3]{x^2+20x+320}}$ ppm/yr

Answer: c.

14. Let $f(x) = \frac{2x}{\left(x^2+5\right)^2}$. Find the x values where the tangent line is horizontal to the graph of f.

a. $\pm\frac{\sqrt{15}}{3}$

b. ± 5

c. $\pm\frac{5}{3}$

d. $\pm\sqrt{3}$

Answer: a.

15. If $f(x) = \sqrt{x^3+5x+121}\left(x^2+x+11\right)$, then $f'(0) =$

a. $\frac{5}{2}$

b. $\frac{27}{2}$

c. $\frac{247}{2}$

d. 22

Answer: b.

16. Compute the derivative of $g(x) = x^3\left(2+\sqrt{x}\right)$ at $x = 4$.

a. 36

b. 152

c. 17

d. 208

Answer: d.

17. An equation of the line normal to the graph of $y = \sqrt{3x^2 + 2x}$ at (2, 4) is

a. $-4x + y = 20$

b. $4x + 7y = 20$

c. $-7x + 4y = 2$

d. $4x + 7y = 36$

Answer: d.

Section 3.4

1. The cost C, in dollars, for a company to produce a total of x refrigerators is $C(x) = 30{,}000 + 700x - 0.01x^2$.
   (a) Find the actual cost incurred in producing the 150th refrigerator.
   Answer: \$697.01
   (b) Find the marginal cost when $x = 149$
   Answer: \$697.02

2. The cost, in dollars, for a company to produce a total of x souvenirs is $C(x) = 100 + 3.25x - 0.002x^2$.
   (a) Find the actual cost incurred in producing the 50th souvenir.
   Answer: \$3.05
   (b) Find the marginal cost when $x = 49$
   Answer: \$3.05

3. The cost, in dollars, for a company to produce a total of x shirts is $C(x) = 340 + 8.25x - 0.008x^2$.
   (a) Find the actual cost incurred in producing the 100th shirt.
   Answer: \$6.66
   (b) Find the marginal cost when $x = 99$
   Answer: \$6.67

4. The cost, in dollars, for a company to produce a total of x personal stereos is $C(x) = 20{,}000 + 120x$.
   (a) Find the average cost function $\overline{C}$. Answer: $\overline{C}(x) = \dfrac{20{,}000}{x} + 120$
   (b) Find the marginal average cost function $\overline{C}'$ Answer: $-\dfrac{20{,}000}{x^2}$

5. The weekly demand for apartments in a large city is $p = -0.5x + 1200$, where p denotes the monthly rent for the apartment in dollars and x denotes the number of apartments rented. The monthly cost associated with renting a total of x apartments is $C = 30{,}000 + 400x$.
   (a) Find the revenue function R. Answer: $R(x) = 1200x - 0.5x^2$
   (b) Find the profit function P. Answer: $P(x) = -30{,}000 + 800x - 0.5x^2$
   (c) Find the marginal profit function P'. Answer: $P'(x) = 800 - x$

6. For the demand equation $x = -\dfrac{4}{3}p + 15$, compute the elasticity of demand and determine whether the demand is elastic, unitary, or inelastic if $p = 8$.
   Answer: $-\dfrac{4p}{4p - 45}$; elastic

7. For the demand equation $x+\frac{1}{4}p-15=0$, compute the elasticity of demand and determine whether the demand is elastic, unitary, or inelastic if $p=20$.

Answer: $-\frac{p}{p-60}$; inelastic

8. For the demand equation $p=324-x^2$, compute the elasticity of demand and determine whether the demand is elastic, unitary, or inelastic if $p=216$.

Answer: $-\frac{p}{2p-648}$; unitary

9. A certain moth population *P* can be approximated by $P(t)=3\sqrt{t^2+2t}\quad(t\geq 2)$, where *t* is measured in days. Find the rate at which the population is changing at the end of 6 days.
Answer: ≈ 3 moths/day

10. A child is flying a kite at a height of 40 ft, which is moving horizontally at a rate of 3 ft/sec. If the string is taut, at what rate is the string being paid out when the length of the string released is 50 ft?
Answer: 1.8 ft/sec

11. A travel company plans to sponsor a special tour to Asia. There will be accommodations for no more than 40 people, and the tour will be canceled if no more than 10 people book reservations. Based on the past experience, the manager determines that if *n* people book the tour, the profit (in dollars) may be modeled by the function:
$P(n)=-n^3+27.6n^2+970.2n-4{,}235$. For what size tour group is the profit maximized?
Answer: When 29 people book the tour and the profit is $22,723.40.

Section 3.4 Multiple Choice Questions

1. Suppose the total cost in dollars incurred each week by Polaraire for manufacturing *x* refrigerators is given by the total cost function
$C(x)=1000+300x-0.5x^2,\ (0\leq x\leq 400)$. Find the rate of change of the total cost function with respect to *x* when *x* = 200.
a. $1100
b. $400
c. $300
d. $100
Answer: d.

2. The total cost of producing x units of a certain commodity is given by $C(x) = x^2 + 6x - 17$. Find the average cost function.
   a. $\dfrac{2x+6}{x}$
   b. $2x+6$
   c. $\dfrac{x^2+6x-17}{x}$
   d. $\dfrac{x^2+6x-17}{x^2}$

   Answer: c.

3. If $C(x)$ is the total cost of producing x units of a product, then $C'(x)$ represents:
   a. the rate of change of units produced with respect to cost
   b. the average cost of producing x items
   c. the approximate cost of producing one additional item after the xth item is produced
   d. the number of units, x, to minimize cost

   Answer: c.

4. Find the marginal cost function for the cost function given by $C(x) = 1423 + 32x - 0.6x^2$.
   a. $C'(x) = 32 - 12x$
   b. $C'(x) = 1.2x + 32$
   c. $C'(x) = \dfrac{-1.2}{x} + 32$
   d. $C'(x) = -1.2x + 32$

   Answer: d.

5. A DVD manufacture company finds its cost function is $C(x) = 200\sqrt{x} + 600$ dollars, where x is the number of DVD players produced. Estimate the cost of producing the 501th DVD player.
   a. \$4.47
   b. \$1.58
   c. \$17.89
   d. \$10.14

   Answer: a.

6. If the revenue function is $R(x) = 5x - 0.001x^2$ dollars and the cost function is $C(x) = 1.2x + 1040$ dollars, where x is the number of units produced. How many units should be produced to make the marginal cost equal to the marginal revenue?
   a. 3100
   b. 1040
   c. 5310
   d. 1900

Answer: d.

7. The cost, in dollars, of producing x thermostats is given by $C(x) = 0.04x^2 - 18x + 1000$ and the revenue, in dollars, from the sale of x thermostats is $R(x) = 0.03x^2 - 6x$. Find the marginal profit function.

a. $P'(x) = 0.02x - 12$

b. $P'(x) = 12 - 0.02x$

c. $P'(x) = 12 - 0.01x$

d. $P'(x) = 12 - 0.08x$

Answer: b.

8. The cost, in dollars, of producing x snow blowers is given by $C(x) = 200 + 8x - \frac{x^2}{3}$. Find the marginal cost function.

a. $8 + \frac{2}{3}x$

b. $8 - \frac{2}{3}x$

c. $208 - \frac{2}{3}x$

d. $192 - \frac{2}{3}x$

Answer: b.

9. The quantity of Sicard wristwatches demanded each month is related to the unit price by the equation $p = 170 - \frac{x}{100}$, $(0 \le x \le 15{,}000)$, where p is measured in dollars. Find the revenue function.

a. $R(x) = 170x - \frac{x^2}{100}$

b. $R(x) = -\frac{1}{100}$

c. $R(x) = 170x + \frac{x^2}{100}$

d. $R(x) = -170x + \frac{x^2}{100}$

Answer: a.

10. Suppose a certain economy's consumption function is $C(x) = 0.826x^{1.2} + 21.78$, where $C(x)$ and x are measured in billions of dollars. Find the marginal propensity to consume when $x = 12$. (Hint: $\frac{dC}{dx}$ is called the marginal propensity to consume.)

a. 0.95 billion/billion dollars
b. 2.12 billion/billion dollars
c. 1.23 billion/billion dollars
d. 1.63 billion/billion dollars

Answer: d.

11. The demand function for a certain make of exercise bicycle sold exclusively through cable television is $p = \sqrt{9 - 0.02x}, \ (0 \le x \le 450)$, where p is the unit price in hundreds of dollars and x is the quantity demanded per week. Compute the elasticity of demand.

a. $\frac{p^2}{9 - p^2}$

b. $\frac{2p^2}{9 - p^2}$

c. $\frac{2p^2}{p^2 - 9}$

d. $\frac{2p^2}{18 - p^2}$

Answer: b

12. The weekly demand for Pulsar VCRs is given by the demand equation $p = -0.03x + 400, \ (0 \le x \le 15{,}000)$, where p is the unit price in dollars and x is the quantity demanded per week. Find the revenue function.

a. $R(x) = -0.03x$
b. $R(x) = -0.03x^2 + 400x$
c. $R(x) = -0.03 + 400x$
d. $R(x) = 0.03x^2 - 400x$

Answer: b.

Section 3.5

1. Find the first and second derivatives of $f(x) = 2x^3 - 4x^2 + 7$.
   Answer: $6x^2 - 8x,\ 12x - 8$

2. Find the first and second derivatives of $f(x) = 2x^4 - 3x^{5/3} + \sqrt{x}$.
   Answer: $8x^3 - 5x^{2/3} + \frac{1}{2}x^{-1/2},\ 24x^2 - \frac{10}{3}x^{-1/3} - \frac{1}{4}x^{-3/2}$

3. Find the first and second derivatives of $f(x) = -0.2x^4 + 8.1x^2 + 24.5x$.
   Answer: $-0.8x^3 + 16.2x + 24.5,\ -2.4x^2 + 16.2$

4. Find the first and second derivatives of $f(x) = x^2(3x - 1)$.
   Answer: $9x^2 - 2x,\ 18x - 2$

5. Find the first and second derivatives of $f(x) = (x^2 + 1)(x^2 - 2x + 4)$.
   Answer: $4x^3 - 6x^2 + 10x - 2,\ 12x^2 - 12x + 10$

6. Find the first and second derivatives of $f(x) = (x^2 + 2)\left(3x^2 - \frac{1}{x}\right)$.
   Answer: $12x^3 + 12x - 1 + 2x^{-2},\ 36x^2 + 12 - 4x^{-3}$

7. Find the first and second derivatives of $f(x) = \frac{x+4}{x+7}$.
   Answer: $\frac{3}{(x+7)^2},\ -\frac{6}{(x+7)^3}$

8. Find the first and second derivatives of $f(t) = 2(t^2 - 2)^4$.
   Answer: $16t(t^2 - 2)^3,\ 96t^2(t^2 - 2)^2 + 16(t^2 - 2)^3$

9. Find the first and second derivatives of $f(x) = (2x + 3)^{-3}$.
   Answer: $-6(2x + 3)^{-4},\ 48(2x + 3)^{-5}$

10. Find the first and second derivatives of $f(x) = (3x^2 + 4x - 2)^{3/2}$.
    Answer: $3(3x + 2)\sqrt{3x^2 + 4x - 2},\ 6(9x^2 + 12x - 1)(3x^2 + 4x - 2)^{-1/2}$

11. Find the first and second derivatives of $f(x)=\left(\frac{x-2}{x-3}\right)^4$.

Answer: $-4\frac{(x-2)^3}{(x-3)^5}$, $4\frac{(x-2)^2(2x-1)}{(x-3)^6}$

12. Find the second derivative of $f(x)=-\frac{9}{2}(x+7)^{2/3}$. Answer: $(x+7)^{-4/3}$

13. Find the second derivative of $s(t)=\frac{t+2}{t-3}$. Answer: $\frac{10}{(t-3)^3}$

14. Find the second derivative of $f(x)=4\sqrt{x+1}$. Answer: $-(x+1)^{-3/2}$

15. Find the third derivative of $f(x)=\frac{3}{x^3}$. Answer: $-180x^{-6}$

16. Let $f(x)=3x^3-2x^2+6x-1$. Find
(a) the first derivative of f. Answer: $9x^2-4x+6$

(b) the second derivative of f. Answer: $18x-4$

(c) the third derivative of f. Answer: 18

Section 3.5 Multiple Choice Questions

1. Find the second derivative of the function $C(x)=1000x+300x^2-0.5x^4$.
   a. $C(x)=1000+600x-2x^3$
   b. $C(x)=600x-6x^2$
   c. $C(x)=600-2x^2$
   d. $C(x)=600-6x^2$

   Answer: d.

2. Find the third derivative of the function $f(x)=x^2+6x-17$.
   a. $2x$
   b. $2x+6$
   c. 0
   d. 2

   Answer: c.

3. Find the third derivative of the function $g(x) = x^{5/2} + \frac{1}{3}x^3$.

a. $-\frac{15}{8}x^{-1/2} + 2$

b. $\frac{5}{8}x^{-1/2} + 2$

c. $\frac{15}{8}x^{-1/2} + 2$

d. $\frac{15}{4}x^{-1/2} + 2$

Answer: c.

4. Find the second derivative of the function $C(x) = \left(2x^2 + 3\right)^{3/2}$.

a. $\frac{6\left(2x^2+3\right)}{\sqrt{2x^2+3}}$

b. $\frac{2\left(4x^2+3\right)}{\sqrt{2x^2+3}}$

c. $\frac{12\left(4x^2+3\right)}{\sqrt{2x^2+3}}$

d. $\frac{6\left(4x^2+3\right)}{\sqrt{2x^2+3}}$

Answer: d.

5. Let $C(x) = \left(200\sqrt{x^7} + 600x^2\right)^3$. Find $C''(0)$.

a. 0
b. 800
c. 2400
d. 1200

Answer: a.

6. A particle's position is given by $s = t^3 - 6t^2 + 9t$ where s is measured in feet and t in seconds. What is its acceleration at time $t = 4$ seconds?

a. 42 ft/sec^2
b. 6 ft/sec^2
c. 24 ft/sec^2
d. 12 ft/sec^2

Answer: d.

7. A ball is thrown straight up into the air from the roof of a building. The height of the ball as measured from the ground is given by $s(t) = -16t^2 + 24t + 100$ where s is measured in feet and t in seconds. Find the acceleration of the ball 2 seconds after it is thrown into the air.

a. -8 ft/sec^2
b. 8 ft/sec^2
c. -16 ft/sec^2
d. -32 ft/sec^2

Answer: d.

8. Find the second derivative of the function $f(x) = \left(2x^3 + 3\right)^5$.

a. $60x(2x^3 + 3)^3(14x^3 + 3)$
b. $10x(2x^3 + 3)^3(14x^3 + 3)$
c. $10x(2x^3 - 3)^3(14x^3 + 3)$
d. $30x(2x^3 + 3)^3(14x^3 + 3)$

Answer: a.

9. Find the second derivative of the function $C(x) = 200x + 8x^3 - \dfrac{(x-1)^6}{3}$.

a. $10(x-1)^4 + 48x$
b. $-10(x-1)^4 + 48x$
c. $-10(x-1)^4 + 24x$
d. $-5(x-1)^4 + 48x$

Answer: b.

10. Find the second derivative of the function $f(x) = x^2(3x+1)^5$.

a. $2(3x+1)^3(189x^2 + 36x + 1)$
b. $(3x+1)^3(189x^2 + 36x + 1)$
c. $-2(3x+1)^3(189x^2 + 36x + 1)$
d. $2(3x+1)^4(189x^2 + 36x + 1)$

Answer: a.

11. Let $P(x) = 175x - x^2 + kx^3$. Find the constant k such that $P''(4) = 22$.

a. 1
b. 2
c. 7
d. 12

Answer: a.

12. Let $f(x) = \sqrt{9-8x}$, find $f''(1)$.
   a. -4
   b. -16
   c. -32
   d. 16
   Answer: b

13. Let $f(x) = \left(\frac{x}{x-1}\right)^3$, find $f''(2)$.
   a. -36
   b. 36
   c. 12
   d. 16
   Answer: b.

14. Let $f(0) = 3$, $f'(0) = 7$, and $f''(0) = 12$, find $g''(0)$ where $g(x) = f(2x)$.
   a. 14
   b. 12
   c. 48
   d. 28
   Answer: c.

15. If $f(x) = \left(1 + \frac{x}{20}\right)^5$, find $f''(40)$.
   a. 0.068
   b. 1.350
   c. 5.400
   d. 540,000
   Answer: b.

16. Let $f(0) = 3$, $f'(0) = 7$, and $f''(0) = 12$, find $g''(0)$ where $g(x) = 3x\,f(x)$.
   a. 21
   b. 48
   c. 42
   d. 6
   Answer: c.

Section 3.6

1. If $x^2 + y^2 = 25$, find $\frac{dy}{dx}$ by implicit differentiation. Answer: $\frac{-x}{y}$

2. If $x^3 + y^3 + y - 5 = 0$, find $\frac{dy}{dx}$ by implicit differentiation. Answer: $\frac{-3x^2}{3y^2+1}$

3. If $x^2y^2 - 3xy = 4$, find $\frac{dy}{dx}$ by implicit differentiation. Answer: $-\frac{3y-2xy^2}{3x-2x^2y}$

4. If $x^{2/3} + y^{2/3} = 4$, find $\frac{dy}{dx}$ by implicit differentiation. Answer: $\frac{-y^{1/3}}{x^{1/3}}$

5. If $(4x+y)^{1/2} = 5x$, find $\frac{dy}{dx}$ by implicit differentiation. Answer: $10(4x+y)^{1/2} - 4$

6. If $\frac{1}{x^3} + \frac{1}{y^3} = 1$, find $\frac{dy}{dx}$ by implicit differentiation. Answer: $\frac{-y^4}{x^4}$

7. If $\sqrt{xy} = 3x + 2y^2$, find $\frac{dy}{dx}$ by implicit differentiation. Answer: $\frac{6\sqrt{xy} - y}{x - 8y\sqrt{xy}}$

8. Find the slope of the line tangent to the graph of $y^3 + 2x^2 = 3$ at the point (1, 1).

   Answer: $-\frac{4}{3}$

9. Find the slope of the line tangent to the graph of $2xy + 3\sqrt{y} = 3$ at the point $(0,1)$.

   Answer: $-\frac{4}{3}$

10. Find the second derivative $\frac{d^2y}{dx^2}$ of the function defined implicitly by $xy^2 = 1$.

    Answer: $\frac{3y}{4x^2}$

11. Find the second derivative $\frac{d^2y}{dx^2}$ of the function defined implicitly by

    $x^2y^2 - 2xy = 0$.

Answer: $\frac{2y}{x^2}$

12. A can in the shape of a right circular cylinder with radius 8 in. is being filled at a constant rate. If the fluid is rising at a rate of 0.1 in/sec, what is the rate at which the fluid is flowing into the can?
Answer: $6.4\pi \text{ in}^3/\text{sec}$

13. A can in the shape of a right circular cone with radius 9 in. is being filled at a constant rate. If the fluid is rising at a rate of 0.5 in/sec, what is the rate at which the fluid is flowing into the can?
Answer: $13.5\pi \text{ in}^3/\text{sec}$

14. An automobile traveling at a rate of 30 ft/sec is approaching an intersection. When the automobile is 120 ft from the intersection, a truck traveling at the rate of 40 ft/sec crosses the intersection. The automobile and the truck are on roads that are at right angles to each other. How fast are the automobile and the truck separating 2 seconds after the truck leaves the intersection?
Answer: 14 ft/sec

15. A man 6 ft tall is walking toward a building at the rate of 5 ft/sec. If there is a light on the ground 50 ft from the building, how fast is the man's shadow on the building shrinking when he is 30 ft from the building?
Answer: -3.75 ft/sec

16. Oil spilled from a ruptured tank spreads in a circular pattern whose radius increases at a constant rate of 2 ft/sec. How fast the area of the spill increasing when the radius of the spill is 60 ft?
Answer: $240\pi \text{ ft}^2/\text{sec}$

Section 3.6 Multiple Choice Questions

1. Consider the equation $x^2 - 0.5y^4 = 25$. Find $\frac{dy}{dx}$ by implicit differentiation.

a. $\frac{dy}{dx} = \frac{x}{y^3}$

b. $\frac{dy}{dx} = -\frac{x}{y^3}$

c. $\frac{dy}{dx} = \frac{y^3}{x}$

d. $\frac{dy}{dx} = -\frac{y^3}{x}$

Answer: a.

2. Consider the equation $y^2 + x^2 + xy - x = 100$. Find $\frac{dy}{dx}$ by implicit differentiation.

a. $\frac{dy}{dx} = \frac{1-2x+y}{2y+x}$

b. $\frac{dy}{dx} = \frac{1+2x-y}{2y-x}$

c. $\frac{dy}{dx} = \frac{1-2x+y}{2y-x}$

d. $\frac{dy}{dx} = \frac{1-2x-y}{2y+x}$

Answer: d.

3. Consider the equation $x^2y^2 + x^3y - \frac{1}{y^2} = 3x$. Find $\frac{dy}{dx}$ by implicit differentiation.

a. $\frac{dy}{dx} = \frac{3+2xy^2+3x^2y}{2x^2y+x^3+2y^{-3}}$

b. $\frac{dy}{dx} = \frac{3-2xy^2+3x^2y}{2x^2y+x^3+2y^{-3}}$

c. $\frac{dy}{dx} = \frac{3-2xy^2-3x^2y}{2x^2y+x^3+2y^{-3}}$

d. $\frac{dy}{dx} = \frac{3-2xy^2-3x^2y}{2x^2y+x^3+2y^{-1}}$

Answer: c.

4. Consider the equation $3xy^2 - y + x = 7$. Find $\frac{dy}{dx}$ by implicit differentiation.

a. $-\frac{1+3y^2}{6xy+1}$

b. $\frac{1-3y^2}{6xy-1}$

c. $\frac{1+3y^2}{6xy-1}$

d. $-\frac{1+3y^2}{6xy-1}$

Answer: d.

5. Consider the equation $xy + y^3 = 4x - 7$. Find $\frac{dy}{dx}$ by implicit differentiation.

a. $\frac{4-y}{x+3y^2}$

b. $\frac{4+y}{x+3y^2}$

c. $\frac{y}{x+3y^2}$

d. $\frac{4}{x+3y^2}$

Answer: a.

6. Consider the equation $y^3 - 3x + 2 = 0$. Find $\frac{dy}{dx}$ at (1, 1).

a. $-\frac{1}{3}$

b. $\frac{1}{3}$

c. -1

d. 1

Answer: d.

7. Consider the equation $x^2 - 4xy + 3y^2 - 12 = 0$. Find $\frac{dy}{dx}$ at (0, -2).

a. $\frac{2}{3}$

b. $-\frac{2}{3}$

c. 1

d. $\frac{2}{5}$

Answer: a.

8. Consider the equation $(x-5)^2 + (y+3)^2 = 100$. Find $\frac{dy}{dx}$ at (-1, 5).

a. $-\frac{3}{4}$

b. $\frac{3}{4}$

c. $-\frac{3}{8}$

d. $-\frac{5}{8}$

Answer: b.

9. An ellipse has the equation $\frac{x^2}{a^2}+\frac{y^2}{b^2}=1$, where $a>b>0$. Find a formula for the slope of the tangent line to the graph of the equation at any point.

a. $\frac{dy}{dx}=-\frac{xb^2}{ya^2}$

b. $\frac{dy}{dx}=-\frac{yb^2}{xa^2}$

c. $\frac{dy}{dx}=\frac{xb^2}{ya^2}$

d. $\frac{dy}{dx}=-\frac{xa^2}{yb^2}$

Answer: a.

10. Find the value(s) of $\frac{dy}{dx}$ of $x^2y+y^2=5$ at $y = 1$.

a. $\pm\frac{3}{2}$

b. $-\frac{2}{3}$ only

c. $\frac{2}{3}$ only

d. $\pm\frac{2}{3}$

Answer: d.

11. Find the equation of the tangent line to the graph of $9x^2+16y^2=52$ through (2, -1).

a. $9x+8y=26$

b. $9x-8y=26$

c. $-9x+8y=26$

d. $9x+8y=-26$

Answer: b.

12. Water is draining at the rate of 48π ft^3 / minute from the vertex at the bottom of a conical tank whose diameter at its base is 40 feet and whose height is 60 feet. At what rate is the radius of the water in the tank shrinking when the radius is 16 feet? ($V=\frac{1}{3}\pi r^2h$)

a. $\frac{1}{4}$ ft/minute

b. $\frac{3}{32}$ ft/minute

c. $\frac{\pi}{16}$ ft/minute

d. $\frac{3\pi}{16}$ ft/minute

Answer: b.

13. Consider the curve given by $xy - 4x^5 + y^2 = 25$, find $\frac{d^2y}{dx^2}$ at (0, 5).

a. 0

b. $-\frac{1}{20}$

c. $\frac{1}{20}$

d. $\frac{1}{10}$

Answer: c.

14. The side of a square is increasing at a constant rate of 0.4 cm/sec. In terms of the perimeter, P, what is the rate of change of the area of the square, in cm^2/sec?

a. $51.2P$

b. $0.4P$

c. $0.2P$

d. $6.4\,P$

Answer: c.

15. A 17-foot ladder is sliding down a wall at a rate of -5 feet/second. When the top of the ladder is 8 feet from the ground, how fast is the foot of the ladder sliding from the wall (in feet/second)?

a. $\frac{8}{3}$

b. $\frac{75}{8}$

c. $\frac{3}{8}$

d. -16

Answer: a.

Section 3.7

1. Find the differential of the function $f(x) = 3x^3$. Answer: $9x^2dx$

2. Find the differential of the function $f(x) = 3x^2 + 2x$. Answer: $(6x+2)dx$

3. Find the differential of the function $f(x) = 3x^{3/2} - x^{1/2}$.
   Answer: $\left(\frac{9}{2}x^{1/2} - \frac{1}{2}x^{-1/2}\right)dx$

4. Find the differential of the function $f(x) = \frac{2}{x-2}$. Answer: $-\frac{2}{(x-2)^2}dx$

5. Find the differential of the function $f(x) = \sqrt{2x^2 - 3x}$.
   Answer: $\frac{4x-3}{2\sqrt{2x^2-3x}}dx$

6. Find the differential of the function $f(t) = \sqrt{5-7t}$.
   Answer: $-\frac{7}{2}(5-7t)^{-1/2}\,dt$

7. Let *f* be the function defined by $y = f(x) = 4x^2 - 3x + 5$.
   (a) Find the differential of *f*. Answer: $(8x-3)dx$

   (b) Use your result from (a) to find the approximate change in *y* if *x* changes from 1 to 1.02.
   Answer: 0.1

   (c) Find the actual change in *y* if *x* changes from 1 to 1.02 and compare your result with that obtained in part (b)
   Answer: 0.1016; larger

8. Use differentials to approximate $\sqrt{15}$. Answer: 3.875

9. Use differentials to approximate $\sqrt{101}$. Answer: 10.05

10. Use differentials to approximate $\sqrt[3]{60}$. Answer: 3.917

11. Approximate the volume of a spherical shell whose inner radius is 4 inches and whose thickness is one-sixteenth of an inch.
    Answer: 4π in^2

12. A closed container in the form of a cube having a volume of 1000 in^3 is to be made by using six equal squares of material costing 20 cents per square inch. How accurately must the side of each square be measured so that the total cost of material will be correct to within \$3.00?
Answer: Within 0.125 inches.

13. Find the differential of the function $f(x)=\sqrt{3x^2-5x}$. Answer: $\dfrac{(6x-5)dx}{2\sqrt{3x^2-5x}}$

Section 3.7 Multiple Choice Questions

1. Find the differential of the function $y=3x^2+9$.
   a. $dy=6xdx$
   b. $dy=\left(3x^2+9\right)dx$
   c. $dy=(6x+9)dx$
   d. $dy=9dx$
   Answer: a.

2. Find the differential of the function $y=\dfrac{1}{x}$.
   a. $dy=-\dfrac{1}{x}dx$
   b. $dy=xdx$
   c. $dy=\dfrac{1}{x^2}dx$
   d. $dy=-\dfrac{1}{x^2}dx$
   Answer: d.

3. Find the differential of the function $y=-x^2+10x+3$.
   a. $dy=2xdx$
   b. $dy=(-2x+10)dx$
   c. $dy=(2x-2)dx$
   d. $dy=10dx$
   Answer: b.

4. Find the differential of the function $y=\dfrac{x+1}{x-1}$.
   a. $dy=-\dfrac{1}{(x-1)^2}dx$

b. $dy = \frac{2}{(x-1)^2}dx$

c. $dy = -\frac{2}{(x-1)^2}dx$

d. $dy = \frac{4}{(x-1)^2}dx$

Answer: c.

5. Find the differential of the function $y = (x+2)(3x-1)$.

a. $dy = (3x-1)dx$

b. $dy = (x+2)dx$

c. $dy = (6x+5)dx$

d. $dy = (6x+4)dx$

Answer: c.

6. Use differentials to approximate $\sqrt{17}$.

a. 4.125

b. 4.120

c. 4.216

d. 4.135

Answer: a.

7. Use differentials to approximate $\sqrt{48.9}$.

a. 6.998

b. 6.993

c. 6.991

d. 7.001

Answer: b.

8. Use differentials to approximate $\sqrt[3]{28}$.

a. 3.025

b. 3.042

c. 3.012

d. 3.037

Answer: d.

9. Let f be the function defined by $f(x) = \sqrt{3x+1}$. Use the differential of f to find the approximate change in y if x changes from 5 to 5.1.

a. -0.0375

b. 4.0375

c. 0.0375

d. 0.375

Answer: c.

10. Let f be the function defined by $f(x) = \frac{1}{x}$. Use the differential of f to find the approximate change in y if x changes from 1 to 1.1.

a. 0.9
b. 1.1
c. 0.1
d. -0.1

Answer: d.

11. Kathy deposits a sum of \$10,000 into an account that pays interest at the rate of r/year compounded monthly. Her investment at the end of 20 yr is given by $A = 10{,}000\left(1+\frac{r}{12}\right)^{240}$. Find the differential of A.

a. $dA = 20{,}000\left(1+\frac{r}{12}\right)^{239} dr$
b. $dA = 200{,}000\left(1+\frac{r}{12}\right)^{239} dr$
c. $dA = 100{,}000\left(1+\frac{r}{12}\right)^{239} dr$
d. $dA = 240{,}000\left(1+\frac{r}{12}\right)^{239} dr$

Answer: b.

12. The demand function for the Sentinel smoke alarm is given by $p = d(x) = \frac{30}{0.02x^2+1}$ where x is the quantity demanded (in units of a thousand) and p is the unit price in dollars. Find the differential of p.

a. $dp = \frac{-1.2x}{\left(0.02x^2+1\right)^2} dx$
b. $dp = \frac{-x}{\left(0.02x^2+1\right)^2} dx$
c. $dp = \frac{1.2x}{\left(0.02x^2+1\right)^2} dx$
d. $dp = \frac{-1.2x}{\left(0.02x^2+1\right)} dx$

Answer: a.

Exam 3A

Name:
Instructor:
Section:

Write your work as neatly as possible.

1. Find the derivative of the function $f(x) = 3x + 10$.

2. Find the derivative of the function $f(x) = \dfrac{x^2 + 1}{x - 3}$.

3. Find the derivative of the function $f(x) = \sqrt{5x - 2}$.

4. Find the slope and an equation of the tangent line to the graph of the function $f(x) = 3x^2 + 2x - 1$ at the point $(1,4)$.

5. Find the derivative of the function $f(x) = \left(x^2 + \dfrac{2}{x^2}\right)(3x + 2)$.

6. Find the slope and an equation of the tangent line to the graph of the function $f(x) = 3x^2 - 6x + 1$ at the point $(0,1)$.

7. Find the derivative of the function $f(x) = \left(8x^2 + x\right)^7$.

8. Find the derivative of the function $f(t) = \left(-t^{-2} + t^{-4}\right)^3$.

9. For the demand equation $x = -\dfrac{5}{3}p + 20$, compute the elasticity of demand and determine whether the demand is elastic, unitary, or inelastic if $p = 5$.

10. Find the first and second derivatives of $f(x) = 5x^3 + 2x^2 + 7x + 2$.

11. A company manufactures a product with cost function $C(x) = 600 + 200x - 0.2x^2$, where $C(x)$ is the cost of manufacturing a total of x units of the product.
    (a) Find the average cost function $\overline{C}$.

    (b) Find the marginal cost function C'.

12. If $x^3 + 3y^2 = 2$, find $\frac{dy}{dx}$ by implicit differentiation.

13. A can in the shape of a right circular cylinder with radius 6 in. is being filled at a constant rate. If the fluid is rising at a rate of 0.2 in/sec, what is the rate at which the fluid is flowing into the can?

14. Find the differential of the function $f(x) = 8x^3 + 1$.

Exam 3B

Name:
Instructor:
Section:

Write your work as neatly as possible.

1. Find the derivative of the function $f(x) = 1 - 5x + x^2$.

2. Find the derivative of the function $f(x) = 12x^{2/3} - 9x^{1/3}$.

3. Find the derivative of the function $f(x) = \dfrac{x^2}{x^2 - 3}$.

4. Find the derivative of the function $f(x) = \sqrt{x^2 + 2}$.

5. Find the slope and an equation of the tangent line to the graph of the function $f(x) = \sqrt{x} + 1$ at the point $(4, 3)$.

6. Find the derivative of the function $f(x) = \left(3x^2 - \dfrac{2}{x}\right)\left(3x^2 + 2\right)$.

7. Find the slope and an equation of the tangent line to the graph of the function $f(x) = x^3 - 9x + 1$ at the point (0, 1).

8. Find the derivative of the function $f(x) = (12x - 2)^{-3}$.

9. Find the derivative of the function $f(x) = (3x + 2)^4 (3x - 1)^3$.

10. For the demand equation $x + \dfrac{1}{5}p - 16 = 0$, compute the elasticity of demand and determine whether the demand is elastic, unitary, or inelastic if $p = 50$.

11. Find the first and second derivatives of $f(x) = 3x^4 - 2x^{5/3} + \sqrt{2x}$.

12. A company manufactures a product with cost function
$C(x) = 3000 + 600x - 0.3x^2$, where $C(x)$ is the cost of manufacturing a total of x units of the product
(a) Find the average cost function $\overline{C}$.

(b) Find the marginal cost function C'.

13. A rock is tossed into a pond creating an expanding circular ripple. If the radius of the ripple is increasing at a rate of 1.5 ft/sec, find out how fast the area is increasing when the radius is 2 feet.

14. If $2xy = 3x + 5y^2$, find $\frac{dy}{dx}$ by implicit differentiation.

15. Find the differential of the function $f(x) = 12x^3 - 2x$.

16. Let f be a function defined by $y = f(x) = 5x^2 - 2x + 1$.
(a) Find the differential of f.

(b) Use your result from (a) to approximate the change in y if x changes from 2 to 2.02.

(c) Find the actual change in y if x changes from 2 to 2.02 and compare your result with that obtained in (b)

Exam 3C

Name:
Instructor:
Section:

Write your work as neatly as possible.

1. Find the derivative of the function $f(x)=7x^2+1$.

2. Find the derivative of the function $f(x)=4x^{5/3}+7x^{2/3}$.

3. Find the derivative of the function $f(x)=\dfrac{3x^2}{x^2+2}$.

4. Find the derivative of the function $f(x)=\sqrt{5-2x^2}$.

5. Let $f(x)=3x^3+2$.
(a) Find the point(s) on the graph of f where the slope of the tangent line is equal to 4.

(b) Find the equation(s) of the tangent line(s) of part (a).

6. Find the point(s) on the graph of $f(x)=\dfrac{2x}{x^2-2x+3}$ where the tangent line is horizontal.

7. Find the derivative of the function $f(x)=\sqrt[5]{2+x^2}$.

8. Find the derivative of the function $f(x)=\sqrt{\dfrac{7x}{2x-1}}$.

9. For the demand equation $p=220-x^2$, compute the elasticity of demand and determine whether the demand is elastic, unitary, or inelastic if $p=104$.

10. Find the first and second derivatives of $f(x) = -0.8x^3 + 7.1x^2 + 32.5x + 0.6^2$.

11. A company manufactures a product with cost function $C(x) = 2000 + 800x - 0.4x^2$, where $C(x)$ is the cost of manufacturing a total of x units of the product.
(a) Find the average cost function $\overline{C}$.

(b) Find the marginal cost function C'.

12. If $x^2y^2 - 2xy + x = 2$, find the slope of the tangent line at $(2,1)$ by implicit differentiation.

13. Find the second derivative $\dfrac{d^2y}{dx^2}$ of the function defined implicitly by $x^2y = 2$.

14. Find the differential of the function $f(x) = 4x^{5/2} - x^{-1/2}$.

15. Use differentials to approximate $\sqrt{82}$.

Exam 3D

Name:
Instructor:
Section:

Write your work as neatly as possible.

1. Find the derivative of the function $f(x)=\frac{1}{8}x+1$.

2. Find the derivative of the function $f(x)=\sqrt{x}-\frac{1}{x}$.

3. Find the derivative of the function $f(x)=\frac{4x^3}{x^2+1}$.

4. Find the derivative of the function $f(x)=\sqrt{x^2-4x}$.

5. Let $f(x)=\frac{2}{3}x^3-3x+1$. Find the x-values of the point(s) on the graph of f where the slope of the tangent line is equal to
(a) −3

(b) 0

(c) 5

6. Find the derivative of the function $f(x)=\frac{-x}{x^2+2x-1}$.

7. Let $f(x)=\frac{1}{4}(x^2+2)(2x+3)$. Find the point(s) on the graph of f where the slope of the tangent line is equal to
(a) 1

(b) 10

8. Find the derivative of the function $f(x) = \dfrac{3}{(2x^3 + 3x)^{3/2}}$.

9. Find $\dfrac{dy}{du}, \dfrac{du}{dx}$, and $\dfrac{dy}{dx}$ if $y = u^{-5/3}$ and $u = x^3 - 2x + 1$.

10. Find $F'(3)$ if $F(x) = f(g(x))$ and
$f(3) = 2,\ f'(3) = 5,\ f'(4) = 6,\ g(3) = 4,$ and $g'(3) = -2$.

11. Find the first and second derivatives of $f(x) = x^4(3x^2 + 1)$.

12. A company manufactures a product with cost function
$C(x) = 1200 + 600x - 0.8x^2$, where $C(x)$ is the cost of manufacturing a total of x units of the product
(a) Find the average cost function $\overline{C}$.

(b) Find the marginal cost function C'.

13. If $x^{5/3} + y^{1/3} = 3x$, find $\dfrac{dy}{dx}$ by implicit differentiation.

14. Find the differential of the function $f(x) = \dfrac{3}{x-1}$.

15. Use differentials to approximate $\sqrt[3]{128}$.

Answers to Chapter 3 Exams

Exam 3A

1. 3
2. $\dfrac{x^2-6x-1}{(x-3)^2}$
3. $\dfrac{5}{2\sqrt{5x-2}}$
4. $8;\ y=8x-4$
5. $9x^2+4x-\dfrac{6}{x^2}-\dfrac{8}{x^3}$
6. $-1;\ y=-x+13$
7. $7(16x+1)(8x^2+x)^6$
8. $3(-t^{-2}+t^{-4})^2(2t^{-3}-4t^{-5})$
9. $\dfrac{-p}{p-12}$; inelastic
10. $15x^2+4x+7,\ 30x+4$
11. (a) $\overline{C}(x)=\dfrac{600}{x}+200-0.2x$

    (b) $C'(x)=200-0.4x$
12. $\dfrac{-x^2}{2y}$
13. $7.2\pi\ \text{in}^3/\text{sec}$
14. $24x^2dx$

Exam 3B

1. $-5+2x$
2. $\dfrac{8}{x^{1/3}}-\dfrac{3}{x^{2/3}}$
3. $\dfrac{-6x}{(x^2-3)^2}$
4. $\dfrac{x}{\sqrt{x^2+2}}$
5. $\dfrac{1}{4};\ y=\dfrac{1}{4}x+2$
6. $36x^3+12x+\dfrac{4}{x^2}-6$
7. $-9,\ y=-9x+1$
8. $-36(12x-2)^{-4}$
9. $3(21x+2)(3x+2)^3(3x-1)^2$
10. $\dfrac{-p}{p-80}$; elastic
11. $12x^3-\dfrac{10}{3}x^{2/3}+\dfrac{\sqrt{2}}{2}x^{-1/2}$

    $36x^2-\dfrac{20}{9}x^{-1/3}-\dfrac{\sqrt{2}}{4}x^{-3/2}$
12. (a) $\overline{C}(x)=\dfrac{3000}{x}+600-0.3x$

    (b) $C'(x)=600-0.6x$
13. $6\pi\ \text{ft}^2/\text{sec}$
14. $\dfrac{3-2y}{2x-10y}$
15. $(36x^2-2)dx$
16. (a) $(10x-2)dx$ (b) 0.36

    (c) 0.362; larger

Exam 3C

1. $14x$

2. $\frac{20}{3}x^{2/3}+\frac{14}{3}x^{-1/3}$

3. $\frac{12x}{\left(x^2+2\right)^2}$

4. $\frac{-2x}{\sqrt{5-2x^2}}$

5. (a) $\left(-\frac{2}{3},\frac{10}{9}\right),\left(\frac{2}{3},\frac{26}{9}\right)$

   (b) $y=4x+\frac{34}{9},\ y=4x+\frac{2}{9}$

6. $\left(-\sqrt{3},\frac{-\sqrt{3}}{3+\sqrt{3}}\right),\left(\sqrt{3},\frac{\sqrt{3}}{3-\sqrt{3}}\right)$

7. $\frac{2}{5}x\left(2+x^2\right)^{-4/5}$

8. $-\frac{7}{2}\left(\frac{7x}{2x-1}\right)^{-1/2}(2x-1)^{-2}$

9. $-\frac{p}{2p-440}$; inelastic

10. $-2.4x^2+14.2x+32.5, -4.8x+14.2$

11. (a) $\overline{C}(x)=\frac{2000}{x}+800-0.4x$

    (b) $C'(x)=800-0.8x$

12. $-\frac{3}{4}$

13. $\frac{12}{x^4}$

14. $\left(10x^{3/2}+\frac{1}{2}x^{-3/2}\right)dx$

15. $\frac{163}{18}=9.0\overline{5}$

Exam 3D

1. $\frac{1}{8}$

2. $\frac{1}{2\sqrt{x}}+\frac{1}{x^2}$

3. $\frac{4x^4+12x^2}{\left(x^2+1\right)^2}$

4. $\frac{x-2}{\sqrt{x^2-4x}}$

5. (a) 0; (b) $\pm\sqrt{6}/2$; (c) ± 2

6. $\frac{x^2+1}{\left(x^2+2x-1\right)^2}$

7. (a) $\left(0,\frac{3}{2}\right),\left(-1,\frac{3}{4}\right)$;

   (b) $\left(-3,-\frac{33}{4}\right),\left(2,\frac{21}{2}\right)$

8. $-\frac{27\left(2x^2+1\right)}{2\left(2x^3+3x\right)^{5/2}}$

9. $-\frac{5}{3}u^{-8/3}, 3x^2-2,$

   $-\frac{5}{3}\left(x^3-2x+1\right)^{-8/3}\left(3x^2-2\right)$

10. -12

11. $18x^5+4x^3, 90x^4+12x^2$

12. (a) $\overline{C}(x)=\frac{1200}{x}+600-0.8x$

    (b) $C'(x)=600-1.6x$

13. $\left(9-5x^{2/3}\right)y^{2/3}$

14. $-\frac{3dx}{(x-1)^2}$

15. 5.04

Chapter 4 ■ Applications of the Derivative

Section 4.1

1. Find the interval(s) where $f(x)=-3x+10$ is increasing and the interval(s) where it is decreasing.
   Answer: Decreasing: $(-\infty,\infty)$; never increasing

2. Find the interval(s) where $f(x)=\frac{1}{5}x-1$ is increasing and the interval(s) where it is decreasing.
   Answer: Increasing: $(-\infty,\infty)$; never decreasing

3. Find the interval(s) where $f(x)=x^2+4x+8$ is increasing and the interval(s) where it is decreasing.
   Answer: Increasing: $(-2,\infty)$; decreasing: $(-\infty,-2)$

4. Find the interval(s) where $f(x)=5-2x^2$ is increasing and the interval(s) where it is decreasing.
   Answer: Increasing: $(-\infty,0)$; decreasing: $(0,\infty)$

5. Find the interval(s) where $f(x)=2x^2-3x+4$ is increasing and the interval(s) where it is decreasing.
   Answer: Increasing: $\left(\frac{3}{4},\infty\right)$; decreasing: $\left(-\infty,\frac{3}{4}\right)$

6. Find the interval(s) where $f(x)=2x^3-6x^2-18x$ is increasing and the interval(s) where it is decreasing.
   Answer: Increasing: $(-\infty,-1)\cup(3,\infty)$; decreasing: $(-1,3)$

7. Find the interval(s) where $f(x)=\frac{1}{3}x^3-4x^2+4x-12$ is increasing and the interval(s) where it is decreasing.
   Answer: Increasing: $\left(-\infty,4-2\sqrt{3}\right)\cup\left(4+2\sqrt{3},\infty\right)$; decreasing: $\left(4-2\sqrt{3},4+2\sqrt{3}\right)$

8. Find the interval(s) where $s(t)=\frac{t}{t-2}$ is increasing and the interval(s) where it is decreasing.
   Answer: Decreasing: $(-\infty,2)\cup(2,\infty)$; never increasing

9. Find the interval(s) where $s(t)=\dfrac{3t}{t^2+2}$ is increasing and the interval(s) where it is decreasing.
Answer: Increasing: $(-\sqrt{2},\sqrt{2})$; decreasing: $(-\infty,-\sqrt{2})\cup(\sqrt{2},\infty)$

10. Find the interval(s) where $f(x)=\sqrt{x+4}$ is increasing and the interval(s) where it is decreasing.
Answer: Increasing: $(-4,\infty)$; never decreasing

11. Find the interval(s) where $f(x)=x\sqrt{x+12}$ is increasing and the interval(s) where it is decreasing.
Answer: Increasing: $(-8,\infty)$; decreasing: $(-12,-8)$

12. Find the interval(s) where $f(x)=\sqrt{25-x^2}$ is increasing and the interval(s) where it is decreasing.
Answer: Increasing: $(-5,0)$; decreasing: $(0,5)$

13. Find the interval(s) where $f(x)=\dfrac{x^2}{x+1}$ is increasing and the interval(s) where it is decreasing.
Answer: Increasing: $(-\infty,-2)\cup(0,\infty)$; decreasing: $(-2,-1)\cup(-1,0)$

14. Find the interval(s) where $f(x)=\dfrac{2x}{(x+2)^2}$ is increasing and the interval(s) where it is decreasing.
Answer: Increasing: $(-2,2)$; decreasing: $(-\infty,-2)\cup(2,\infty)$

15. Given the graph of f determine the interval(s) where f is increasing, decreasing, or constant.

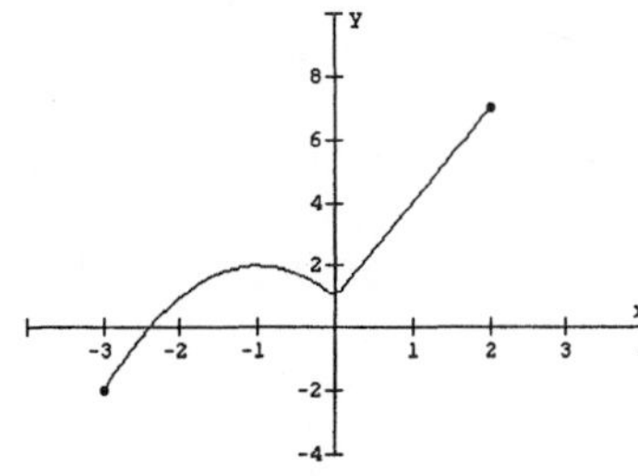

Answer: Increasing: $(-3,-1)\cup(0,2)$; decreasing: $(-1,0)$

16. Given the graph of *f*, determine the interval(s) where f is increasing, decreasing, or constant.

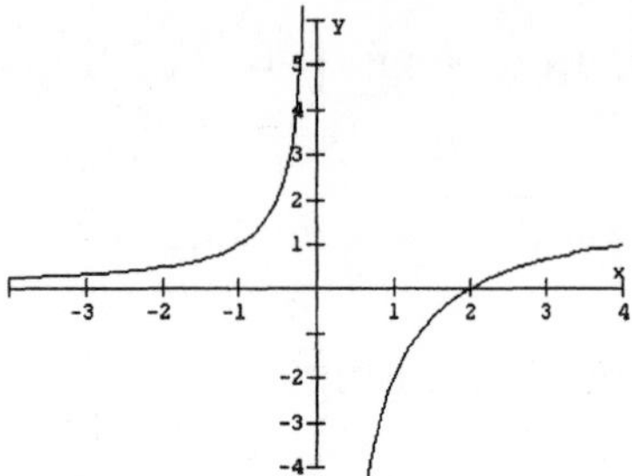

Answer: Increasing: $(-\infty,0)\cup(0,\infty)$; decreasing: nowhere

17. Given the graph of *f*, determine the interval(s) where f is increasing, decreasing, or constant.

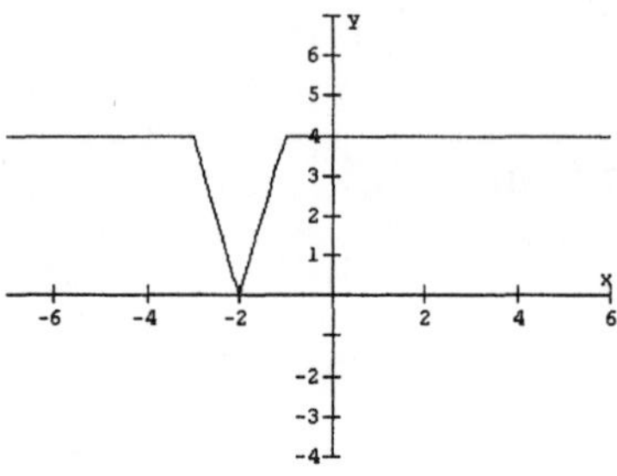

Answer: Constant $(-\infty,-3)\cup(-1,\infty)$; Increasing: $(-2,-1)$; Decreasing: $(-3,-2)$

18. A stone is thrown straight up from the roof of a 192-foot building. The distance of the stone from the ground (in feet) at any time t (in seconds) is given by $h(t)=-16t^2+64t+192$. When is the stone rising and when is it falling? If the stone were to miss the building, when would it hit the ground?
Answer: Rising when $0<t<2$, falling when $2<t<4$; after 6 seconds

19. The concentration (in milligrams per cubic centimeter) of a certain drug in a patient's body t hours after injection is given by $C(t)=\dfrac{t^2}{3t^3+1}$, $0\le t\le 5$. When is the concentration of the drug increasing and when is it decreasing?
Answer: Increasing when $0<t<\frac{1}{3}\sqrt[3]{18}$, decreasing when $\frac{1}{3}\sqrt[3]{18}<t<5$.

20. Find the relative maxima and relative minima, if any, of $f(x)=x^2-8x$.
Answer: Relative minimum $f(4)=-16$; no relative maximum

21. Find the relative maxima and relative minima, if any, of $f(x)=x^{4/3}$.

Answer: Relative minimum $f(0)=0$; no relative maximum

22. Find the relative maxima and relative minima, if any, of $f(x)=3-x^{2/3}$.
Answer: Relative maximum $f(0)=3$; no relative minimum

23. Find the relative maxima and relative minima, if any, of $g(t)=-t^2+4t+4$.
Answer: Relative maximum $g(2)=8$; no relative minimum

24. Find the relative maxima and relative minima, if any, of $g(x)=x^3-x^2-5x+6$.
Answer: Relative minimum $g\left(\frac{5}{3}\right)=-\frac{13}{27}$; relative maximum $g(-1)=9$

25. Find the relative maxima and relative minima, if any, of $g(x)=-\frac{1}{4}x^4+2x^2$.
Answer: Relative minimum $g(0)=0$; relative maxima $g(\pm 2)=4$

26. Find the relative maxima and relative minima, if any, of $g(x)=3x^4-4x^3+5$.
Answer: Relative minimum $g(1)=4$; no relative maximum

27. Find the relative maxima and relative minima, if any, of $f(x)=\frac{x}{2x+3}$.
Answer: No relative extremum

28. Find the relative maxima and relative minima, if any, of $f(x)=\frac{2x+3}{x}$.
Answer: No relative extremum

29. Find the relative maxima and relative minima, if any, of $g(x)=x+3x^{-1}$.
Answer: Relative minimum $g\left(\sqrt{3}\right)=2\sqrt{3}$; relative maximum $g(-\sqrt{3})=-2\sqrt{3}$

30. Find the relative maxima and relative minima, if any, of $f(x)=x\sqrt{x-9}$.
Answer: No relative extremum

31. Given the graph of *f*, determine the relative maxima and relative minima.

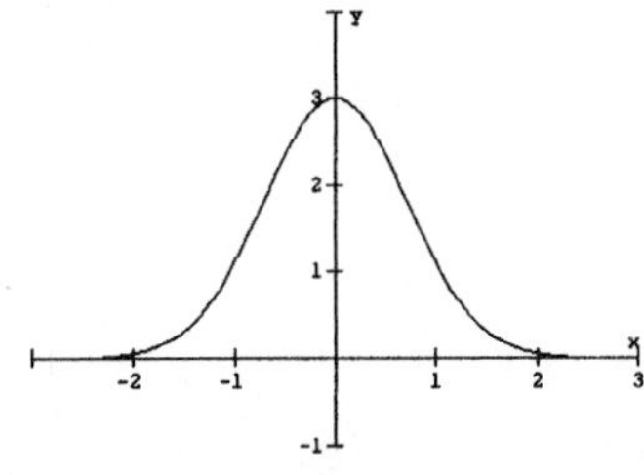

Answer: relative max: $(0,3)$; relative min: none

32. Given the graph of f, determine the relative maxima and relative minima.

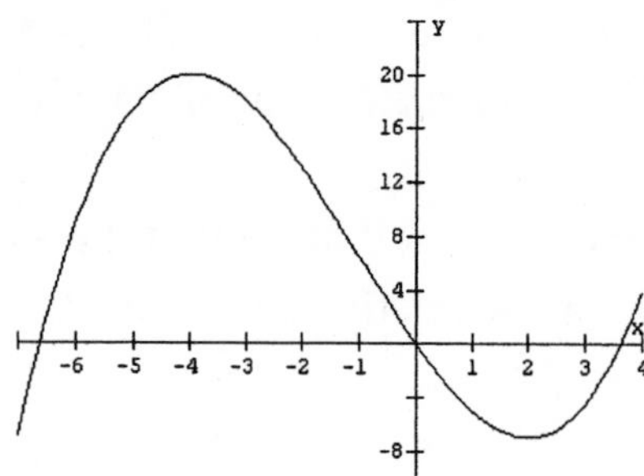

Answer: relative max: $(-4,20)$; relative min: $(2,-7)$

33. Given the graph of f, determine the relative maxima and relative minima.

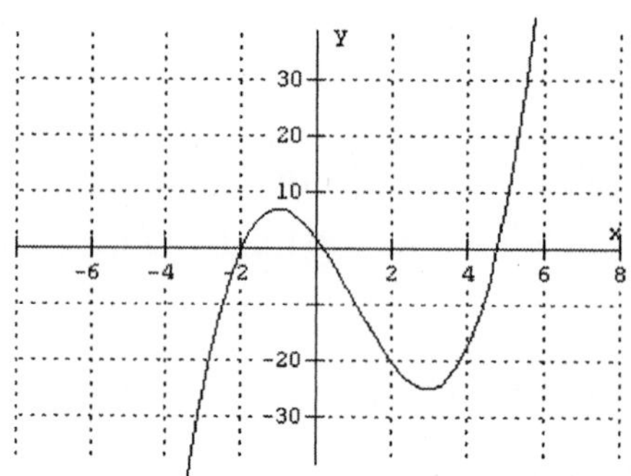

Answer: relative max (-1, 7); relative min: (3, -25).

34. Given the graph of f, determine the relative maxima and relative minima.

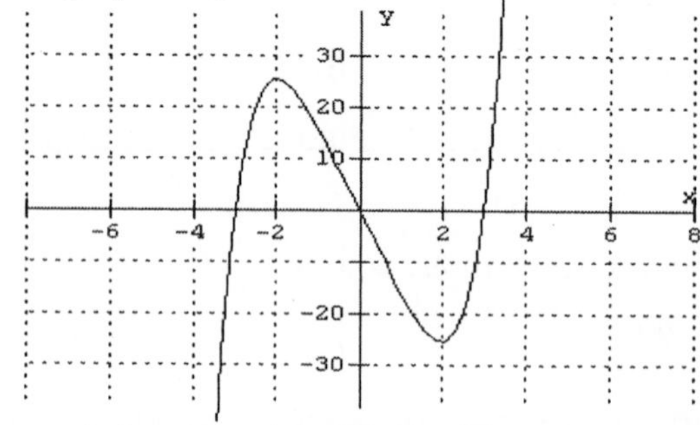

Answer: relative max (-2, 25.6); relative min: (2, 25.6).

Section 4.1 Multiple Choice Questions

1. Let $f(x) = x^4 + 4x^3$. On which of the following intervals is *f* increasing?
   a. $(-3,\ 0)\cup(0,\ \infty)$
   b. $(-3,\ 0)$
   c. $(0,\ \infty)$
   d. $(-\infty,\ -3)$

   Answer: a.

2. Let $f(x) = \dfrac{1}{x-5}$. On which of the following intervals is *f* decreasing?
   a. $(-5,\ \infty)$
   b. $(-\infty,\ 0)$
   c. $(5,\ \infty)$
   d. $(-\infty,\ 5)\cup(5,\ \infty)$

   Answer: d.

3. Let $f(x) = \sqrt{x^2 - 16}$. On which of the following intervals is *f* decreasing?
   a. $(-\infty,\ \infty)$
   b. $(-\infty,\ -4)$
   c. $(4,\ \infty)$
   d. $(-\infty,\ -4)\cup(4,\ \infty)$

   Answer: b.

4. Let $f(x) = \sqrt{x^2 - 16}$. On which of the following intervals is *f* increasing?
   a. $(-\infty,\ \infty)$
   b. $(-\infty,\ 4)$
   c. $(4,\ \infty)$
   d. $(-\infty,\ -4)\cup(4,\ \infty)$

   Answer: c.

5. Let $f(x) = x^4 + 4x^3$. On which of the following intervals is *f* decreasing?
   a. $(-3,\ \infty)$
   b. $(-3,\ 0)$
   c. $(0,\ \infty)$

d. $(-\infty, -3)$

Answer: d.

6. The graph of $y = x^3 - 5x^2 + 4x + 2$ has a relative minimum at
   a. (2.87, –4.06)
   b. (0.46, 2.87)
   c. (4.06, 2.87)
   d. (0.46, 0)

   Answer: a.

7. For what value of x does the function $f(x) = x^3 - 9x^2 - 120x + 6$ have a relative minimum?
   a. 3
   b. 4
   c. 10
   d. –10

   Answer: c.

8. The graph of $f(x) = x^3 - 2x^2 - 5x + 2$ has a relative maximum at
   a. (0.666, -1.926)
   b. (-0.786, 0)
   c. (-0.786, 4.209)
   d. (2.120, 0)

   Answer: c.

9. A particle's height for $t \geq 0$ is given by $h(t) = 100t - 16t^2$, where h is measured in feet and t is measured in seconds. What is the maximum height?
   a. 312.25 ft
   b. 156.25 ft
   c. 78.125 ft
   d. 6.250 ft

   Answer: b.

10. The graph of the function $f(x) = x^3 + 12x^2 + 15x + 3$ has a relative maximum at $x =$
    a. -0.248
    b. -7.317
    c. -1.138
    d. -10.613

    Answer: b.

11. If $f'(x) = (x+1)^3(x-3)$, at which of the following values of x does f have a relative minimum value?
    a. 3
    b. -3

c. 1
d. -1
Answer: a.

12. The relative minimum value of the function $f(x) = x^3 - 7x + 11,\ x \geq 0$, is approximately
    a. 18.128
    b. 6.698
    c. 5.513
    d. 3.872
    Answer: d.

13. Consider the function $f(x) = 2x^4 - 4x^2 + 1$. Find the *x*- and *y*-coordinate(s) of the relative maxima.
    a. $(0, 1)$
    b. $(-1, -1)$
    c. $(1, -1)$
    d. $(0, -1)$
    Answer: a.

14. Consider the function $f(x) = 2x^4 - 4x^2 + 1$. Find the *x*-coordinate(s) of the relative minima.
    a. 0
    b. 1 and -1
    c. 1 only
    d. -1 only
    Answer: b.

15. A stone is thrown straight up from the roof of a 100-feet building. The distance (in feet) of the stone from the ground at any time *t* (in seconds) is given by $h(t) = -16t^2 + 64t + 100$. Over what time interval is the stone rising?
    a. $(0, 4)$
    b. $(0, 2)$
    c. $(0, 3)$
    d. $(0, 8)$
    Answer: b.

Section 4.2

1. Determine where $f(x) = x^2 + 4x + 8$ is concave upward and where it is concave downward.
   Answer: Concave upward: $(-\infty, \infty)$; never concave downward

2. Determine where $f(x) = x^3 - 3x$ is concave upward and where it is concave downward.
   Answer: Concave downward: $(-\infty, 0)$; concave upward $(0, \infty)$

3. Determine where $f(x) = -2x^2 - 3x + 4$ is concave upward and where it is concave downward.
   Answer: Concave downward: $(-\infty, \infty)$; never concave upward

4. Determine where $g(x) = 2x^3 - 6x^2 - 18x$ is concave upward and where it is concave downward.
   Answer: Concave upward: $(1, \infty)$; concave downward: $(-\infty, 1)$.

5. Determine where $g(x) = \frac{1}{3}x^3 - 4x^2 + 4x - 12$ is concave upward and where it is concave downward.
   Answer: Concave upward: $(4, \infty)$; concave downward: $(-\infty, 4)$.

6. Determine where $s(t) = \frac{t}{t-2}$ is concave upward and where it is concave downward.
   Answer: Concave upward: $(2, \infty)$; concave downward: $(-\infty, 2)$.

7. Determine where $s(t) = \frac{3t}{t^2 + 2}$ is concave upward and where it is concave downward.

   Answer: Concave upward: $(-\sqrt{6}, 0) \cup (\sqrt{6}, \infty)$; concave downward: $(-\infty, -\sqrt{6}) \cup (0, \sqrt{6})$

8. Determine where $f(x) = \sqrt{x+4}$ is concave upward and where it is concave downward.

   Answer: Concave downward: $(-4, \infty)$; never concave upward

9. Determine where $f(x) = x\sqrt{x+12}$ is concave upward and where it is concave downward.
Answer: Concave upward: $(-12, \infty)$; never concave downward

10. Determine where $f(x) = \sqrt{25 - x^2}$ is concave upward and where it is concave downward.
Answer: Concave downward: $(-5, 5)$; never concave upward

11. Determine where $f(x) = \dfrac{x^2}{x+1}$ is concave upward and where it is concave downward.
Answer: Concave upward: $(-1, \infty)$; concave downward: $(-\infty, -1)$

12. Determine where $f(x) = \dfrac{2x}{(x+2)^2}$ is concave upward and where it is concave downward.
Answer: Concave upward: $(4, \infty)$; concave downward: $(-\infty, -2) \cup (-2, 4)$

13. Given the graph of f, determine the interval(s) where f is concave upward and concave downward.

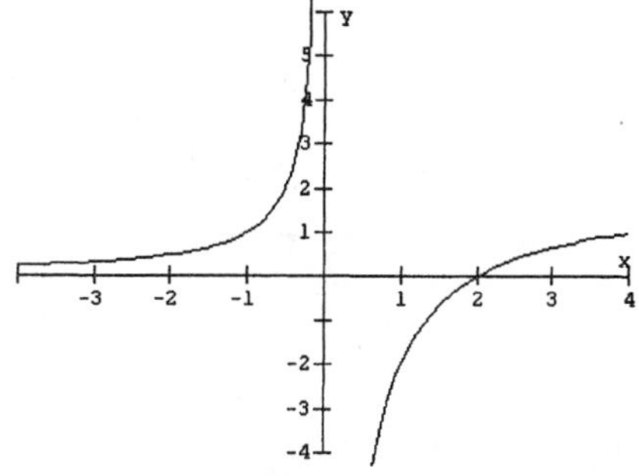

Answer: Concave upward: $(-\infty, 0)$; Concave downward: $(0, \infty)$

14. Given the graph of f, determine the interval(s) where f is concave upward and concave downward.

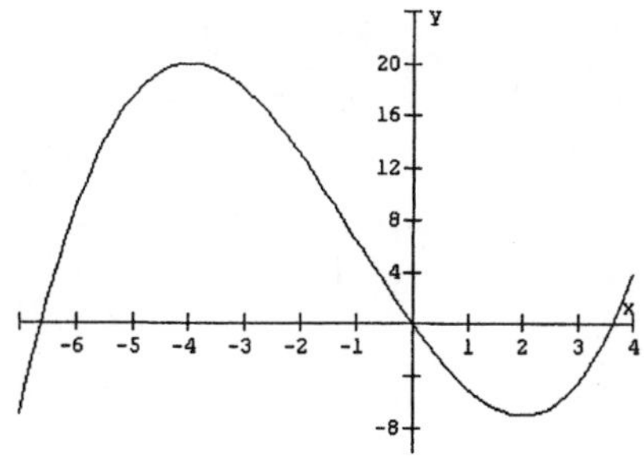

Answer: Concave upward: $(-1, \infty)$; Concave downward: $(-\infty, -1)$

15. Find the inflection points, if any, of $g(t) = -t^2 + 4t + 4$.
Answer: None

16. Find the inflection points, if any, of $g(x) = x^3 - x^2 - 5x + 6$.
Answer: $\left(\frac{1}{3}, \frac{115}{27}\right)$

17. Find the inflection points, if any, of $g(x) = -\frac{1}{4}x^4 + 2x^2$.
Answer: $\left(\pm\frac{2\sqrt{3}}{3}, \frac{20}{9}\right)$

18. Find the inflection points, if any, of $g(x) = 3x^4 - 4x^3 + 5$.
Answer: $(0,5)$, $\left(\frac{2}{3}, \frac{119}{27}\right)$

19. Find the inflection points, if any, of $f(x) = x^3 - 17x$.
Answer: $(0,0)$

20. Find the inflection points, if any, of $h(t) = \sqrt[5]{t}$.
Answer: $(0,0)$

21. Find the inflection points, if any, of $f(x) = \frac{x}{2x+3}$.
Answer: None

22. Find the inflection points, if any, of $g(x) = x + 3x^{-1}$.
Answer: None

23. Find the inflection points, if any, of $s(t) = \frac{3t}{t^2 + 2}$.
Answer: $\left(-\sqrt{6}, \frac{-3\sqrt{6}}{8}\right)$, $(0,0)$, $\left(\sqrt{6}, \frac{3\sqrt{6}}{8}\right)$

24. Find the inflection points, if any, of $f(x) = \frac{2x}{(x+2)^2}$.
Answer: $\left(4, \frac{2}{9}\right)$

25. An efficiency study conducted for the Cassiopeia Cabbage Company showed that the number of cases of cabbage packed by the average worker t hours after starting work at 8 a.m. is given by $-t^3+4t^2+12t,\ 0 \le t \le 4$. At what time during the morning shift is the average worker at peak efficiency?
Answer: At 9:20 a.m.

26. Let $f(x)=x^3+x$.
(a) Find the interval(s) on which $f(x)$ is concave upward.
Answer: $(0,\infty)$
(b) Find the interval(s) on which $f(x)$ is concave downward.
Answer: $(-\infty,0)$
(c) Find the x-coordinate(s) of any point(s) of inflection of f.
Answer: $x=0$

27. Let $f(x)=x^4-4x^3-48x^2-64x-32$.
(a) Find the interval(s) on which $f(x)$ is concave upward.
Answer: $(-\infty,-2)\cup(4,\infty)$
(b) Find the interval(s) on which $f(x)$ is concave downward.
Answer: $(-2,4)$
(c) Find the x-coordinate(s) of any point(s) of inflection of f.
Answer: $x=-2$ and $x=4$

28. Let $f(x)=2x\sqrt{x-4}$.
(a) Find the interval(s) on which $f(x)$ is concave upward.
Answer: $\left(\frac{16}{3},\infty\right)$
(b) Find the interval(s) on which $f(x)$ is concave downward.
Answer: $\left(4,\frac{16}{3}\right)$
(c) Find the x-coordinate(s) of any point(s) of inflection of f.
Answer: $x=\frac{16}{3}$

Section 4.2 Multiple Choice Questions

1. Determine the interval(s) where the function $y = x^4 + 4x^3$ is concave up.
   a. $(-2,0)$
   b. $(0,\infty)$ only
   c. $(-\infty,-2)\cup(0,\infty)$
   d. $(-\infty,-2)$ only

   Answer: c.

2. Determine the interval(s) where the function $y = \sqrt{x^2 - 25}$ is concave down.
   a. $(-5,0)$
   b. $(5,\infty)$ only
   c. $(-\infty,-5)\cup(5,\infty)$
   d. $(-\infty,-5)$ only

   Answer: c.

3. Determine the interval(s) where the function $y = \dfrac{1}{x+4}$ is concave down.
   a. $(-4,0)$
   b. $(-4,\infty)$ only
   c. $(-\infty,-4)\cup(-4,\infty)$
   d. $(-\infty,-4)$ only

   Answer: d.

4. Consider the curve defined by $y = x^4 + 4x^3$. Find the coordinates of the relative minimum.
   a. (-3, -27)
   b. (-3, 189)
   c. (-3, 36)
   d. (3, -189)

   Answer: a.

5. Consider the curve defined by $y = x^4 + 4x^3$. Find the coordinates of the inflection point(s).
   a. There are no inflection point(s)
   b. (-2, -16) only
   c. (0, 0) only
   d. (0, 0) and (-2, -16)

   Answer: d.

6. The graph of $f(x) = x^3 - 2x^2 - 5x + 2$ has a relative maximum at
   a. (0.666, -1.926)
   b. (-0.786, 0)
   c. (-0.786, 4.209)
   d. (2.120, 0)
   Answer: c.

7. The graph of $g(x) = \sqrt{11 + x^2}$ has an inflection point at
   a. $\left(\sqrt{11},\ 0\right)$
   b. $\left(0,\ -\sqrt{11}\right)$
   c. $\left(0,\ \sqrt{11}\right)$
   d. There is no inflection point
   Answer: d.

8. Consider the function $f(x) = 2x^4 - 4x^2 + 1$. Find the x-coordinate(s) of the inflection point(s).
   a. $-\dfrac{\sqrt{3}}{3}$ only
   b. $\pm\dfrac{\sqrt{3}}{3}$
   c. $\dfrac{\sqrt{3}}{3}$ only
   d. $\dfrac{1}{3}$
   Answer: b.

9. Describe the graph of $y = x^3 + 3x$.
   a. Concave up when $x < -3$, concave down when $x > 3$
   b. Concave up for all x, relative minimum at $x = 0$
   c. Concave down when $x < 0$, concave up when $x > 0$, the inflection point is (0, 0)
   d. Concave down for all x, relative maximum at $x = 1$
   Answer: c.

10. Find the inflection point(s), if any, of the function $f(x) = 12x^3 - 36x + 10$.
    a. (0, 0)
    b. (0, 10)
    c. $(1, -14)$
    d. $(-1, 34)$
    Answer: b.

11. Given that the derivative of a function is $f'(x) = x^3 - 27x + 6$, find the x-coordinate(s) of the inflection point(s), if any, of the function.
a. 0
b. −3 only
c. 3 only
d. ±3
Answer: d.

12. Find the inflection point(s), if any, of the function $f(x) = \frac{x^4}{12} + \frac{x^3}{3} + x + 5$.
a. (0, 5) only
b. (5, 5) and $\left(-2, \frac{5}{3}\right)$
c. $\left(-2, \frac{5}{3}\right)$ only
d. $\left(-2, \frac{5}{3}\right)$ and (0, 5)
Answer: d.

13. Find the inflection point(s), if any, of the function $f(x) = \sqrt{x-4}$.
a. (5, 1)
b. (4, 0)
c. There is no inflection point
d. (20, 4)
Answer: c.

14. An economy's consumer price index (CPI) is described by the function $I(t) = -3t^3 + 18t^2 + 120 \quad (0 \le t \le 9)$, where $t = 0$ corresponds to the year 2000. Find the point of inflection of the function I.
a. (1, 135)
b. (0, 120)
c. (2, 168)
d. None of the above
Answer: c.

15. The function $S(t) = -t^2 + 20t + 1, \; (0 \le t \le 20)$, represents the intensity of the symptoms of a person suffering from viral pneumonia t days after the onset of the infection. How many days will it take for the symptoms to be at their worst?
a. 10
b. 20
c. 4
d. 5
Answer: a.

Section 4.3

1. Find the horizontal and vertical asymptotes of the following graph.

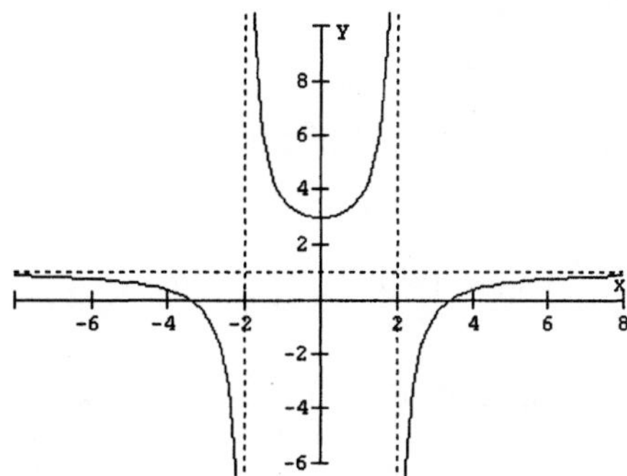

Answer: Horizontal: $y = 1$; vertical: $x = \pm 2$

2. Find the horizontal and vertical asymptotes of the following graph.

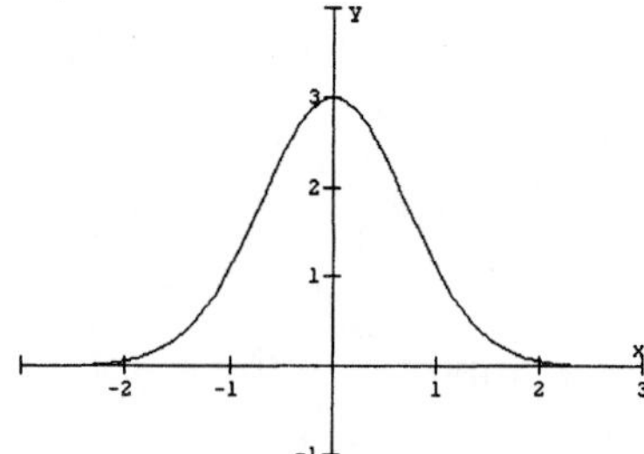

Answer: Horizontal: $y = 0$; vertical: none

3. Find the horizontal and vertical asymptotes of the following graph.

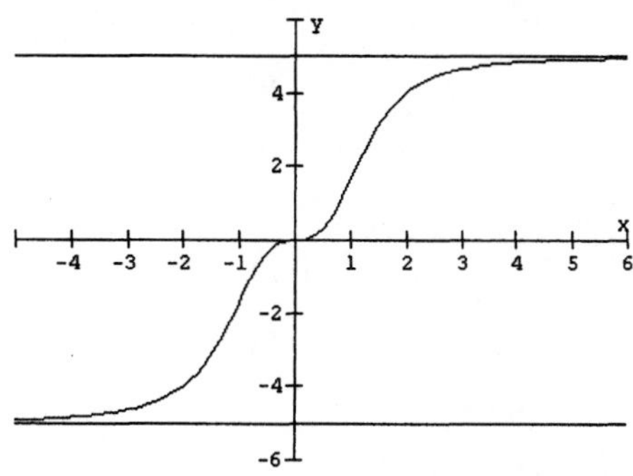

Answer: Horizontal: $y = -5$, $y = 5$; vertical: none

4. Find the horizontal and vertical asymptotes of the graph of $f(x) = \dfrac{2}{2x+1}$.

Answer: Horizontal: $y = 0$; vertical: $x = -\dfrac{1}{2}$

5. Find the horizontal and vertical asymptotes of the graph of $h(x) = \frac{4}{x^2}$.

Answer: Horizontal: $y = 0$; vertical: $x = 0$

6. Find the horizontal and vertical asymptotes of the graph of $f(x) = \frac{1}{1+3x^2}$.

Answer: Horizontal: $y = 0$; vertical: none

7. Find the horizontal and vertical asymptotes of the graph of $h(x) = 3x^3 - 4x + 2$.

Answer: Horizontal: none; vertical: none

8. Find the horizontal and vertical asymptotes of the graph of
$f(x) = \frac{-3x^2 + 2x - 1}{x^2 + 2x - 15}$.

Answer: Horizontal: $y = -3$; vertical: $x = -5$, $x = 3$

9. Find the horizontal and vertical asymptotes of the graph of $h(x) = 2 + \frac{1}{1-x}$.

Answer: Horizontal: $y = 2$; vertical: $x = 1$

10. Sketch the graph of $f(x) = x^3 + 6x^2 + 9x$.

Answer:

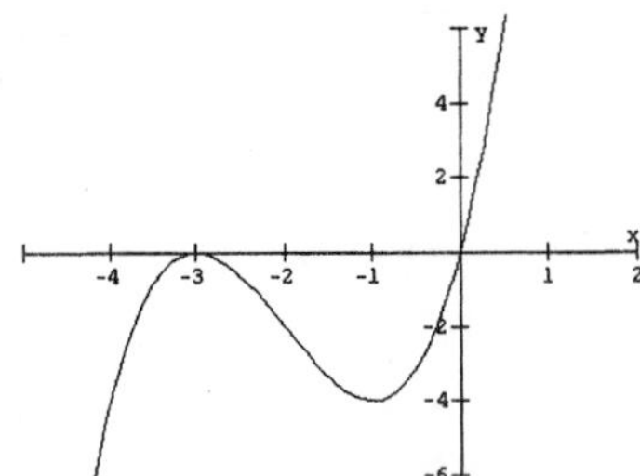

11. Sketch the graph of $h(x) = 2x^3 - 4x + 1$.
Answer:

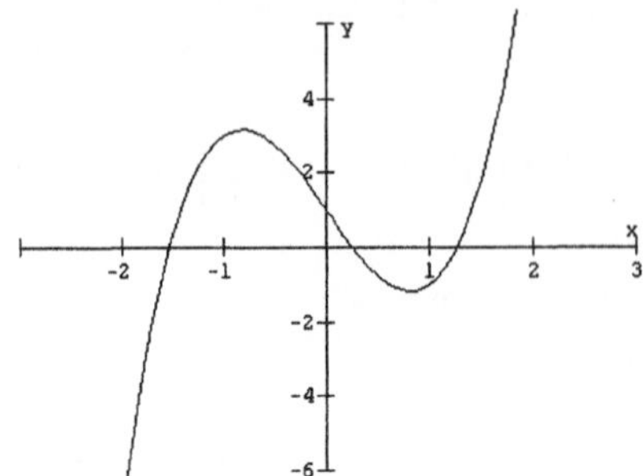

12. Sketch the graph of $f(x) = -x^3 + 2x^2 + 2$.
Answer:

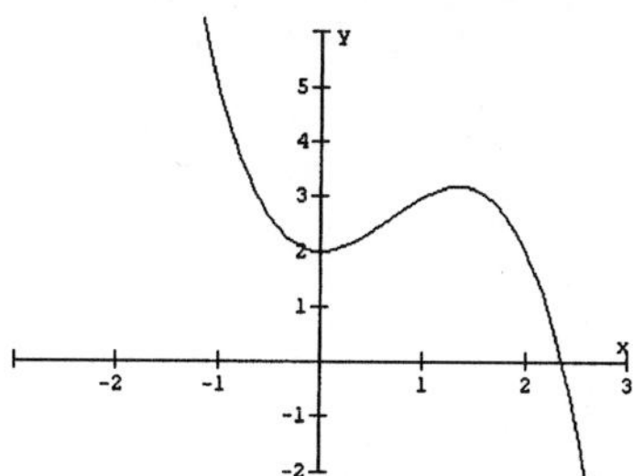

13. Sketch the graph of $f(x) = \dfrac{x^2 - 8}{x^2 - 4}$.

Answer:

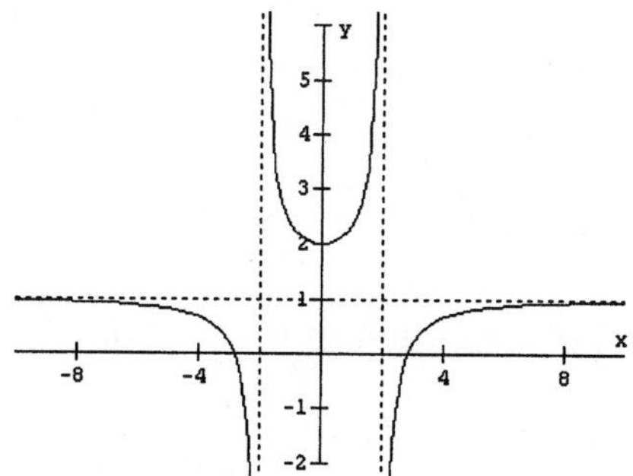

14. Sketch the graph of $h(x) = x^2 - 4\sqrt{x}$.
Answer:

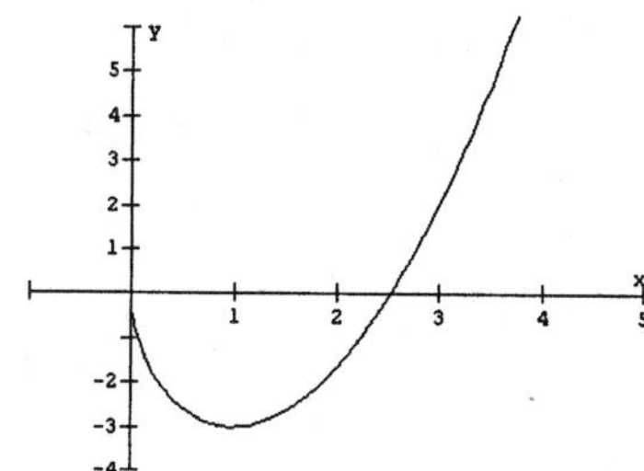

15. Sketch the graph of $h(x) = \dfrac{x}{2x - 5}$.

Answer:

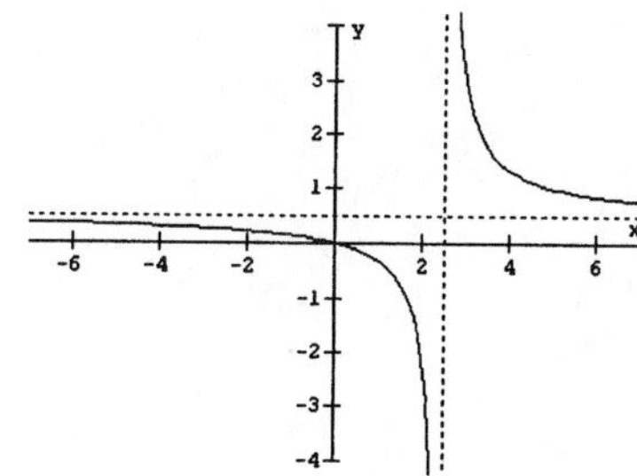

Section 4.3 Multiple Choice Questions

1. Find the horizontal asymptote(s) of the graph of the function $f(x)=\dfrac{3}{x+4}$.

   a. $y=0$
   b. $x=0$
   c. $y=4$
   d. $x=4$
   Answer: a.

2. Find the vertical asymptote(s) of the graph of the function $f(x)=\dfrac{3x}{(x+4)(x-1)}$.

   a. $y=4$ and $y=-1$
   b. $x=4$ and $x=-1$
   c. $y=-4$ and $y=1$
   d. $x=-4$ and $x=1$
   Answer: d.

3. Find the vertical asymptote(s) of the graph of the function $f(x)=\dfrac{3x+15}{(x-4)(x+5)}$.

   a. $y=-4$ and $y=-5$
   b. $x=4$ only
   c. $y=4$ and $y=-5$
   d. $x=-5$ and $x=4$
   Answer: b.

4. Find the horizontal asymptote(s) of the graph of the function
   $f(x)=\dfrac{x^2+1}{(x-3)(x+1)}$.

   a. $y=-1$ and $y=3$
   b. $x=1$ only
   c. $y=1$
   d. $x=-1$ and $x=3$
   Answer: c.

5. Find the vertical asymptote(s) of the graph of the function $f(x)=\dfrac{3x+8}{x^2-2x-8}$.

   a. $y=0$
   b. $x=4$ only
   c. $y=4$ and $y=-2$
   d. $x=-2$ and $x=4$
   Answer: d.

6. Find the horizontal asymptote(s) of the graph of the function
$f(x) = \dfrac{(4x-5)(3x-1)}{x^2-2x-8}$.
   a. $y=0$
   b. $x=4$ only
   c. $y=12$
   d. $x=-2$ and $x=4$

   Answer: c.

7. Find the vertical asymptote(s) of the graph of the function $f(x) = \dfrac{x^2-25}{x^2-2x-15}$.
   a. $y=0$
   b. $x=-3$ only
   c. $y=1$
   d. $x=-3$ and $x=5$

   Answer: b.

8. The average cost per disc (in dollars) incurred by Herald Records in pressing x videodiscs is given by the average cost function $y = \overline{C}(x) = 3 + \dfrac{2000}{x+1}$. Find the horizontal asymptote of the graph of $\overline{C}(x)$.
   a. $y=3$
   b. $x=3$
   c. $y=2000$
   d. $x=0$

   Answer: a.

9. The average cost per disc (in dollars) incurred by Herald Records in pressing x videodiscs is given by the average cost function $y = \overline{C}(x) = 3 + \dfrac{7x+2000}{x^2+2}$. Find the horizontal asymptote of the graph of $\overline{C}(x)$.
   a. $y=0$
   b. $y=3$
   c. $y=2010$
   d. 2

   Answer: b.

10. The concentration (in milligrams/cubic centimeter) of a certain drug in a patient's bloodstream t hr after injection is given by $C(t) = \dfrac{0.3t}{t^2+2}$. Find the horizontal asymptote of the graph of $C(t)$.
    a. $y=0$

b. $y = 0.3$
c. $y = 2.3$
d. $x = 0$
Answer: a.

11. Given the function $f(x) = \dfrac{x^2 - 100}{x^2 - 64}$, which of the following statements is true?
a. The domain of the function is all real numbers
b. The vertical asymptote(s) of the function are $x = \pm 10$
c. The horizontal asymptote of the function is $y = 1$
d. The horizontal asymptote of the function is $x = 1$
Answer: c.

12. Given the function $f(x) = \dfrac{x^2 - 10x + 25}{x^2 - 25}$, which of the following statements is true?
a. The domain of the function is all real numbers except -5
b. The vertical asymptote(s) of the function are $x = \pm 5$
c. The horizontal asymptote of the function is $y = 10$
d. The domain of the function is all real numbers except -5 and 5
Answer: d.

13. Given the function $f(x) = \dfrac{x^3 - 1}{x - 1}$, which of the following statements is true?
a. The domain of the function is all real numbers
b. (1, 3) is a point on the graph of the function
c. The function is continuous everywhere
d. The domain of the function is all real numbers except $x = 1$
Answer: d.

Section 4.4

1. Find the absolute maximum and the absolute minimum of $f(x) = 2x^2 - 6x + 6$.

   Answer: Absolute minimum: $f\left(\frac{3}{2}\right) = \frac{3}{2}$; no absolute maximum

2. Find the absolute maximum and the absolute minimum of $f(x) = 4 - x^{2/3}$.
   Answer: Absolute maximum: $f(0) = 4$; no absolute minimum

3. Find the absolute maximum and the absolute minimum of $f(x) = 3x + 4$.
   Answer: No absolute maximum: no absolute minimum

4. Find the absolute maximum and the absolute minimum of
   $f(x) = x^2 - 6x + 6$ on $[-2,4]$.
   Answer: Absolute maximum: $f(-2) = 22$; absolute minimum: $f(3) = -3$

5. Find the absolute maximum and the absolute minimum of
   $f(x) = -x^2 + 2x$ on $[-2,2]$.
   Answer: Absolute maximum: $f(1) = 1$; absolute minimum: $f(-2) = -8$

6. Find the absolute maximum and the absolute minimum of $f(x) = -2x + 6$ on [0,5].
   Answer: Absolute maximum (0,6): Absolute minimum (5, -4)

7. Find the absolute maximum and the absolute minimum of $f(x) = x^3 + 3x^2$ on $[-2,3]$.
   Answer: Absolute maximum: $f(3) = 54$; absolute minimum: $f(0) = 0$

8. Find the absolute maximum and the absolute minimum of $g(x) = \frac{x+2}{x-2}$ on $[-4,4]$.
   Answer: Absolute maximum: none; absolute minimum: none

9. Find the absolute maximum and the absolute minimum of
   $g(x) = \frac{x+2}{x-2}$ on $[-4,1]$.

   Answer: Absolute maximum: $g(-4) = \frac{1}{3}$; absolute minimum: $g(1) = -3$

10. Find the absolute maximum and the absolute minimum of $f(x)=3x^{2/3}-6x+6$ on $[1,8]$.

Answer: Absolute maximum: $f(1)=3$; absolute minimum: $f(8)=-30$

11. Find the absolute maximum and the absolute minimum of $f(x)=\dfrac{x}{x^2+4}$ on $[-4,8]$.

Answer: Absolute maximum: $f(2)=\dfrac{1}{4}$; absolute minimum: $f(-2)=-\dfrac{1}{4}$

12. Find the absolute maximum and the absolute minimum of $f(x)=\dfrac{1}{x^2+3x+4}$ on $[-2,2]$.

Answer: Absolute maximum: $f\left(-\dfrac{3}{2}\right)=\dfrac{4}{7}$; absolute minimum: $f(2)=\dfrac{1}{14}$

13. Find the absolute maximum and the absolute minimum of $f(x)=\dfrac{x}{x^2+3x+4}$ on $[-3,3]$.

Answer: Absolute maximum: $f(2)=\dfrac{1}{7}$; absolute minimum: $f(-2)=-1$

14. Given the graph of *f*, determine the absolute maximum and absolute minimum.

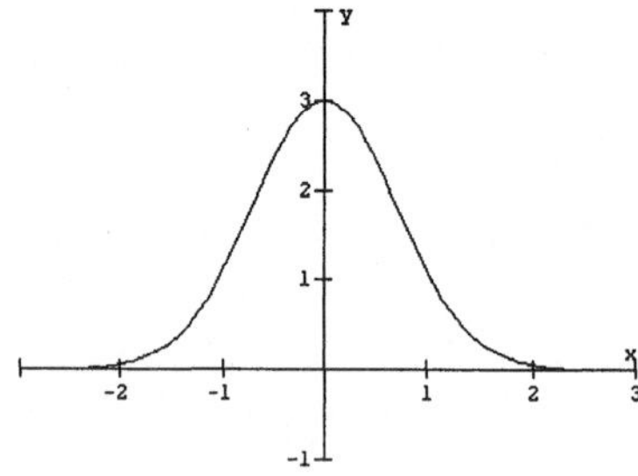

Answer: Absolute max: $(0,3)$; Absolute min: none

15. Given the graph of *f*, determine the absolute maximum and absolute minimum.

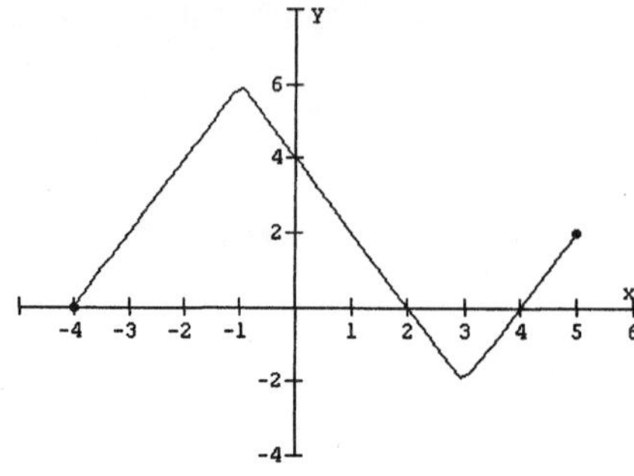

Answer: Absolute max: $(-1,6)$; Absolute min: $(3,-2)$

16. Given the graph of f, determine the absolute maximum and absolute minimum.

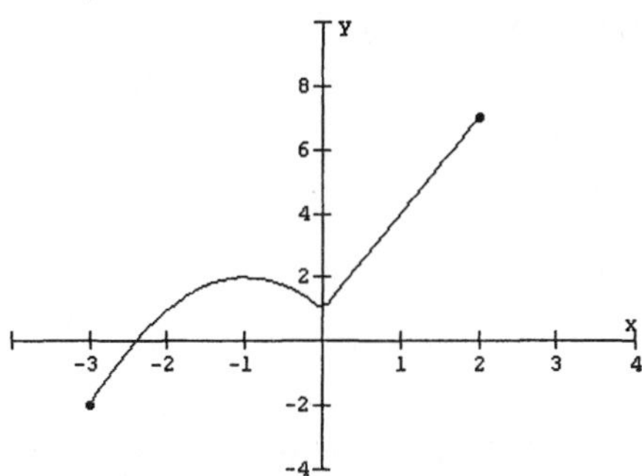

Answer: Absolute max: $(2,7)$; Absolute min: $(-3,-2)$

17. Given the graph of f, determine the absolute maximum and absolute minimum.

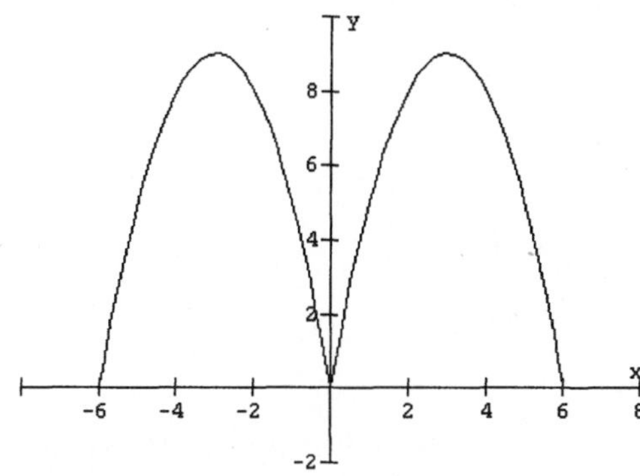

Answer: Absolute max: $(\pm 3,9)$; Absolute min: $(\pm 6,0)$ and $(0,0)$

Section 4.4 Multiple Choice Questions

1. Given $f(x)=2x^2-7x-10$, find the x value of the absolute maximum of $f(x)$ on $[-1, 3]$.
   a. -1
   b. -13
   c. $\frac{7}{4}$
   d. 0
   Answer: a.

2. A rectangle is to be inscribed between the parabola $y=4-x^2$ and the x-axis, with its base on the x-axis. A value of x that maximizes the area of the rectangle is
   a. $\frac{\sqrt{3}}{3}$
   b. $\frac{2\sqrt{3}}{3}$
   c. $\frac{2}{3}$
   d. $\frac{\sqrt{3}}{2}$
   Answer: b.

3. Suppose the total cost function for manufacturing a certain product is $C(x)=300+5x+0.001x^2$, where x is the number of units produced per day. The product can be sold at a price of p dollars, where $p=8-0.003x$. If all the products produced are sold, find the daily level of production that will yield a maximum profit for the manufacturer.
   a. 350
   b. 375
   c. 400
   d. 425
   Answer: b.

4. The function $g(x)=4x^3-8x^2+1$ on the interval [-1, 1] has an absolute minimum at $x=$
   a. -11
   b. 0
   c. 1
   d. -1
   Answer: d.

5. The *GrassChomper Lawnmower Company* can produce up to 200 lawnmowers per week. If the weekly cost function is $C(x)=3\left(0.02x^2+150\right)$, where C is measured in dollars, how many lawnmowers should be made to minimize the average weekly cost?
a. 92 lawnmowers
b. 87 lawnmowers
c. 70 lawnmowers
d. 50 lawnmowers
Answer: b.

6. In order to sell x thousand new novels each month, the price p must be $p=\sqrt{576-2x^2}$ dollars. How many novels must be sold each month to maximize revenue and what must the price of each novel at that sale level be?

a. 9,000 novels selling at $20.23 each
b. 10,000 novels selling at $19.35 each
c. 12,000 novels selling at $16.97 each
d. 15,000 novels selling at $11.22 each
Answer: c.

7. The concentration C of a particular blood pressure medication t hours after it is swallowed is given by $C(t)=\dfrac{0.3t}{(t+2.5)^2}$. How long will it take for the concentration to be at its highest?
a. 1.0 hours
b. 2.0 hours
c. 1.5 hours
d. 2.5 hours
Answer: d.

8. The management of Trappee and Sons, producers of the famous TezaPep hot sauce, estimate that their profit (in dollars) from the daily production and sale of x cases (each case consisting of 24 bottles) of the hot sauce is given by $P(x)=-0.0003x^3+9x-420$. What is the largest possible profit Trappee can make in 1 day?
a. $100
b. $180
c. $300
d. $420
Answer: a.

9. A stone is thrown straight up from the roof of a 90-ft building. The height (in feet) of the stone at any time t (in seconds), measured from the ground, is given by $h(t) = -16t^2 + 64t + 90$. What is the maximum height the stone reaches?
   a. 90 ft
   b. 282 ft
   c. 26 ft
   d. 154 ft
   Answer: d.

10. The function $g(x) = \sqrt{x^2 - 36}$ on the interval [6, 100] has an absolute minimum at $x =$
    a. 0
    b. 100
    c. 6
    d. –6
    Answer: c.

11. The function $g(x) = \sqrt{x^2 + 4}$ on the interval [-1, 1] has an absolute minimum at $x =$
    a. There is no absolute minimum
    b. 0
    c. 1
    d. –1
    Answer: b.

12. The function $g(x) = \dfrac{1}{x+5}$ on the interval [-1, 1] has an absolute maximum at $x =$
    a. There is no absolute maximum
    b. 0
    c. 1
    d. –1
    Answer: d.

Section 4.5

1. An arrow is shot from a cliff 100 feet above the ground. The height of the arrow above the ground at any time t (measured in seconds) is given by $h(t) = -16t^2 + 320t + 100$ (with h measured in feet). Find the maximum height of the arrow above the ground.
   Answer: 1,700 feet

2. A company has determined that its profit (P) depends on the amount of money spent on advertising (x). The relationship is given by the equation $P(x) = \dfrac{2x}{x^2 + 4} + 70$, where P and x are measured in thousands of dollars.
   (a) What amount should the company spend on advertising to assure maximum profit?
   Answer: $2,000
   (b) What is the maximum profit?
   Answer: $70,500

3. The price of a certain stock, measured in dollars, at time t, measured in hours, is estimated by $P(t) = 0.1t^3 + 0.05t^2 - 3t + 10$, $(0 \le t \le 5)$. When will the stock price be at a maximum, and when will it reach a minimum?
   Answer: Maximum price at $t = 0$; Minimum price at $t = 3$ hours

4. A farmer has 300 feet of fencing with which to enclose a rectangular grazing pen next to a barn. The farmer will use the barn as one side of the pen, and will use the fencing for the other three sides. Find the dimensions of the pen with the maximum area.
   Answer: 75 feet by 150 feet

5. A farmer has 460 feet of fencing with which to enclose a rectangular grazing pen next to a barn. The farmer will use the barn as one side of the pen, and will use the fencing for the other three sides. Find the dimensions of the pen with the maximum area.
   Answer: 115 feet by 230 feet

6. By cutting away identical squares from each corner of a rectangular piece of cardboard and folding up the resulting flaps, an open box may be made. If the cardboard is 10 inches long and 10 inches wide, find the dimensions of the box that will yield the maximum volume.
   Answer: $\dfrac{20}{3}$ inches by $\dfrac{20}{3}$ inches by $\dfrac{5}{3}$ inches

7. By cutting away identical squares from each corner of a rectangular piece of cardboard and folding up the resulting flaps, an open box may be made. If the

cardboard is 30 inches long and 14 inches wide, find the dimensions of the box that will yield the maximum volume.
Answer: 24 inches by 8 inches by 3 inches

8. A property management company manages 200 apartments renting for $800 each with all the apartments rented. For each $10 per month increase in rent there will be two vacancies with no possibility of filling them. What rent per apartment will maximize the total monthly revenue?
Answer: $900

9. The window below is to have a perimeter of 20 feet. Find the dimensions that will maximize the area (to let the most light in).

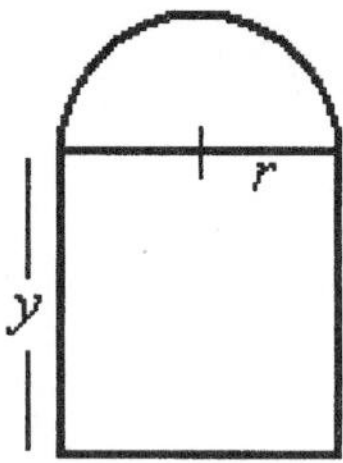

Answer: $r = \dfrac{20}{4+\pi} \approx 2.8$ feet, $y \approx 2.8$ feet

10. An editorial assistant at Bloke/Coors Publishing Company arbitrarily decided that the pages of a book should have three-quarter-inch margins at the top and bottom and half-inch margins on the sides. She further stipulated that each page should have an area of 40 square inches. Determine the page dimensions that will result in the maximum printed area on the page.
Answer: Height: $2\sqrt{15}$; width: $\dfrac{4}{3}\sqrt{15}$

11. You wish to construct an open rectangular box with a volume of 18 cubic feet. The length of the base of the box is to be twice as long as the width. The material for the bottom of the box costs 10 cents per square foot, while the material for the sides of the box costs 20 cents per square foot. Find the dimensions of the least expensive box which can be constructed.
Answer: width = 3 feet, length = 6 feet, height = 1 foot

Section 4.5 Multiple Choice Questions

1. A gardener has 1,600 feet of fence to enclose a rectangular parcel of land. The gardener also wants to use fence to divide the garden into two equal sections so he can share half the space with his neighbor. What dimensions should the entire parcel be to maximize the area?
   a. Length = 500 ft, width = 200 ft
   b. Length = 600 ft, width = $\frac{400}{3}$ ft
   c. Length = 400 ft, width = $\frac{800}{3}$ ft
   d. Length = 575 ft, width = 150 ft
   Answer: c.

2. An arrow is shot from a cliff 200 feet above the ground. The height of the arrow above the ground at any time t (measured in seconds) is given by $h(t) = -16t^2 + 320t + 200$ (with h measured in feet). Find the maximum height of the arrow above the ground.
   a. 200 ft
   b. 1800 ft
   c. 3400 ft
   d. 3000 ft
   Answer: b.

3. A basketball is thrown from a cliff 120 feet above the ground. The height of the basketball above the ground at any time t (measured in seconds) is given by $h(t) = -16t^2 + 32t + 120$ (with h measured in feet). Find the maximum height of the basketball above the ground.
   a. 136 ft
   b. 120 ft
   c. 152 ft
   d. 16 ft
   Answer: a.

4. The price of a certain stock at time t ($0 \le t \le 5$) is estimated by $P(t) = 0.1t^2 - 0.4t + 10$, where p is measured in dollars and t is measured in days. When will the stock price be at a minimum?
   a. 5 days
   b. 3 days
   c. 1 day
   d. 2 days
   Answer: d.

5. The price of a certain stock at time t ($0 \le t \le 10$) is estimated by $P(t) = -0.4t^2 + 0.8t + 45$, where p is measured in dollars and t is measured in days. When will the stock price be at a maximum?
   a. 5 days
   b. 3 days
   c. 1 day
   d. 2 days
   Answer: c.

6. A company has determined that its profit (P) depends on the amount of money spent on advertising (x). The relationship is given by the equation $P(x) = \dfrac{3x}{x^2 + 25} + 90$, where P and x are measured in thousands of dollars. What amount should the company spend on advertising to assure maximum profit?
   a. $5,000
   b. $25,000
   c. $10,000
   d. $7,000
   Answer: a.

7. The owner of a company has 1000 yd of fencing material with which to enclose a rectangular piece of grazing land along the straight portion of a river. If fencing is not required along the river, what are the dimensions of the largest area that he can enclose? What is this area?
   a. $250 \text{ yd} \times 500 \text{ yd}$; $500{,}000 \text{ yd}^2$
   b. $250 \text{ yd} \times 500 \text{ yd}$; $125{,}000 \text{ yd}^2$
   c. $250 \text{ yd} \times 250 \text{ yd}$; $625{,}000 \text{ yd}^2$
   d. $250 \text{ yd} \times 400 \text{ yd}$; $100{,}000 \text{ yd}^2$
   Answer: b.

8. By cutting away identical squares from each corner of a rectangular piece of cardboard and folding up the resulting flaps, an open box may be made. If the cardboard is 24 in. long and 9 in. wide, find the dimensions of the box that will yield the maximum volume.
   a. $20 \text{ in.} \times 5 \text{ in.} \times 2 \text{ in.}$
   b. $20 \text{ in.} \times 15 \text{ in.} \times 2 \text{ in.}$
   c. $10 \text{ in.} \times 10 \text{ in.} \times 2 \text{ in.}$
   d. $20 \text{ in.} \times 12 \text{ in.} \times 5 \text{ in.}$
   Answer: a.

9. If an open box is made from a tin sheet 10 in. square by cutting out identical squares from each corner and bending up the resulting flaps, determine the dimensions of the largest box that can be made.

a. $\frac{20}{2}$ in.$\times\frac{20}{2}$ in.$\times\frac{5}{2}$ in.

b. $\frac{10}{3}$ in.$\times\frac{10}{3}$ in.$\times\frac{10}{3}$ in.

c. $\frac{20}{3}$ in.$\times\frac{20}{3}$ in.$\times\frac{10}{3}$ in.

d. $\frac{20}{3}$ in.$\times\frac{20}{3}$ in.$\times\frac{5}{3}$ in.

Answer: d.

10. What are the dimensions of a closed rectangular box that has a square cross section, a capacity of 108 in^3, and is constructed using the least amount of materials?

a. 3.76 in.$\times$3.76 in.$\times$3.76 in.

b. 4 in.$\times$4 in.$\times$4 in.

c. 4.76 in.$\times$4.76 in.$\times$4.76 in.

d. 5 in.$\times$5 in.$\times$5 in.

Answer: c.

11. If an open box has a square base and a volume of 256 in^3, and is constructed from a tin sheet, find the dimensions of the box, assuming a minimum amount of material is used in its construction.

a. 8 in.$\times$8 in.$\times$4 in.

b. 4 in.$\times$4 in.$\times$4 in.

c. 10 in.$\times$10 in.$\times$2 in.

d. 5 in.$\times$5 in.$\times$5 in.

Answer: a.

12. A ball is thrown from a cliff 150 feet above the ground. The height of the ball above the ground at any time t (measured in seconds) is given by $h(t) = -16t^2 + 32t + 150$ (with h measured in feet). Find the maximum height of the ball above the ground.

a. 136 ft

b. 182 ft

c. 150 ft

d. 166 ft

Answer: d.

13. A manufacturer can produce a color pen at a cost of \$3. The color pens have been selling for \$5 per pen and at this price, consumers have been buying 4,000 pens per month. The manufacturer is planning to raise the price of the pens and estimates that for each \$1 increase in the price, 400 fewer pens will be sold each month. At what price should the manufacturer sell the pen to maximize profit? What is the maximized profit?

a. \$ 4 per pen; the maximized profit is \$14,400

b. $ 9 per pen; the maximized profit is $14,400
c. $ 6 per pen; the maximized profit is $12,800
d. $ 8 per pen; the maximized profit is $8,000
Answer: b.

14. A manufacturer estimates that when x units of a particular commodity are produced each month, the total cost (in dollars) will be $C(x)=\frac{1}{8}x^2+4x+200$ and all units can be sold at a price of $p(x)=49-x$ dollars per units. Determine the price that corresponds to the maximum profit?
a. $ 49 per unit
b. $ 20 per unit
c. $ 29 per unit
d. $ 8 per unit
Answer: c.

Exam 4A

Name:
Instructor:
Section:

Write your work as neatly as possible.

1. Find the interval(s) where $f(x) = x^3 + 12x^2 + 21x + 1$ is increasing and the interval(s) where it is decreasing.

2. Given the graph of f below, find the interval(s) where f is increasing and the interval(s) where it is decreasing.

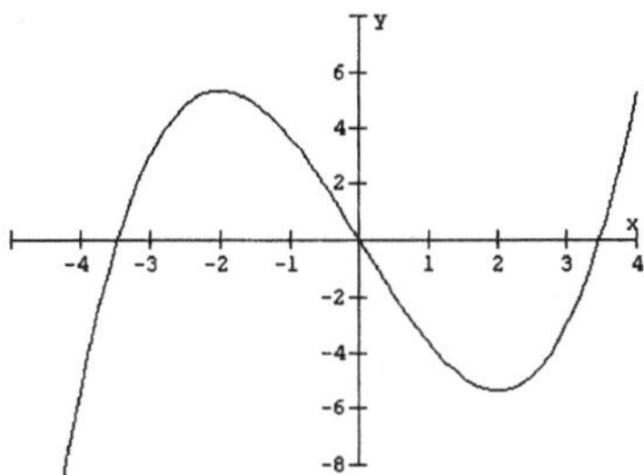

3. Find the relative maxima and minima, if any, of $g(x) = \frac{1}{3}x^3 - \frac{3}{2}x^2 + 2$.

4. Find the relative maxima and minima, if any, of $h(t) = 3 - t^{2/3}$.

5. Let $f(x) = x^3 + 12x^2 + 21x + 1$.
   (a) Find the interval(s) where $f(x)$ is concave upward.

   (b) Find the interval(s) where $f(x)$ is concave downward.

   (c) Find the x-coordinate(s) of any point(s) of inflection.

6. Let $f(x) = \dfrac{x+3}{x+2}$.
   (a) Find the interval(s) where $f(x)$ is concave upward.

   (b) Find the interval(s) where $f(x)$ is concave downward.

   (c) Find the x-coordinate(s) of any point(s) of inflection.

7. Find the horizontal and vertical asymptotes of the graph of the function shown below.

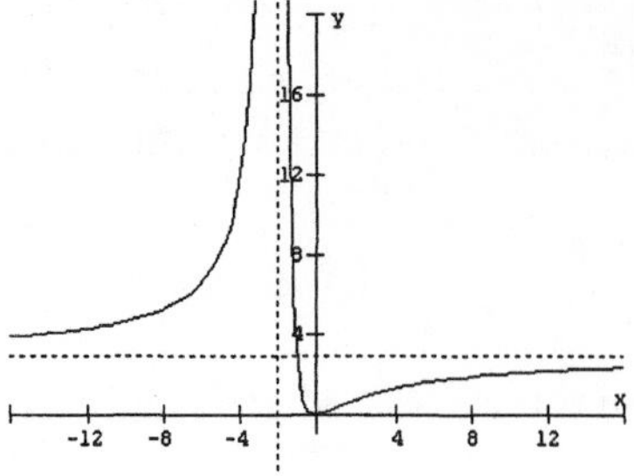

8. Sketch the graph of $y = \dfrac{1}{x+3}$.

9. Sketch the graph of $y = x^3 - 6x$.

10. Find the absolute maximum and the absolute minimum of $f(x) = 36x - 3x^2$ on $[0,7]$.

11. Find the absolute maximum and the absolute minimum of $f(x) = x^2 + 3x^3$ on $[-2,3]$.

12. The mosquito population is a function of rainfall, and can be approximated by the formula $N(x) = 1000 + 30x + 44.5x^2 - x^3$, where x is the number of inches of rainfall $(0 \le x \le 43)$. What amount of rainfall will result in a maximum number of mosquitoes?

13. A farmer wants to create a divided grazing area like the one shown below. The barn will be one side of the grazing area. The farmer has a total of 1200 feet of fencing material to enclose the grazing area and provide the dividing fence down the middle. What is the maximum area that can be enclosed?

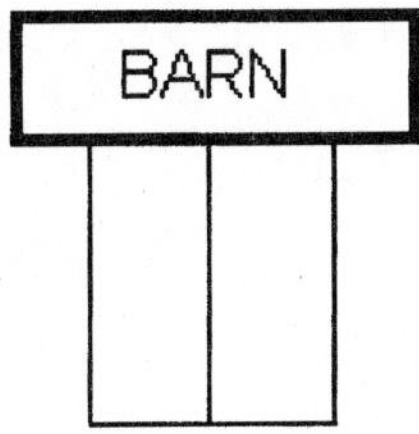

14. The window below is to have a perimeter of 32 feet. Find the dimensions that will maximize the area (to let the most light in).

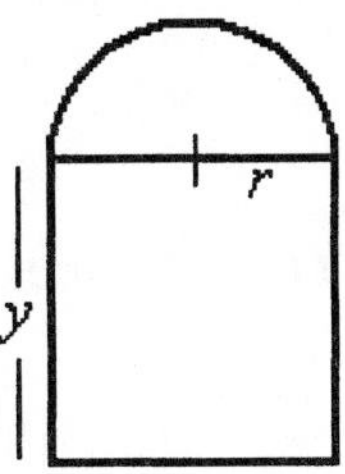

15. An apple orchard has an average yield of 40 bushels of apples per tree if the tree density is 10 trees per acre. For each unit increase in tree density, the average yield decreases by 2 bushels per acre. Find how many trees should be planted per acre to maximize the number of apples produced per acre.

Exam 4B

Name:
Instructor:
Section:

Write your work as neatly as possible.

1. Find the interval(s) where $f(x) = x^3 + x^2 - 5x + 2$ is increasing and the interval(s) where it is decreasing.

2. Find the interval(s) where $f(x) = \sqrt{2 - 4x}$ is increasing and the interval(s) where it is decreasing.

3. Find the relative maxima and minima, if any, of $g(x) = x^3 - 12x^2$.

4. Find the relative maxima and minima, if any, of $h(t) = 3 + \sqrt{t - 2}$.

5. Let $f(x) = x^3 + 5x^2 - 1$.
   (a) Find the interval(s) where $f(x)$ is concave upward.

   (b) Find the interval(s) where $f(x)$ is concave downward.

   (c) Find the x-coordinate(s) of any point(s) of inflection.

6. Let $f(x) = \dfrac{x - 2}{x + 1}$.
   (a) Find the interval(s) where $f(x)$ is concave upward.

   (b) Find the interval(s) where $f(x)$ is concave downward.

   (c) Find the x-coordinate(s) of any point(s) of inflection.

7. Find the horizontal and vertical asymptotes of the graph of $y = \dfrac{3x^2}{x^2 - 5x - 6}$.

8. Sketch the graph of $y = \dfrac{2-x}{x+3}$.

9. Sketch the graph of $y = x^4 - 4x^2$.

10. Find the absolute maximum and the absolute minimum of
$f(x) = 2x^2 + 1$ on $[-2,3]$.

11. Find the absolute maximum and the absolute minimum of
$f(x) = \dfrac{x}{x^2+4}$ on $[0,3]$.

12. The quantity demanded per month, x, of a certain brand of electric shavers is related to the price, p, per shaver by the equation $p = -0.1x + 10{,}000$ $(0 \le x \le 20{,}000)$, where p is measured in dollars. The total monthly cost for manufacturing the shavers is given
$$C(x) = 0.00002x^3 - 0.4x^2 + 10{,}000x + 20{,}000.$$
How many shavers should be produced per month in order to maximize the company's profit? What is the maximum profit?

13. A farmer wants to create a pen inside a barn like the one shown below. The sides of the barn will form two sides of the pen, while fencing material will be used for the other two sides. The farmer has a total of 80 feet of fencing material to enclose the pen. What is the maximum area that can be enclosed?

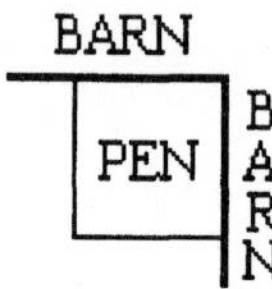

14. To make a rectangular trough, you bend the sides of a 32-inch wide sheet of metal to obtain the cross section pictured below. Find the dimensions of the cross section with the maximum area (this will result in the trough with the largest possible volume).

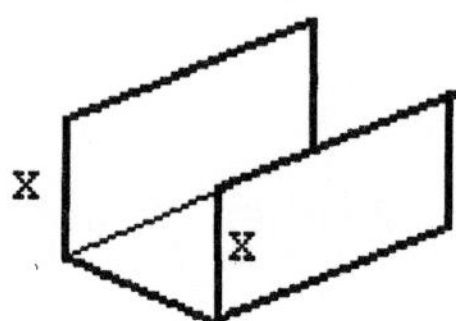

15. An apple orchard has an average yield of 64 bushels of apples per tree if the tree density is 24 trees per acre. For each unit increase in tree density, the average yield decreases by 2 bushels per acre. Find how many trees should be planted per acre to maximize the number of apples produced per acre.

Exam 4C

Name:
Instructor:
Section:

Write your work as neatly as possible.

1. Find the interval(s) where $f(x) = x^2 + 4x - 3$ is increasing and the interval(s) where it is decreasing.

2. Find the interval(s) where $f(x) = \sqrt{6-2x}$ is increasing and the interval(s) where it is decreasing.

3. Given the graph of f below, find the relative maxima and minima, if any.

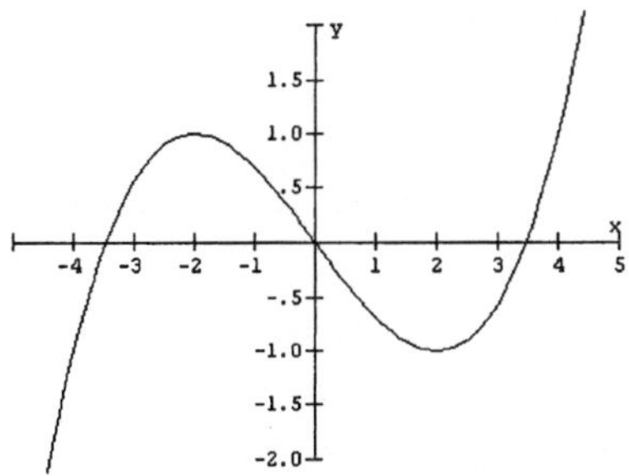

4. Find the relative maxima and minima, if any, of $h(t) = 4 - \sqrt{t}$.

5. Let $f(x) = 3x^3 + x + 1$.
   (a) Find the interval(s) where $f(x)$ is concave upward.

   (b) Find the interval(s) where $f(x)$ is concave downward.

   (c) Find the x-coordinate(s) of any point(s) of inflection.

6. Let $f(x) = x^4 - 4x^3 - 48x^2 - 64x - 32$.
   (a) Find the interval(s) where $f(x)$ is concave upward.

   (b) Find the interval(s) where $f(x)$ is concave downward.

   (c) Find the x-coordinate(s) of any point(s) of inflection.

7. Find the horizontal and vertical asymptotes of the graph below.

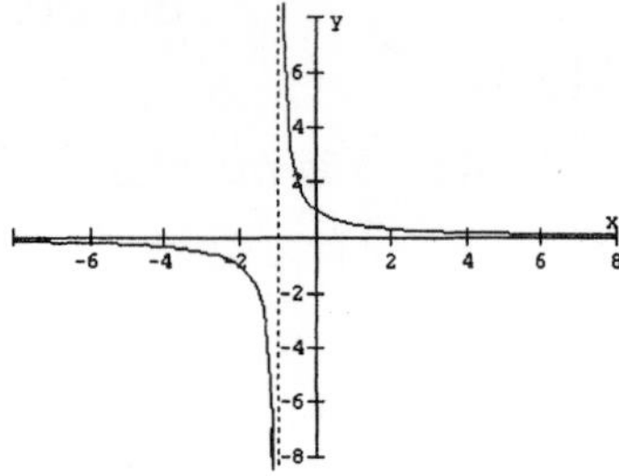

8. Sketch the graph of $y = \dfrac{-2}{x^2 - 9}$.

9. Sketch the graph of $y = 3\sqrt{x} - x$.

10. Find the absolute maximum and the absolute minimum of $f(x) = 3x^3 - 4x$ on $[-1, 0]$.

11. Find the absolute maximum and the absolute minimum of $f(x) = \dfrac{x+2}{x-2}$ on $[-4, 4]$.

12. A farmer wants to create a grazing area beside a river like the one shown below. The river will form one side of the area, while fencing will be used for the other sides. The farmer has a total of 680 feet of fencing to enclose the area. What is the maximum area that can be enclosed?

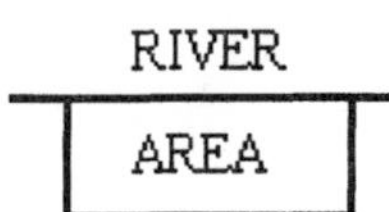

13. By cutting away identical squares from each corner of a rectangular piece of cardboard and folding up the resulting flaps, an open box may be made. If the cardboard is 16 inches long and 16 inches wide, find the dimensions of the box that will yield the maximum volume.

14. A landlord owns an apartment building. When the rent for each apartment is \$400 per month, all 50 apartments are rented. The landlord estimates that each \$50 increase in the monthly rent will result in 5 apartments becoming vacant with no chance of being rented. What monthly rent amount will maximize the total monthly revenue?

Exam 4D

Name:
Instructor:
Section:

Write your work as neatly as possible.

1. Find the interval(s) where $f(x) = x^3 + \frac{9}{2}x^2 + 6x - 3$ is increasing and the interval(s) where it is decreasing.

2. Find the interval(s) where $f(x) = \sqrt{1 + \frac{1}{5}x}$ is increasing and the interval(s) where it is decreasing.

3. Find the relative maxima and minima, if any, of $g(x) = 4x - x^4$.

4. Find the relative maxima and minima, if any, of $h(t) = t^{1/3} - 3t$.

5. The graph of *f* follows. Given that the point of inflection is (0,-1), find the interval(s) where *f* is concave upward and where *f* is concave downward.

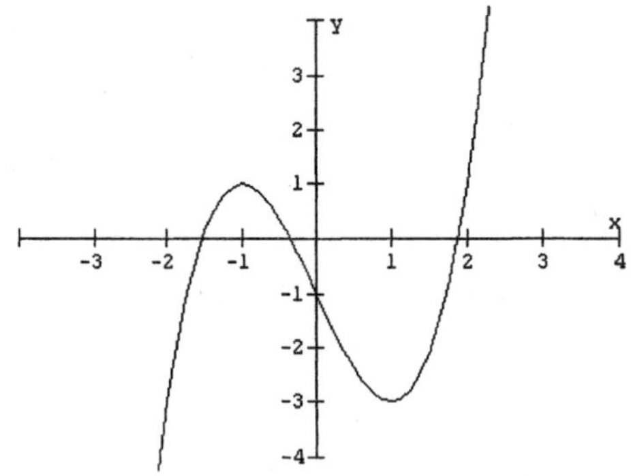

6. Let $f(x) = \sqrt[3]{x+1}$.
   (a) Find the interval(s) where $f(x)$ is concave upward.

   (b) Find the interval(s) where $f(x)$ is concave downward.

   (c) Find the *x*-coordinate(s) of any point(s) of inflection.

7. Find the horizontal and vertical asymptotes of the graph of $y = \dfrac{x^2+2x+1}{x^2-6x+8}$.

8. Sketch the graph of $y = 3x - 2x^3$. Label at least three points on the graph.

9. Sketch the graph of $y = \dfrac{4x^2}{x^2-4}$. Label at least three points in the graph.

10. Find the absolute maximum and the absolute minimum of
$f(x) = x^3 - 3x + 2$ on $[-2,4]$.

11. Find the absolute maximum and the absolute minimum of the graph below.

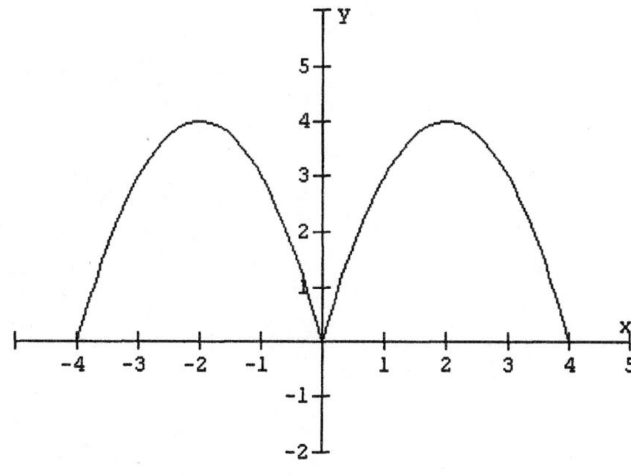

12. A farmer wants to create a pen inside a barn like the one shown below. The barn will form two sides of the pen, while fencing material will be used for the other side. The farmer wants the walls of the pen to take up a total of only 80 feet of the barn walls. What is the maximum area that can be enclosed?

13. The window below is to have a perimeter of 36 feet. Find the dimensions that will maximize the area (to let the most light in).

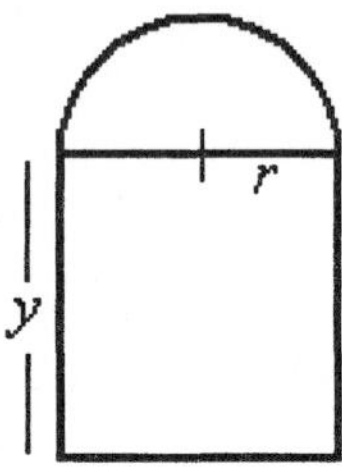

14. A landlord owns an apartment building. When the rent for each apartment is \$700 per month, all 100 apartments are rented. The landlord estimates that each \$100 increase in the monthly rent will result in 10 apartments becoming vacant with no chance of being rented. What monthly rent amount will maximize the total monthly revenue?

Answers to Chapter 4 Exams

Exam 4A

1. Increasing: $(-\infty,-7)\cup(-1,\infty)$;

   Decreasing: $(-7,-1)$

2. Inc: $(-\infty,-2)\cup(2,\infty)$; dec (-2,2)

3. Relative maximum $g(0)=2$;

   relative minimum $g(3)=-\dfrac{5}{2}$

4. Relative maximum $h(0)=3$;
   No relative minimum

5. (a) $(-4,\infty)$

   (b) $(-\infty,-4)$

   (c) $x=-4$

6. (a) $(-2,\infty)$

   (b) $(-\infty,-2)$

   (c) None

7. Horizontal: $y=3$;
   vertical: $x=-2$

8.

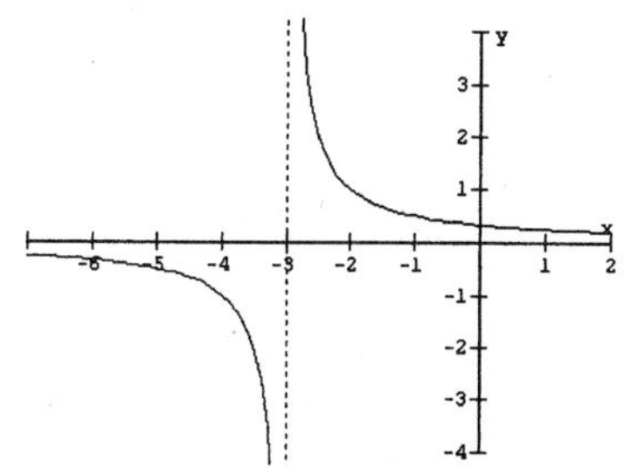

Exam 4B

1. Increasing: $\left(-\infty,-\dfrac{5}{3}\right)\cup(1,\infty)$;

   Decreasing: $\left(-\dfrac{5}{3},1\right)$

2. Inc: never ; dec $(-\infty,1/2]$

3. Relative maximum $g(0)=0$;

   relative minimum $g(8)=-256$

4. No relative maximum;
   relative minimum $h(2)=3$

5. (a) $\left(-\dfrac{5}{3},\infty\right)$

   (b) $\left(-\infty,-\dfrac{5}{3}\right)$

   (c) $x=-\dfrac{5}{3}$

6. (a) $(-\infty,-1)$

   (b) $(-1,\infty)$

   (c) None

7. Horizontal: $y=3$;
   vertical: $x=6$, $x=-1$

8.

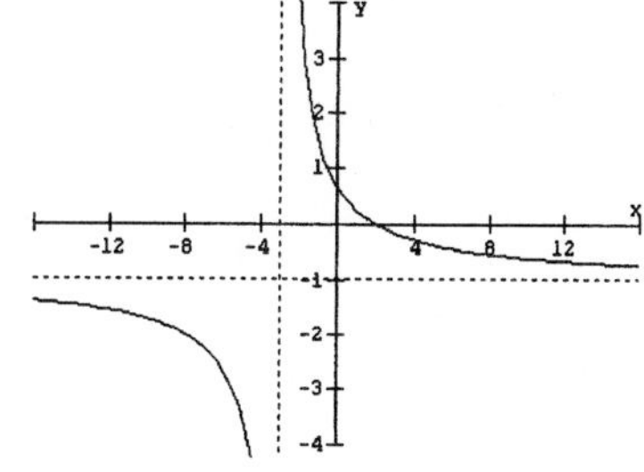

9.

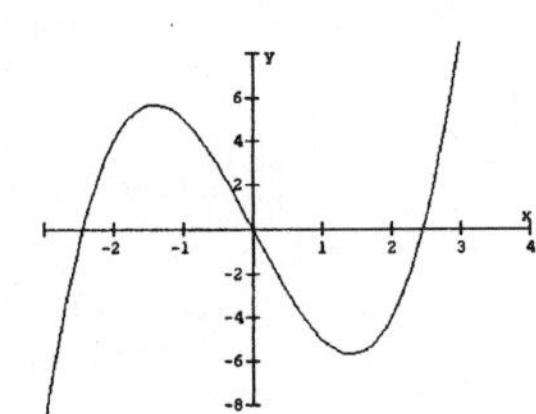

10. Absolute maximum $f(6)=108$; absolute minimum $f(0)=0$
11. Absolute maximum $f(3)=90$; absolute minimum $f(-2)=-20$
12. 30 inches
13. 120,000 square feet
14. $r=\dfrac{32}{4+\pi}\approx 4.48$ ft, $y\approx 4.48$ ft
15. 15 trees per acre

9.

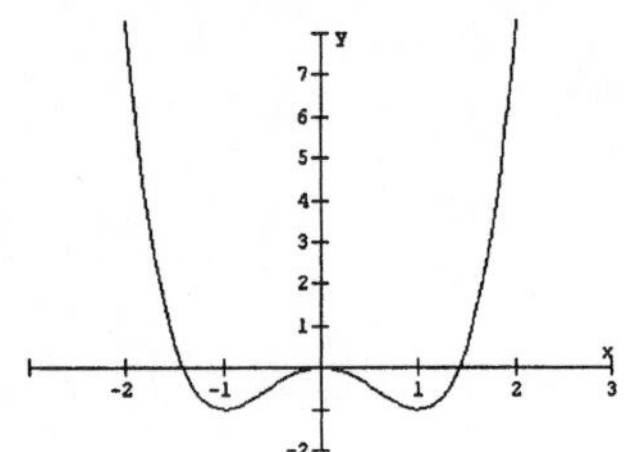

10. Absolute maximum $f(3)=19$; absolute minimum $f(0)=1$
11. Absolute maximum $f(2)=\dfrac{1}{4}$; absolute minimum $f(0)=0$
12. 10,000; $9,980,000
13. 1600 square feet
14. 8 inches by 16 inches
15. 28 trees per acre

Exam 4C

1. Increasing: $(-2,\infty)$; Decreasing: $(-\infty,-2)$
2. Inc: nowhere; dec $(-\infty,3]$
3. Relative maximum $f(-2)=1$; relative minimum $f(2)=-1$
4. Relative maximum $h(0)=4$; No relative minimum
5. (a) $(0,\infty)$; (b) $(-\infty,0)$; (c) $x=0$
6. (a) $(-\infty,-2)\cup(4,\infty)$ (b) $(-2,4)$ (c) $x=-2$ and $x=4$
7. Horizontal: $y=0$; vertical: $x=-1$

Exam 4D

1. Increasing: $(-\infty,-2)\cup(-1,\infty)$; Decreasing: $(-2,-1)$
2. Increasing: $[-5,\infty)$; never decreasing
3. Rel maximum (1, 3) rel minimum none
4. relative maximum; $g(\frac{1}{27})=\frac{2}{9}$ rel minimum $g(-\frac{1}{27})=-\frac{2}{9}$
5. concave down $(-\infty,0)$ concave upward $(0,\infty)$
6. (a) $(-\infty,-1)$ (b) $(-1,\infty)$ (c) $x=-1$
7. Horizontal: $y=1$; vertical: $x=2$, $x=4$

8.

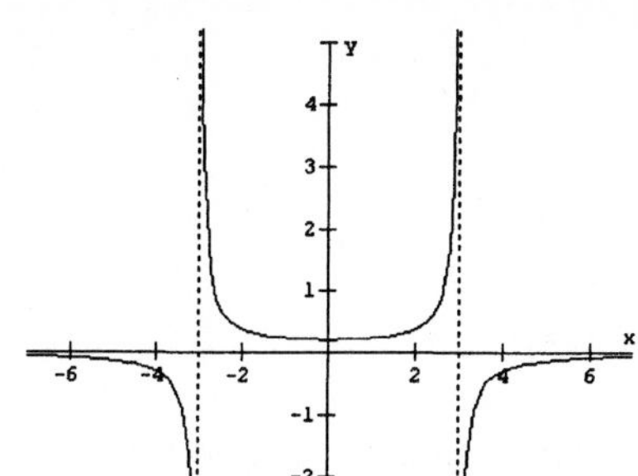

8.

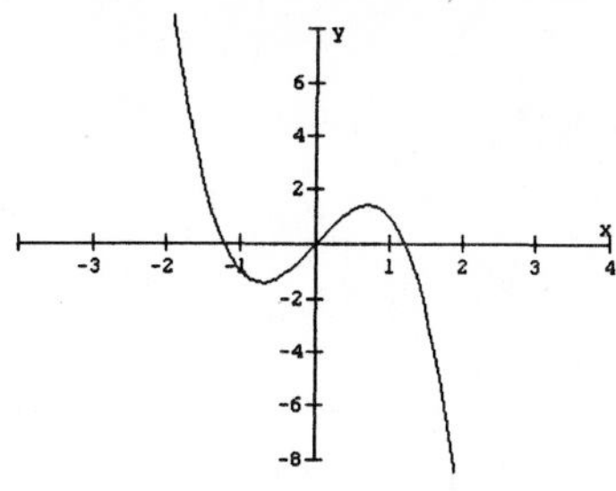

9.

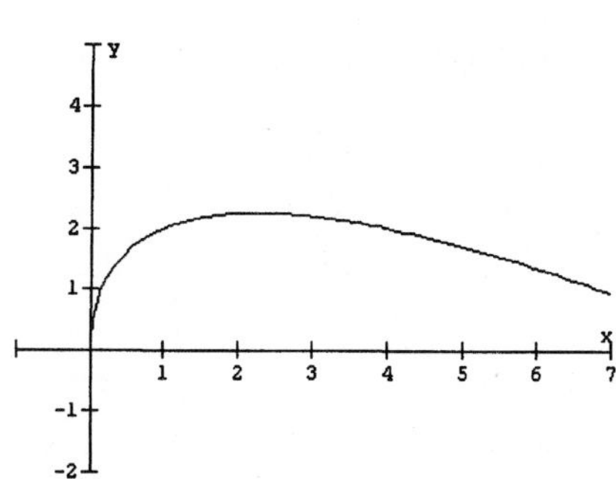

9.

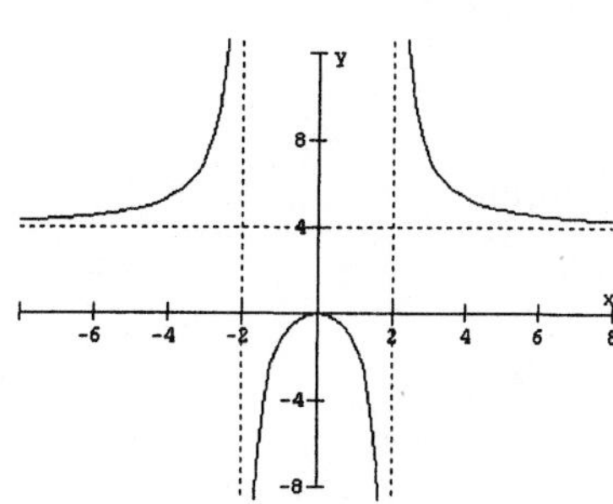

10. Absolute maximum $f(-\frac{2}{3}) = \frac{16}{9}$;

Abs min $f(0) = 0$

11. No absolute maximum, nor minimum

12. 57,800 square feet

13. $\frac{32}{3}$ in. by $\frac{16}{3}$ in. by $\frac{8}{3}$ in.

14. \$450

10. Absolute maximum $f(4) = 54$;

abs minimum $f(1) = f(-2) = 0$

11. Abs max $(\pm 2,\ 4)$;

Abs min $(\pm 4, 0), (0, 0)$

12. 800 square feet

13. $r = \frac{36}{4+\pi} \approx 3.88$ ft, $y \approx 8.03$ ft

14. \$850

Chapter 5 ■ Exponential and Logarithmic Functions

Section 5.1

1. Evaluate

(a) $3^{-2} \cdot 3^5$ Answer: 27

(b) $\left(\frac{1}{4}\right)^{-1/2}\left(\frac{1}{3}\right)^{-2}$ Answer: 18

2. Evaluate $9^{3/2}27^{-1/3}$. Answer: 9

3. Evaluate $\left(\frac{125}{8}\right)^{-1/3} 81^{-1/4}$. Answer: $\frac{2}{15}$

4. Evaluate

(a) $\left(9^{-1/2}\right)^3$ Answer: $\frac{1}{27}$

(b) $3^{1/3}\left(9^{1/6}\right)^2$ Answer: 3

5. Evaluate

(a) $\dfrac{5^{2.2} \cdot 5^{-1.3}}{5^{-0.1}}$ Answer: 5

(b) $\left[\left(-\frac{2}{3}\right)^2\right]^{-2}$ Answer: $\frac{81}{16}$

6. Simplify

(a) $\left(16x^4\right)^{1/2}$ Answer: $4x^2$

(b) $\left(2x^2y^3\right)^2$ Answer: $4x^4y^6$

7. Simplify

(a) $\left(2x^4\right)\left(-3x^{-1}\right)$ Answer: $-6x^3$

(b) $\dfrac{8a^{-4}}{2a^{-2}}$ Answer: $\frac{4}{a^2}$

8. Simplify

(a) $\dfrac{7^0}{\left(3^{-2}x^{-1}y\right)^2}$ Answer: $\frac{81x^2}{y^2}$

(b) $\dfrac{\left(a^{-m} \cdot a^{n}\right)^{2}}{\left(a^{m-n}\right)^{-2}}$ Answer: 1

9. Simplify $\left(5x^3y^2z^4\right)^3$. Answer: $125x^9y^6z^{12}$

10. Simplify $x^{-5/2}x^{10/3}$. Answer: $x^{5/6}$

11. Solve the equation $5^{2x} = 5^4$ for x. Answer: $x = 2$

12. Solve the equation $2.4^{-2x+1} = 2.4^{-3}$ for x. Answer: $x = 2$

13. Solve the equation $7^{3x-2} = 7^{5x+1}$ for x. Answer: $x = -\dfrac{3}{2}$

14. Solve the equation $8.6^{x^2-5x} = 8.6^6$ for x. Answer: $x = -1, 6$

15. Solve the equation $5^{3x+1} = 5^{-5}$ for x. Answer: $x = -2$

16. Sketch the graph of $f(x) = 3^x$.
Answer:

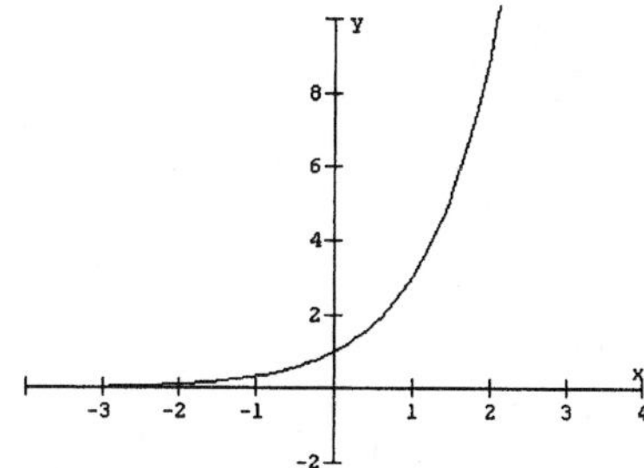

17. Sketch the graph of $f(x) = \left(\dfrac{1}{3}\right)^x$.

Answer:

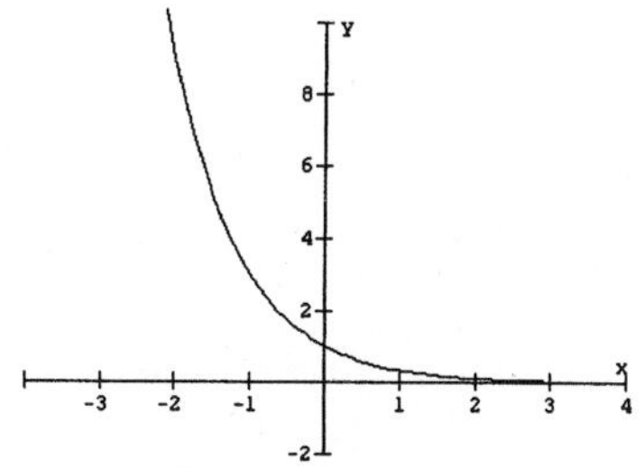

18. Sketch the graph of $f(x) = 2e^{-x}$.

Answer:

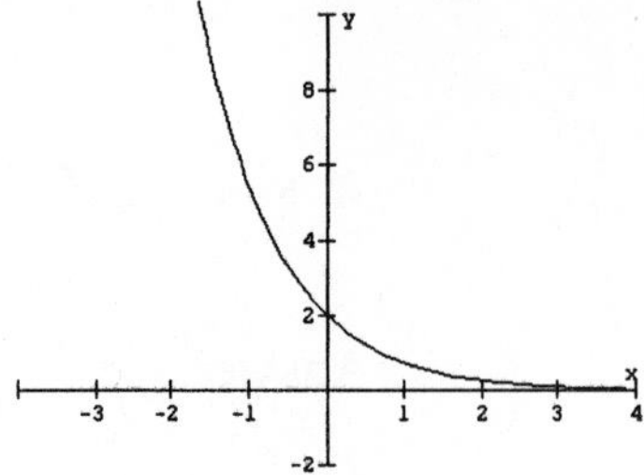

19. Sketch the graph of $f(x) = 5^{0.75x}$.

Answer:

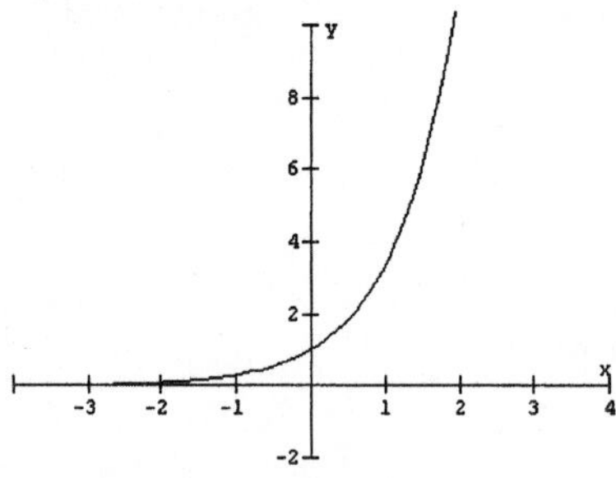

20. Sketch the graph of $y = 2 - e^{-x}$.

Answer:

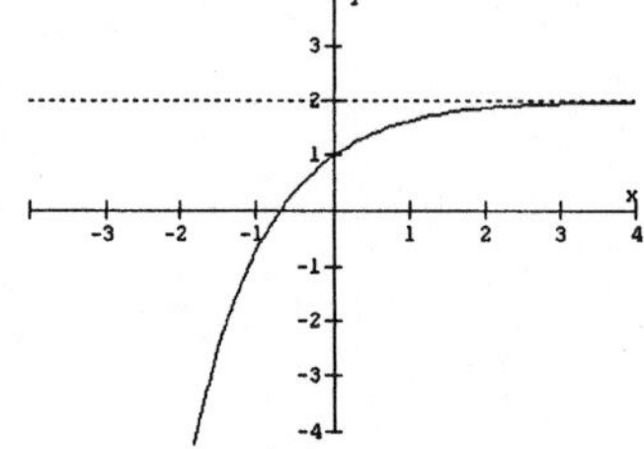

21. Sketch the graph of $y = \dfrac{e^{x} - e^{-x}}{2}$.

Answer:

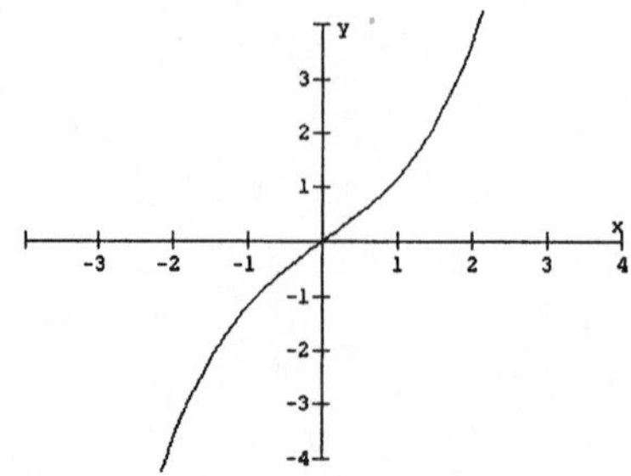

Section 5.1 Multiple Choice Questions

1. Evaluate the expression $\dfrac{7^{2.3} \cdot 7^{3.7}}{7^{-5}}$.

   a. 7^{11}
   b. 7
   c. 7^{6}
   d. None of the above
   Answer: a.

2. Simplify the expression $\left(27x^{9}y^{-12}\right)^{1/3}$.

   a. $\dfrac{9x^{3}}{y^{4}}$
   b. $\dfrac{3x^{3}}{y^{4}}$
   c. $\dfrac{9x^{3}}{y^{-4}}$
   d. None of the above
   Answer: b.

3. Simplify the expression $\left(64x^{3}y^{-12}\right)^{1/3}\left(15^{0}\right)$.

   a. $\dfrac{60x^{2}}{y^{4}}$
   b. $\dfrac{60x}{y^{4}}$
   c. $\dfrac{4x}{y^{4}}$
   d. None of the above
   Answer: c.

4. Simplify the expression $\left(2x^{-3}y^{-12}\right)^{0}\left(9x^{-5}y^{7}\right)$.

   a. $\dfrac{18y^{5}}{x^{8}}$
   b. $18x^{8}y^{5}$
   c. $18x^{-8}y^{5}$
   d. $9x^{-5}y^{7}$
   Answer: d.

5. Find the solution of the equation $11^{2x-3} = 11^{x-5}$.
   a. $x = -2$
   b. $x = 2$
   c. $x = -1$
   d. $x = -3$
   Answer: a.

6. Find the solution of the equation $(3)^{2x-3} = \left(\frac{1}{9}\right)^{x-5}$.
   a. $x = -2$
   b. $x = 3.25$
   c. $x = -3.25$
   d. $x = 4$
   Answer: b.

7. Find the solution of the equation $4^x - 5 \cdot 2^x + 4 = 0$.
   a. $x = -2$ and $x = 0$
   b. $x = 2$ and $x = 0$
   c. $x = 2$ and $x = 1$
   d. $x = 1$ and $x = 0$
   Answer: b.

8. The concentration of a drug in an organ at any time t (in seconds) is given by $C(t) = 0.25\left(1 - e^{-0.159t}\right)$. What is the initial concentration of the drug in the organ?
   a. 0
   b. 0.25
   c. 0.75
   d. –0.25
   Answer: a.

9. The concentration of a drug in an organ at any time t (in seconds) is given by $C(t) = 0.25\left(1 - e^{-0.159t}\right)$. What is the concentration of the drug in the organ after 30 seconds?
   a. 0
   b. 0.24788
   c. 0.25
   d. 0.35782
   Answer: b.

10. The concentration of a drug in an organ at any time t (in seconds) is given by $C(t) = 0.25\left(1 - e^{-0.159t}\right)$. What will be the concentration of the drug in the organ in the long run?
   a. 0.75

b. 0.23
c. 0.25
d. 1
Answer: c.

11. The concentration of a drug in an organ at any time t (in seconds) is given by $C(t) = 0.0075 + 0.25\left(1 - e^{-0.159t}\right)$. What is the initial concentration of the drug in the organ?
a. 0.0075
b. 0.2575
c. 1.2575
d. 1
Answer: a.

12. The concentration of a drug in an organ at any time t (in seconds) is given by $C(t) = 0.0075 + 0.25\left(1 - e^{-0.159t}\right)$. What is the concentration of the drug in the organ after 30 seconds?
a. 0
b. 0.24788
c. 0.25538
d. 0.35782
Answer: c.

13. The concentration of a drug in an organ at any time t (in seconds) is given by $C(t) = 0.0075 + 0.25\left(1 - e^{-0.159t}\right)$. What will be the concentration of the drug in the organ in the long run?
a. 0.75
b. 0.25
c. 0.2575
d. 1
Answer: c.

14. The temperature of a cup of coffee t minutes after it is poured is given by $T(t) = 100 + 35\left(e^{-0.469t} - 1\right)$, where T is measured in degrees Fahrenheit. What is the temperature of the coffee when it was poured?
a. 75 degrees
b. 175 degrees
c. 100 degrees
d. 125 degrees
Answer: c.

Section 5.2

1. Express in logarithmic form: $4^2 = 16$. Answer: $\log_4 16 = 2$

2. Express in logarithmic form: $\left(\frac{1}{3}\right)^4 = \frac{1}{81}$. Answer: $\log_{1/3} \frac{1}{81} = 4$

3. Express in logarithmic form: $3^{-2} = \frac{1}{9}$. Answer: $\log_3 \frac{1}{9} = -2$

4. Express in logarithmic form: $81^{3/4} = 27$. Answer: $\log_{81} 27 = \frac{3}{4}$

5. Express in logarithmic form: $32^{-2/5} = 0.25$. Answer: $\log_{32} 0.25 = -\frac{2}{5}$

6. Use the fact that $\log_6 5 = 0.8982$ and $\log_6 3 = 0.6131$ to find $\log_6 15$.
   Answer: 1.5113

7. Use the fact that $\log_6 5 = 0.8982$ and $\log_6 3 = 0.6131$ to find $\log_6 \frac{5}{3}$.
   Answer: 0.2851

8. Use the fact that $\log_6 5 = 0.8982$ and $\log_6 3 = 0.6131$ to find $\log_6 9$.
   Answer: 1.2262

9. Use the fact that $\log_6 5 = 0.8982$ and $\log_6 3 = 0.6131$ to find $\log_6 75$.
   Answer: 2.4095

10. Use the fact that $\log_6 5 = 0.8982$ and $\log_6 3 = 0.6131$ to find $\log_6 \sqrt{5}$.
    Answer: 0.4491

11. Use the laws of logarithms to expand and simplify the expression: $\log x(x-1)^2$.
    Answer: $\log(x) + 2\log(x-1)$

12. Use the laws of logarithms to expand and simplify the expression: $\log \frac{\sqrt{x-2}}{x^2-3}$.
    Answer: $\frac{1}{2}\log(x-2) - \log(x^2-3)$

13. Use the laws of logarithms to simplify the expression: $\log x^3 \left(x^3+2\right)^{1/3}$.

Answer: $3\log x + \frac{1}{3}\log\left(x^3 + 2\right)$

14. Use the laws of logarithms to expand and simplify the expression: $\ln(xe^x)$.
Answer: $\ln x + x$

15. Use the laws of logarithms to simplify the expression: $\ln\left(\frac{3e^x}{x}\right)$.

Answer: $\ln 3 + x - \ln x$

16. Sketch the graph of $f(x) = \log_2 x$.
Answer:

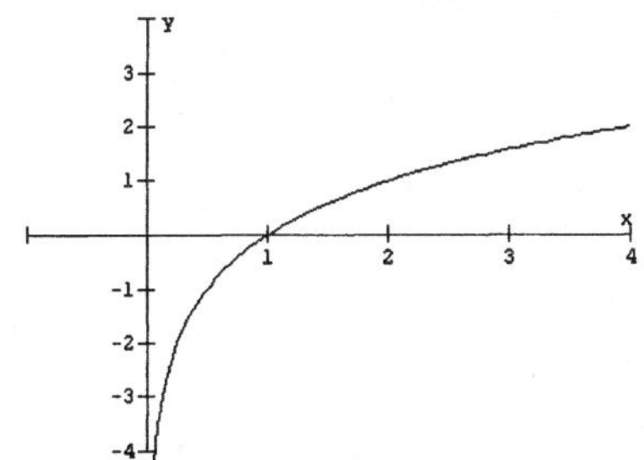

17. Sketch the graph of $g(x) = \ln 3x$.
Answer:

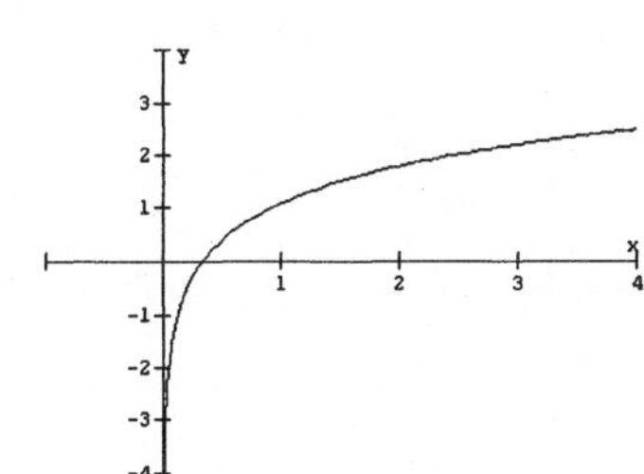

18. Sketch the graph of $g(x) = \log_{2/5} x$.
Answer:

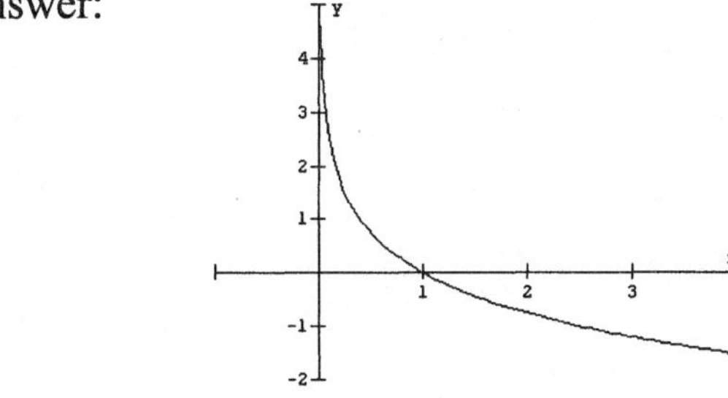

19. Use the laws of logarithms to solve the equation $\log_3 x = 3$.
Answer: $x = 27$

20. Use the laws of logarithms to solve the equation $\log_2 \frac{1}{4} = x$.

Answer: $x = -2$

21. Use the laws of logarithms to solve the equation $\log_x 9 = 2$.
Answer: $x = 3$

22. Use the laws of logarithms to solve the equation $\log(x+2) + \log(3) = 1$.
Answer: $x = \frac{4}{3}$

23. Use the laws of logarithms to solve the equation $\log(x+2) - \log(x-1) = \log 4$.
Answer: $x = 2$

24. Use the laws of logarithms to solve the equation $e^{3x-1} = 5$.
Answer: $x = \frac{1}{3} + \frac{1}{3}\ln 5$

25. Use the laws of logarithms to solve the equation $e^{3x+6} = 9$.
Answer: $x = \frac{1}{3}\ln 9 - 2$

26. Use the laws of logarithms to solve the equation $7e^{3t-1} = 7$.
Answer: $t = \frac{1}{3}$

27. Use the laws of logarithms to solve the equation $5e^{-0.3t} - 3 = 7$.
Answer: $t = -\frac{10\ln 2}{3}$

28. Use the laws of logarithms to solve the equation $\frac{40}{1+2e^{0.3t}} = 10$.
Answer: $t = \frac{10}{3}\ln(3/2)$

29. Use the laws of logarithms to solve the equation $3e^{2-3x} = 19$.
Answer: $x = \frac{2}{3} - \frac{1}{3}\ln 19 + \frac{1}{3}\ln 3$

30. The temperature of a mug of coffee after t minutes is given by $T = 80 + 100e^{-0.182t}$, where T is measured in degrees Fahrenheit.
(a) What is the initial temperature of the coffee?
Answer: 180° F

(b) When (to the nearest hundredth of a minute) will the coffee be at 100°?
Answer: after 8.84 minutes

Section 5.2 Multiple Choice Questions

1. Express the equation $7^{-2} = \frac{1}{49}$ in logarithmic form.

a. $\log_7 \frac{1}{49} = -2$

b. $\log_7(-2) = \frac{1}{49}$

c. $\log_7 \frac{1}{49} = 2$

d. $\log_7 49 = -2$

Answer: a.

2. Express the equation $32^{-3/5} = \frac{1}{8}$ in logarithmic form.

a. $\log_{32} 8 = -\frac{3}{5}$

b. $\log_{32} \frac{1}{8} = \frac{3}{5}$

c. $\log_8 32 = -\frac{3}{5}$

d. $\log_{32} \frac{1}{8} = -\frac{3}{5}$

Answer: d.

3. Simplify the expression $\log\left[(x+4)^3(x^2-3)\right]$.

a. $3\log(x+4)\cdot\log(x^2-3)$

b. $3\log(x+4)+\log(x^2-3)$

c. $3\log(x+4)+2\log(x-3)$

d. $3\log(x+4)+2\log x$

Answer: b.

4. Simplify the expression $\log\left(27x^{15}y^{-12}\right)^{1/3}$.

a. $3\log 3+5\log x-4\log y$

b. $\log 3+5\log x+4\log y$

c. $\log 3 + 5\log x - 4\log y$

d. $\log 27 + 5\log x - 4\log y$

Answer: c.

5. Simplify the expression $\log \frac{1}{27}\sqrt[5]{4x^{10}+9}$.

a. $-3\log 3 + \frac{1}{5}\log\left(4x^{10}+9\right)$

b. $\log 27 + \frac{1}{5}\log\left(4x^{10}+9\right)$

c. $-\log 27 - \frac{1}{5}\log\left(4x^{10}+9\right)$

d. $-3\log 2 + \frac{1}{5}\log\left(4x^{10}+9\right)$

Answer: a.

6. Find the solution of the equation $25e^{t^2-1} = 25$.

a. $t = \pm 1$

b. $t = 1$ only

c. $t = -1$ only

d. $t = \pm\sqrt{2}$

Answer: a.

7. Find the solution of the equation $\frac{30}{1+2e^{-0.5t}} = 10$.

a. $t = \ln 2$

b. $t = 2$

c. $t = 0$

d. $t = 3$

Answer: c.

8. The height (in feet) of a certain kind of tree is approximated by $h(t) = \frac{150}{1+200e^{-0.3t}}$, where t is measured in year. Estimate the age of a 100-ft tree.

a. 17 years old

b. 20 years old

c. 10 years old

d. 26 years old

Answer: b.

9. The concentration of a drug (in gm/cm^3) in an organ at any time t (in seconds) is given by $C(t) = 0.25\left(1 - e^{-0.159t}\right)$. When will the concentration of the drug in the organ be $0.24788\ \text{gm/cm}^3$?
   a. 30 seconds
   b. 10 seconds
   c. 25 seconds
   d. 35 seconds
   Answer: a.

10. The concentration of a drug in an organ at any time t (in seconds) is given by $C(t) = 0.25\left(1 - e^{-0.159t}\right)$. When will the concentration of the drug in the organ be 0.199?
    a. 5 seconds
    b. 10 seconds
    c. 15 seconds
    d. 20 seconds
    Answer: b.

11. The concentration of a drug in an organ at any time t (in seconds) is given by $C(t) = 0.0075 + 0.25\left(1 - e^{-0.159t}\right)$. When will the concentration of the drug in the organ be 0.0075?
    a. $t = 0$ second
    b. $t = 2$ seconds
    c. $t = 3$ seconds
    d. $t = 1$ second
    Answer: a.

12. The concentration of a drug in an organ at any time t (in seconds) is given by $C(t) = 0.0075 + 0.25\left(1 - e^{-0.159t}\right)$. When will the concentration of the drug in the organ be 0.25538?
    a. 5 seconds
    b. 30 seconds
    c. 10 seconds
    d. 20 seconds
    Answer: b.

13. The length (in centimeters) of a typical Pacific halibut t years old is approximately $f(t) = 210\left(1 - 0.967e^{-0.17t}\right)$. Suppose a Pacific halibut caught by Kathy measures 107 cm. What is its approximate age?
    a. 2 years old
    b. 3 years old
    c. 4 years old
    d. 5 years old
    Answer: c.

Section 5.3

1. What is the interest on $20,000, invested at 6.5% for 7 years, and compounded annually?
   Answer: $11,079.73

2. What is the interest on $1 million, invested at 18% for 4 years, and compounded annually?
   Answer: $938,777.76

3. What is the future value of $1250, invested at 9.5% for 5 years, if it is compounded semiannually?
   Answer: $1988.16

4. What is the future value of $4500, invested at 15% for 20 years, if it is compounded quarterly?
   Answer: $85,558.06

5. What is the future value of $20,000, invested at 6.5% for 7 years, if it is compounded monthly?
   Answer: $31,484.79

6. What is the future value of $1 million, invested at 18% for 4 years, if it is compounded daily?
   Answer: $2,054,068.63

7. What is the present value of $25,000 in 2 years, if it is invested at 12% compounded monthly?
   Answer: $19,689.15

8. Find the accumulated amount after 5 years if $1800 is invested at 8% per year compounded quarterly.
   Answer: $2674.71

9. Find the accumulated amount after 5 years if $3200 is invested at 7% per year compounded continuously.
   Answer: $4541.02

10. Find the accumulated amount after 12 years if $800 is invested at 15% per year compounded continuously.
    Answer: $4839.72

11. Find the effective rate of interest corresponding to a nominal rate of 6% compounded quarterly.
    Answer: 6.14%

12. A father wants to be able to provide his newborn baby with a college education. To do this, the father estimates that he will need $120,000 when his child turns 18. How much money should the father invest in an account that pays 7% interest per year compounded daily so that the account is worth $120,000 in 18 years?
Answer: $34,042.60

13. Compute the future value after 10 years on $2000 invested at 8% interest compounded annually.
Answer: $4317.85

14. What interest rate would double your money in 10 years if you earned interest compounded monthly?
Answer: 6.95% per year

15. Find the effective rate of interest corresponding to a nominal rate of 17.5% per year compounded monthly (round to the nearest hundredth of one percent).
Answer: 18.97% per year

16. Find the effective rate of interest corresponding to a nominal rate of 11.5% per year compounded monthly (round to the nearest hundredth of one percent).
Answer: 12.13% per year

17. Find the effective rate of interest corresponding to a nominal rate of 15.5% per year compounded monthly (round to the nearest hundredth of one percent).
Answer: 16.65% per year

18. Find the effective rate of interest corresponding to a nominal rate of 6.5% per year compounded monthly (round to the nearest hundredth of one percent).
Answer: 6.7% per year

19. Find the time, in years, that it will take for an investment to double in value at a rate of 7% per year compounded daily (round to the nearest tenth of a year).
Answer: 9.9 years

20. Find the time, in years, that it will take for an investment to triple in value at a rate of 6% per year compounded daily (round to the nearest tenth of a year).
Answer: 18.3 years

21. How long will it take $800 to grow to $1800 if the investment earns interest at a rate of 10% per year compounded monthly?
Answer: 8.1 years

22. How long will it take $2500 to grow to $40000 if the investment earns interest at a rate of 16% per year compounded quarterly?
Answer: 17.7 years

Section 5.3 Multiple Choice Questions

1. Find the accumulated amount after 5 years if $12,000 is invested at 18% per year compounded monthly.
   a. $27,453.09
   b. $29,127.15
   c. $29,508.69
   d $29,318.64
   Answer: d.

2. Find the accumulated amount after 5 years if $12,000 is invested at 18% per year compounded continuously.
   a. $29,127.15
   b. $27,453.09
   c. $29,515.24
   d $29,318.64
   Answer: c.

3. If $12,000 is invested at interest rate of 18% per year compounded continuously, how long will it take for the money to double?
   a. 3 years and 10 months
   b. 3 years and 2 months
   c. 2 years and 10 months
   d 4 years and 1 month
   Answer: a.

4. Find the accumulated amount after 4 years if $2000 is invested at 8% per year compounded semiannually.
   a. $2737.14
   b. $2745.57
   c. $2751.33
   d $2754.26
   Answer: a.

5. Find the accumulated amount after 4 years if $2000 is invested at 8% per year compounded quarterly.
   a. $2737.14
   b. $2751.33
   c. $2745.57
   d $2754.26
   Answer: c.

6. Find the accumulated amount after 4 years if $2000 is invested at 8% per year compounded monthly.
   a. $2737.14
   b. $2745.57

c. $2754.26
d $2751.33
Answer: d.

7. Find the accumulated amount after 4 years if $2000 is invested at 8% per year compounded daily.
   a. $2751.33
   b. $2754.16
   c. $2745.57
   d $2754.26
   Answer: b.

8. Find the accumulated amount after 4 years if $2000 is invested at 8% per year compounded continuously.
   a. $2745.57
   b. $2751.33
   c. $2754.16
   d. $2754.26
   Answer: d.

9. Find the effective rate of interest corresponding to a nominal rate of 10% per year compounded annually.
   a. 10.38%
   b. 10.00%
   c. 10.25%
   d 10.47%
   Answer: b.

10. Find the effective rate of interest corresponding to a nominal rate of 10% per year compounded semiannually.
    a. 10.25%
    b. 10.47%
    c. 10.00%
    d 10.38%
    Answer: a.

11. Find the effective rate of interest corresponding to a nominal rate of 10% per year compounded quarterly.
    a. 10.25%
    b. 10.00%
    c. 10.38%
    d 10.47%
    Answer: c.

12. Find the effective rate of interest corresponding to a nominal rate of 10% per year compounded monthly.

a. 10.47%
b. 10.38%
c. 10.52%
d. 10.25%
Answer: a.

13. Find the present value of $37,930.55 due in 7 years at an interest rate of 6% per year compounded quarterly.
a. $25,076.56
b. $24,948.24
c. $25,000.00
d $24,974.19
Answer: c.

14. Hong long will it take $10,000 to grow to $40,000 if the investment earns interest at the rate of 6% per year compounded daily?
a. 23.56 years
b. 23.11 years
c. 24.89 years
d 21.27 years
Answer: b.

15. Find the interest rate needed for an investment of $7,000 to grow to an amount of $9,500 in 3 years if interest is compounded monthly?
a. 10.22% per year
b. 5.21% per year
c. 12.00% per year
d. 9.34% per year
Answer: a.

16. Find the interest rate needed for an investment of $8000 to double in 5 years if interest is compounded continuously.
a. 13.21% per year
b. 13.86% per year
c. 13.10% per year
d. 14.01% per year
Answer: b

17. Find the interest rate needed for an investment of $8000 to grow to an amount of $15,000 in 10 years if interest is compounded continuously.
a. 6.3% per year
b. 6.1% per year
c. 6.0% per year
d. 6.5% per year
Answer: a.

18. Dave invested a sum of money 5 years ago in a savings account, for which he was paid interest at a rate of 8% per year compounded monthly. His investment is now worth $21,358.46. How much did he originally invest?
    a. $14,354.90
    b. $14,336.02
    c. $14,429.01
    d $14,317.63

    Answer: b.

Section 5.4

1. Find the derivative of the function $f(x)=e^{4x}$. Answer: $4e^{4x}$

2. Find the derivative of the function $f(x)=3e^{x}-x^{4}$. Answer: $3e^{x}-4x^{3}$

3. Find the derivative of the function $f(x)=e^{-3x}$. Answer: $-3e^{-3x}$

4. Find the derivative of the function $f(x)=x^{2}e^{4x}$. Answer: $4x^{2}e^{4x}+2xe^{4x}$

5. Find the derivative of the function $f(x)=\dfrac{2x}{e^{2x}}$. Answer: $\dfrac{2-4x}{e^{2x}}$

6. Find the derivative of the function $f(t)=18e^{0.5t}+2$. Answer: $9e^{0.5t}$

7. Find the derivative of the function $f(x)=\dfrac{e^{x}+2}{e^{x}}$. Answer: $-2e^{-x}$

8. Find the derivative of the function $f(x)=3e^{2x+2}$. Answer: $6e^{2x+2}$

9. Find the derivative of the function $f(x)=2e^{-3/x}$. Answer: $\dfrac{6}{x^{2}}e^{-3/x}$

10. Find the derivative of the function $f(x)=\left(e^{2x}+1\right)^{12}$. Answer: $24e^{2x}\left(e^{2x}+1\right)^{11}$

11. Find the derivative of the function $f(x)=\dfrac{e^{2x}+1}{e^{2x}-1}$. Answer: $-4\dfrac{e^{2x}}{\left(e^{2x}-1\right)^{2}}$

12. Find the derivative of the function $f(t)=\dfrac{e^{-2t}}{1+4t}$.

    Answer: $\dfrac{-2(1+4t)e^{-2t}-4e^{-2t}}{(1+4t)^{2}}$

13. Find the second derivative of the function $f(t)=3e^{-3t}+4e^{-2t}$.

    Answer: $27e^{-3t}+16e^{-2t}$

14. Find the interval(s) where $h(x)=xe^{x}$ is increasing and the interval(s) where it is decreasing.

Answer: Increasing: $(-1,\infty)$; decreasing: $(-\infty,-1)$

15. Find the absolute maximum and the absolute minimum of $g(x)=e^{x}-x$ on $[-1,1]$.
Answer: Absolute maximum: $g(1)=e-1$; absolute minimum: $g(0)=1$

16. Find the absolute extrema of $f(x)=e^{-x^2+4x}$ on $[0,3]$.
Answer: Absolute maximum: $f(2)=e^{4}$; absolute minimum: $f(0)=1$

17. Find the equation of the tangent line to the graph of the function $y=e^{3x-1}$ at the point $(1/3,1)$.
Answer: $y=3x$

18. Sketch the graph of $f(t)=t-e^{-2t}$.
Answer:

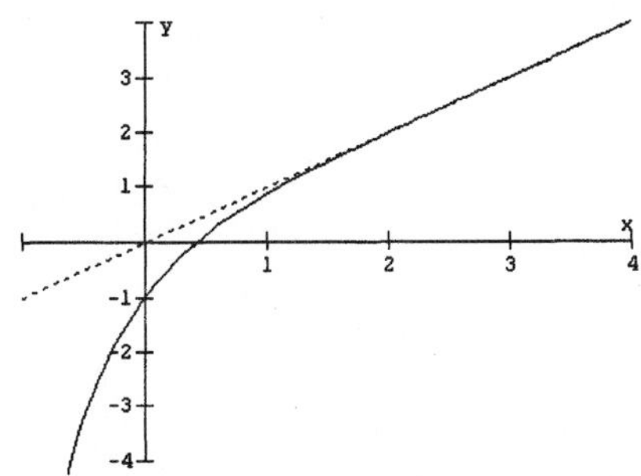

Section 5.4 Multiple Choice Questions

1. Find the derivative of the function given by $f(x)=e^{7x+5}$.
   a. $f'(x)=7e^{7x+5}$
   b. $f'(x)=e^{7x+5}$
   c. $f'(x)=(7x+5)e^{7x+5}$
   d. $f'(x)=7e^{7x+4}$
   Answer: a.

2. Find the derivative of the function given by $f(x)=e^{x^2+5x-100}$.
   a. $f'(x)=(x^2+5x-100)e^{x^2+5x-100}$
   b. $f'(x)=(2x+95)e^{x^2+5x-100}$
   c. $f'(x)=(2x+5)e^{x^2+5x-100}$

d. $f'(x)=(2x-95)e^{x^2+5x-100}$

Answer: c.

3. Find the derivative of the function given by $f(x)=\dfrac{e^x}{x}$.

a. $f'(x)=-\dfrac{e^x}{x^2}+\dfrac{1}{x}$

b. $f'(x)=-\dfrac{e^x}{x^2}$

c. $f'(x)=\dfrac{e^x(x-1)}{x^2}$

d. $f'(x)=\dfrac{e^x}{x^2}$

Answer: c.

4. Find the derivative of the function given by $f(x)=xe^{3x-7}$.

a. $f'(x)=3xe^{3x-7}$

b. $f'(x)=e^{3x-7}+3xe^{3x-7}$

c. $f'(x)=3e^{3x-7}$

d. $f'(x)=9e^{3x-7}$

Answer: b.

5. Find the derivative of the function given by $f(x)=\dfrac{e^{2x}}{x^3}$.

a. $f'(x)=\dfrac{e^{2x}(2x+3)}{x^4}$

b. $f'(x)=\dfrac{e^{2x}(2x-3)}{x^6}$

c. $f'(x)=\dfrac{e^{2x}(2x-3)}{x^4}$

d. $f'(x)=\dfrac{-e^{2x}}{x^4}$

Answer: c.

6. Find the derivative of the function given by $f(x)=e^{\sqrt{x^2+1}}$.

a. $f'(x)=\dfrac{e^{\sqrt{x^2+1}}}{\sqrt{x^2+1}}$

b. $f'(x) = \dfrac{xe^{\sqrt{x^2+1}}}{\sqrt{x^2+1}}$

c. $f'(x) = \dfrac{xe^{\sqrt{x^2+1}}}{2\sqrt{x^2+1}}$

d. $f'(x) = \dfrac{2xe^{\sqrt{x^2+1}}}{\sqrt{x^2+1}}$

Answer: b.

7. If $f(x)$ is the function given by $f(x) = e^{3x} + 1$, at what value of x is the slope of the tangent line to $f(x)$ equal to 2?

a. -0.135
b. 0
c. 0.231
d. 0.693

Answer: a.

8. Find the inflection point(s) of the function $f(x) = xe^{-3x} - 12$

a. $\left(\frac{2}{3}, \frac{2}{3}e^{-1} - 12\right)$

b. $\left(\frac{2}{3}, -\frac{2}{3}e^{-2} + 12\right)$

c. $\left(-\frac{2}{3}, -\frac{2}{3}e^{-2} + 12\right)$

d. $\left(\frac{2}{3}, \frac{2}{3}e^{-2} - 12\right)$

Answer: d.

9. Find the x and y values of the relative extrema of the function $f(x) = xe^{-3x} - 12$.

a. $\left(\frac{1}{3}, \frac{e}{3}\right)$

b. $\left(\frac{1}{3}, \frac{1}{3e} - 12\right)$

c. $\left(\frac{1}{3}, \frac{1}{3e}\right)$

d. $\left(\frac{1}{3}, \frac{e}{3} - 12\right)$

Answer: b.

10. If $3y^2 - e^{xy} = 1$, then $\frac{dy}{dx}$ equals

a. $\frac{e^{xy}}{6y - xe^{xy}}$

b. $-\frac{ye^{xy}}{6y - xe^{xy}}$

c. $\frac{ye^{xy}}{6y - xe^{xy}}$

d. $\frac{ye^{xy}}{6y - e^{xy}}$

Answer: c.

11. If $xy - e^{xy} = 7$, then $\frac{dy}{dx}$ equals

a. $-\frac{e^x}{e^y}$

b. $\frac{e^x}{e^y}$

c. $\frac{e^x\left(y - e^y\right)}{e^y\left(e^x - x\right)}$

d. $-\frac{y}{x}$

Answer: d.

12. If $e^x + e^y = e^{x+y}$, then $\frac{dy}{dx}$ equals

a. $-e^{x-y}$

b. $-e^{y-x}$

c. $\frac{e^x\left(1 - e^y\right)}{e^y\left(e^x - 1\right)}$

d. $\frac{e^x\left(1 - e^y\right)}{e^y\left(1 - e^x\right)}$

Answer: c.

13. Find the derivative of the function $f(x) = \left(2 - 4e^{2x}\right)^3$.

a. $f'(x) = -24\left(e^{2x}\right)\left(2-4e^{2x}\right)^2$

b. $f'(x) = 24\left(e^{2x}\right)\left(2-4e^{2x}\right)^2$

c. $f'(x) = -12\left(e^{2x}\right)\left(2-4e^{2x}\right)^2$

d. $f'(x) = -24\left(2-4e^{2x}\right)^2$

Answer: a.

14. Garfield, the cat, needs to go on a diet. It is estimated that Garfield's weight in pounds t days after he begins his diet is given by $W(t) = 26e^{-0.01t}$. After Garfield has been on the diet for 7 days, what is his rate of weight loss?

a. $-\dfrac{0.26}{e^{0.07}}$ pounds/day

b. $\dfrac{0.26}{e^{0.07}}$ pounds/day

c. $\dfrac{26}{e^{0.07}}$ pounds/day

d. $0.26e^{0.07}$ pounds/day

Answer: b.

15. Find the slope of the tangent line to the curve $y = e^{x^2-5x+10}$ at $(0,\ e^{10})$.

a. $-5e^{-10}$

b. $-e^{10}$

c. $-5e^{10}$

d. $5e^{10}$

Answer: c.

16. The height of a certain kind of tree is approximated by $h(t) = \dfrac{150}{1+200e^{-0.3t}}$, where h is measured in feet and t is measured in years. Find $h'(t)$.

a. $h'(t) = -\dfrac{9000e^{-0.3t}}{\left(1+200e^{-0.3t}\right)^2}$ ft/yr

b. $h'(t) = \dfrac{9000e^{-0.3t}}{\left(1+200e^{-0.3t}\right)^2}$ ft/yr

c. $h'(t) = -\dfrac{300e^{-0.3t}}{\left(1+200e^{-0.3t}\right)^2}$ ft/yr

d. $h'(t) = \dfrac{3000e^{-0.3t}}{\left(1+200e^{-0.3t}\right)^2}$ ft/yr

Answer: b.

17. The concentration of a drug in an organ at any time t (in seconds) is given by $C(t) = 0.0075 + 0.25\left(1 - e^{-0.159t}\right)$. Find $C'(t)$.

a. $C'(t) = 0.03975e^{-0.159t}$

b. $C'(t) = 0.03975e^{-0.159t} + 0.0075$

c. $C'(t) = -0.03975e^{-0.159t} + 0.0075$

d. $C'(t) = -0.03975e^{0.159t} + 0.0075$

Answer: a.

18. Let $f(x) = x^2e^{-x}$. Find the coordinates of the relative extremum that lies in the first quadrant.

a. $\left(2,\ 4e^2\right)$

b. $\left(-2,\ \dfrac{-4}{e^2}\right)$

c. $\left(2,\ \dfrac{4}{e^2}\right)$

d. $\left(-2,\ 4e^2\right)$

Answer: c.

Section 5.5

1. Find the derivative of the function $f(x) = \ln(x^2 + 3)$. Answer: $\frac{2x}{x^2 + 3}$

2. Find the derivative of the function $f(x) = \frac{1}{\ln x}$. Answer: $\frac{-1}{x(\ln x)^2}$

3. Find the derivative of the function $f(x) = x^2 \ln x$. Answer: $x + 2x \ln x$

4. Find the derivative of the function $f(x) = \ln\left(\frac{2}{3x^5}\right)$. Answer: $\frac{-5}{x}$

5. Find the derivative of the function $f(t) = 8\ln(t^6)$. Answer: $\frac{48}{t}$

6. Find the derivative of the function $f(x) = e^{2x} \ln(x+2)$.

   Answer: $\frac{e^{2x}}{x+2} + 2e^{2x} \ln(x+2)$

7. Find the second derivative of the function $f(x) = \ln 3x$. Answer: $\frac{-1}{x^2}$

8. Find the second derivative of the function $f(x) = \frac{1}{\ln x}$. Answer: $\frac{2 + \ln x}{x^2 (\ln x)^3}$

9. Find the second derivative of the function $f(x) = \frac{1}{(\ln x)^2}$. Answer: $\frac{6 + 2\ln x}{x^2 (\ln x)^4}$

10. Use logarithmic differentiation to find the derivative of the function
    $y = (2x+1)^2 (x+3)^3$.
    Answer: $5(2x+3)(2x+1)(x+3)^2$

11. Use logarithmic differentiation to find the derivative of the function
    $y = 7^x$.
    Answer: $7^x \ln 7$

12. Use logarithmic differentiation to find the derivative of the function
    $y = \sqrt[3]{x+4}(2x+3)^3$.

Answer: $\sqrt[3]{x+4}(2x+3)^3\left[\frac{1}{3(x+4)}+\frac{6}{2x+3}\right]$

13. Use logarithmic differentiation to find the derivative of the function
$y=(x-8)^3(x+2)^5$.
Answer: $(8x-34)(x-8)^2(x+2)^4$

14. Use logarithmic differentiation to find the derivative of the function
$y=x^{(\ln x)^2}$.
Answer: $\dfrac{3(\ln x)^2 x^{(\ln x)^2}}{x}$

15. Find the interval(s) on which $f(x)=x-\ln x$ is increasing and the interval(s) on which it is decreasing.
Answer: Increasing: $(1,\infty)$; decreasing: $(0,1)$

16. Find the absolute maximum and the absolute minimum of $g(x)=2\ln x-x$ on $[1,3]$

Answer: Absolute maximum $g(2)=2\ln 2-2$; absolute minimum $g(1)=-1$

17. Let $f(x)=xe^{2x}$.
(a) Find the interval(s) on which $f(x)$ is concave upward.
Answer: $(-1,\infty)$

(b) Find the interval(s) on which $f(x)$ is concave downward.
Answer: $(-\infty,-1)$

(c) Find the x-coordinate(s) of any point(s) of inflection of f.
Answer: $x=-1$

18. Let $f(x)=e^x-\frac{1}{2}x^2$.
(a) Find the interval(s) on which $f(x)$ is concave upward.
Answer: $(0,\infty)$

(b) Find the interval(s) on which $f(x)$ is concave downward.
Answer: $(-\infty,0)$

(c) Find the x-coordinate(s) of any point(s) of inflection of f.
Answer: $x=0$

Section 5.5 Multiple Choice Questions

1. If $f(x)=\ln(2x-5)^2$, then $f'(x)=$

   a. $f'(x)=-\dfrac{4}{2x-5}$

   b. $f'(x)=-\dfrac{2}{2x-5}$

   c. $f'(x)=\dfrac{2}{2x-5}$

   d. $f'(x)=\dfrac{4}{2x-5}$

   Answer: d.

2. If $f(x)=\ln\left(1+3x-x^2\right)$, then $f'(x)=$

   a. $f'(x)=\dfrac{3-2x}{1+3x-x^2}$

   b. $f'(x)=\dfrac{3+2x}{1+3x-x^2}$

   c. $f'(x)=\dfrac{1}{1+3x-x^2}$

   d. $f'(x)=\dfrac{-3-2x}{1+3x-x^2}$

   Answer: a.

3. If $f(x)=\ln\left[\ln(1-x)\right]$, then $f'(x)=$

   a. $f'(x)=-\dfrac{1}{\ln(1-x)}$

   b. $f'(x)=-\dfrac{1}{(1-x)^2}$

   c. $f'(x)=\dfrac{1}{(1-x)\ln(1-x)}$

   d. $f'(x)=-\dfrac{1}{(1-x)\ln(1-x)}$

   Answer: d.

4. If $f(x)=\ln\left(3x^2-1\right)^3$, then $f'(1)=$

   a. $\dfrac{3}{2}$

   b. 3

c. 36
d. 9
Answer: d.

5. If $f(x) = \ln\sqrt{\frac{2x+3}{4x+5}}$, then $f'(0) =$

a. $-\frac{1}{15}$
b. 15
c. -15
d. 8
Answer: a.

6. If $y^2 + \ln\left(\frac{x}{y}\right) - 3x + 2 = 0$, then $\frac{dy}{dx}$ at (1, 1) equals:

a. $\frac{2}{3}$
b. -2
c. 2
d. $\frac{4}{3}$
Answer: c.

7. Find the derivative of the function given by $f(x) = \ln(2x+1)^4 + e^{100}$.

a. $f'(x) = \frac{8}{x+1} + e^{100}$
b. $f'(x) = \frac{8}{2x+1}$
c. $f'(x) = \frac{8}{2x-1}$
d. $f'(x) = \frac{8}{2x+1} + e^{100}$
Answer: b.

8. Find the derivative of the function given by $f(x) = \ln\left(e^{x^2} + 4x - 10\right)$.

a. $f'(x) = \frac{2xe^{x^2} + 14}{e^{x^2} + 4x - 10}$
b. $f'(x) = -\frac{2e^{x^2} + 14}{e^{x^2} + 4x - 10}$

c. $f'(x) = \dfrac{2xe^{x^2} + 4}{e^{x^2} + 4x - 10}$

d. $f'(x) = \dfrac{2xe^{x^2} - 6}{e^{x^2} + 4x - 10}$

Answer: c.

9. Find the slope of the line tangent to the graph of $3x^2 + 5\ln y = 12$ at (2, 1).

a. $-\dfrac{12}{5}$

b. $\dfrac{12}{5}$

c. 12

d. -7

Answer: a.

10. If $f(x) = \ln(x-3)$, at what value of x is the slope of the tangent line to $f(x)$ equal to 2?

a. 3.5

b. 7

c. 2.5

d. 5

Answer: a.

11. If $f(x) = \ln\left(x + \sqrt{x^2 - 1}\right)$, then find $f'(x)$.

a. $f'(x) = -\dfrac{1}{x + \sqrt{x^2 - 1}}$

b. $f'(x) = -\dfrac{1}{\sqrt{x^2 - 1}}$

c. $f'(x) = \dfrac{1}{x + \sqrt{x^2 - 1}}$

d. $f'(x) = \dfrac{1}{\sqrt{x^2 - 1}}$

Answer: d.

12. Find the equation of the tangent line to the graph of $f(x) = \ln x^3$ at (1, 0).

a. $y = -3x + 3$

b. $y = -3x - 3$

c. $y = 3x - 3$

d. $y = 3x + 3$

Answer: c.

13. Find the inflection point(s) of the function $f(x) = \ln(x^2 - 4)$.

a. $(\sqrt{5}, 0)$
b. $(-2, 0)$
c. There is no inflection point
d. $(2, 0)$

Answer: c.

14. Which of the following statements is true?

a. If $f(x) = e^{22}$, then $f'(x) = e^{22}$
b. If $f(x) = \ln 12$, then $f'(x) = \frac{1}{12}$
c. If $f(x) = \ln a^x$, then $f'(x) = \ln x$
d. If $f(x) = \ln a^x$, then $f'(x) = \ln a$

Answer: d.

15. Find the inflection point(s) of the function $f(x) = \ln(x^2 + 1)$.

a. $(1, \ln 2)$ only
b. $(-1, \ln 2)$ and $(1, \ln 2)$
c. $(-1, \ln 2)$ only
d. There is no inflection point

Answer: b.

Section 5.6

1. A quantity $Q(t)$ is described by the exponential growth function $Q(t) = 1{,}200e^{0.05t}$, where t is measured in minutes.
   (a) What is the growth constant?
   Answer: 0.05
   (b) What quantity is initially present?
   Answer: 1200
   (c) What quantity is present after 10 minutes? (Round your answer to a whole year)
   Answer: 1978

2. A nature preserve is being established. A population biologist has estimated that the population of the deer in the preserve is currently 150 and will increase at an annual growth rate of 5%.
   (a) Find the function $Q(t)$ that expresses the deer population as a function of time t (in years).
   Answer: $Q(t) = 150e^{0.05t}$
   (b) Estimate the deer population in 10 years.
   Answer: 247

3. Wood deposits recovered from an archaeological site contain 35% of the carbon 14 they originally contained. How long ago did the tree from which the wood was obtained die? The decay constant of carbon 14 is $k = 0.00012$.
   Answer: 8749 years

4. A radioactive element has a half-life of 400 years. What is the decay constant? (in 5-decimal places)
   Answer: 0.001732868

5. During a flu epidemic, the number of children in a school district who contracted influenza after t days is given by $Q(t) = \dfrac{1500}{1+229e^{-0.5t}}$.
   (a) How many children had contracted influenza after the first day?
   Answer: 11
   (b) How many children had contracted influenza after five days?
   Answer: 76

6. A town had a population of 600 when it built a new school building. Ten years after the school was built, the population of the town was 900. Assuming the same rate of exponential growth, what will be the population of the town twenty years after the school was built?
   Answer: 1350

7. A city currently has a population of 150,000. A city planner estimates that the population of the city will be 200,000 in 15 years. If this is true, what is the annual rate of population growth?
Answer: 0.019 or 1.9%

8. A new car depreciates according to the function $V(t) = 18{,}000e^{-0.6t}$, where $V(t)$ represents the value of the car in dollars t years after it was purchased. How fast will the value of the car be changing three years after purchase?
Answer: Decreasing at a rate of $1785.23 per year

9. The population growth of a certain rodent is approximately 3% per month. Find the time it takes for the population to triple.
Answer: $\approx$ 36.6 months

10. A radioactive substance has a half-life of 20 years. If 200 g of the substance are present initially, find
(a) the amount present after 18 years.
Answer: ≈ 107.2 g
(b) the rate at which the substance will be decaying 18 years later.
Answer: ≈ -3.71 g/year

Section 5.6 Multiple Choice Questions

1. The rate at which snow fell during a recent blizzard is modeled by the equation $s(t) = -\frac{1}{2}t^3 + 3t^2 \ (0 \le t \le 6)$, where t is measured in hours. At what time did the rate of snowfall stop increasing and start to fall off?
   a. 4 hours
   b. 3 hours
   c. 5 hours
   d. 2 hours
   Answer: a.

2. Kathy owns an asset whose market price in dollars t years from now is modeled by $p(t) = 20,000e^{\sqrt{t}}$. If the prevailing rate of interest is 8% per year compounded continuously, when should the asset be sold? (Hint: Consider the function $P(t) = 20,000e^{\sqrt{t}}e^{-0.08t}$.)
   a. 35 years from now
   b. 42 years form now
   c. 80 years from now
   d. 39 years from now
   Answer: d.

3. The unit selling price p (in dollars) and the quantity demanded of a certain product is given by the demand equation $p = 80e^{-0.002x}$ $(0 \le x \le 1000)$. Find the revenue function.

a. $R(x) = 80xe^{-0.002x}$

b. $R(x) = 80x^2e^{-0.002x}$

c. $R(x) = \dfrac{80e^{-0.002x}}{x}$

d. $R(x) = 80xe^{0.002x}$

Answer: a.

4. The unit selling price p (in dollars) and the quantity demanded of a certain product is given by the demand equation $p = 80e^{-0.002x}$ $(0 \le x \le 1000)$. How many units must be sold to yield maximum revenue?

a. 400
b. 480
c. 520
d. 500

Answer: d.

5. It is projected that t years from now, the population in millions of a certain country will be $P(t) = 60e^{0.2t}$. At what rate will the population be changing with respect to time 10 years from now?

a. 60.65 million/yr
b. 88.67 million/yr
c. 78.95 million/yr
d. 70.29 million/yr

Answer: b.

6. It is projected that t years from now, the population in millions of a certain country will be $P(t) = -0.2t^3 + 4.8t^2 + 100$ $(0 \le t \le 10)$. When will the population be growing most rapidly?

a. 8 years
b. 6 years
c. 7 years
d. 9 years

Answer: a.

7. A computer depreciates in such a way that its value (in dollars) after t years is $Q(t) = 3{,}000e^{-0.5t}$. At what rate is the value of the computer changing with respect to time after t years?

a. $-3{,}000e^{-0.5t}$ dollars/yr

b. $1{,}500e^{-0.5t}$ dollars/yr

c. $-1{,}500e^{-0.5t}$ dollars/yr

d. $3{,}000e^{-0.5t}$ dollars/yr

Answer: c.

8. A manufacturer estimates its cost to produce x units of a product is $C(x)=5xe^{-x/40}+20\ \ (0\le x\le 40)$. Find the average cost function.

a. $\bar{C}(x)=5e^{-x/40}+\dfrac{20}{x}$

b. $\bar{C}(x)=5xe^{-x/40}-\dfrac{20}{x^2}$

c. $\bar{C}(x)=-\dfrac{1}{8}xe^{-x/40}+\dfrac{20}{x}$

d. $\bar{C}(x)=5xe^{-x/40}+\dfrac{20}{x}$

Answer: a.

9. A manufacturer estimates its cost to produce x units of the product will be $C(x)=5x^2e^{-x/2}+20\ln(x+1)$. Find the marginal cost.

a. $C'(x)=10xe^{-x/2}-\dfrac{5}{2}x^2e^{-x/2}+\dfrac{20}{x+1}$

b. $C'(x)=-\dfrac{5}{2}x^2e^{-x/2}+\dfrac{20}{x+1}$

c. $C'(x)=10xe^{-x/2}+\dfrac{20}{x+1}$

d. $C'(x)=10xe^{-x/2}+\dfrac{5}{2}x^2e^{-x/2}+\dfrac{20}{x+1}$

Answer: a.

10. A manufacturer estimates its revenue to sale x units of the product will be $R(x)=\dfrac{135}{1+4e^{-0.05x}}-27$. Find the marginal revenue function.

a. $R'(x)=-\dfrac{135e^{-0.05x}}{\left(1+4e^{-0.05x}\right)^2}$

b. $R'(x)=\dfrac{135e^{-0.05x}}{\left(1+4e^{-0.05x}\right)^2}$

c. $R'(x)=-\dfrac{27e^{-0.05x}}{\left(1+4e^{-0.05x}\right)^2}$

d. $R'(x)=\dfrac{27e^{-0.05x}}{\left(1+4e^{-0.05x}\right)^2}$

Answer: d.

11. The world's population (in billions) t years after 1960 is modeled by the function $P(t) = \frac{34}{1+32.5e^{-0.049t}}$. At what rate will it be changing in the year 2006?

a. Decreasing at 0.29 billion/yr
b. Increasing at 0.29 billion/yr
c. Decreasing at 29 billion/yr
d. Increasing at 29 billion/yr

Answer: b.

12. Mike owns a parcel of land whose value (in thousand dollars) t years from now is modeled as $p(t) = 20t$. If the prevailing rate of interest is 10% compounded continuously, when will be the most advantageous time to sell? (Hint: Consider the function $P(t) = 20te^{-0.1t}$.)

a. 4 years
b. 5 years
c. 10 years
d. 20 years

Answer: c.

Exam 5A

Name:
Instructor:
Section:

Write your work as neatly as possible.

1. Evaluate

(a) $\left(\frac{1}{2}\right)^{-4} \cdot 2^{-3}$

(b) $\left(3x^2y^6\right)^3$

2. Sketch the graph of $f(x) = 2 - \left(\frac{1}{3}\right)^x$.

3. Sketch the graph of $f(x) = e^{-x}$.

4. Express in logarithmic form: $49^{-1/2} = \frac{1}{7}$.

5. What is the future value of \$7800, invested at 9% per year for 3 years, if it is compounded monthly?

6. What is the future value of \$200, invested at 5.5% per year for 7 years, if it is compounded continuously?

7. Use the laws of logarithms to expand and simplify the expression: $\log x\sqrt{x+2}$.

8. Use the laws of logarithms to expand and simplify the expression: $\ln x^2 e^{2x}$.

9. Use the laws of logarithms to solve the equation $\log_4 16 = x$.

10. Use the laws of logarithms to solve the equation $\log_3 x = -2$.

11. Sketch the graph of $h(x) = \log_{1/2} x$.

12. Use the laws of logarithms to solve the equation $e^{3x+1} = 18$.

13. Find the derivative of the function $f(x) = e^{7x}$.

14. Find the derivative of the function $f(x) = x \ln x$.

15. Find the absolute maximum and the absolute minimum of $g(x) = \dfrac{\ln x}{x}$ on $[1,3]$.

16. Use logarithmic differentiation to find the derivative of the function $y = (x+7)^4 (x-9)^5$.

17. A quantity $Q(t)$ is described by the exponential growth function $Q(t) = 220e^{0.08t}$, where t is measured in months.
    (a) What is the growth constant?

    (b) What quantity is initially present?

18. A radioactive element has a half-life of 1700 years. What is the decay constant?

19. The population of rabbits in a park is initially 120 and is expected to increase at an annual rate of 5%. Find the expected population in 5 years.

20. How long will it take \$600 to grow to \$1300 if the money is in an account that pays interest at a rate of 6% per year compounded quarterly?

Exam 5B

Name:
Instructor:
Section:

Write your work as neatly as possible.

1. Simplify

   (a) $\left(6x^{8}\right)\left(3x^{-4}\right)$

   (b) $\dfrac{3a^{-5}}{27a^{-7}}$

2. Sketch the graph of $f(x) = 3 - 3^{x}$.

3. Sketch the graph of $f(x) = e^{2x}$.

4. Express in logarithmic form: $\left(\dfrac{1}{4}\right)^{1/2} = \dfrac{1}{2}$.

5. Use the fact that $\log_c a = 0.1101$ and $\log_c b = 2.3444$ to find $\log_c ab$.

6. Use the fact that $\log_c a = 2.6667$ and $\log_c b = 0.5141$ to find $\log_c \left(\dfrac{a}{b}\right)$.

7. Use the laws of logarithms to expand and simplify the expression: $\log \dfrac{x}{3x+1}$.

8. Use the laws of logarithms to expand and simplify the expression: $\ln \sqrt{e^{x}}$.

9. Use the laws of logarithms to solve the equation $\log_5 \frac{1}{25} = x$.

10. Use the laws of logarithms to solve the equation $\log_x 64 = 3$.

11. Sketch the graph of $h(x) = -\ln x + 2$.

12. Use the laws of logarithms to solve the equation $e^{4x-1} = 6$.

13. A quantity $Q(t)$ is described by the exponential growth function $Q(t) = 410e^{0.0035t}$

    (a) What quantity is initially present?

    (b) What quantity is present in 50 minutes?

14. A radioactive element has a half-life of 52 years. What is the decay constant?

15. The population of rabbits in a park is initially 700 and is expected to increase at an annual rate of 4%. Find the expected population in 12 years.

16. A town has a population of 1000. In 7 years, the population is expected to be 1400. What is the annual rate of population growth?

17. What annual interest rate would double your money in 12 years if interest were compounded monthly?

18. Find the derivative of the function $f(x) = \ln\left(x^3 + 2x\right)$.

19. Find the derivative of the function $f(x) = \sqrt{x+1}\left(e^3\right)$.

20. Use logarithmic differentiation to find the derivative of the function $y = e^x x^{2\ln x}$.

Exam 5C

Name:
Instructor:
Section:

Write your work as neatly as possible.

1. Solve the equation $6.3^{2-3x} = 6.3^{x}$ for x.

2. Sketch the graph of $f(x) = 3^{0.5x}$.

3. Sketch the graph of $g(x) = 1 - \frac{1}{2}e^{-x}$.

4. Express in logarithmic form: $64^{-2/3} = \frac{1}{16}$.

5. Use the fact that $\log_c a = 0.475$ and $\log_c b = 0.223$ to find $\log_c a^2 b$.

6. Use the fact that $\log_c a = 0.111$ and $\log_c b = 0.845$ to find $\log_c \sqrt{ab}$.

7. Use the laws of logarithms to expand and simplify the expression: $\log \frac{\sqrt{x}}{x+1}$.

8. Use the laws of logarithms to expand and simplify the expression: $\ln \frac{e^x}{x}$.

9. Use the laws of logarithms to solve the equation $\log_9 1 = x$.

10. Use the laws of logarithms to solve the equation $\log_{1/5} \frac{1}{25} = x$.

11. Sketch the graph of $h(x) = \log_3(x+2)$.

12. Compute the future value after 50 years on \$5 invested at an annual rate of 8% compounded monthly.

13. Use the laws of logarithms to solve the equation $e^{1-3x} = 9$.

14. A quantity $Q(t)$ is described by the exponential growth function $Q(t) = 1000e^{0.007t}$, where t is measured in hours.

    (a) What is the initial quantity?

    (b) What quantity is present after 5 hours?

15. A radioactive element has a half-life of 900 years. What is the decay constant?

16. The population of rabbits in a park is initially 500 and is expected to increase at an annual rate of 7%. Find the expected population in 8 years.

17. A town has a population of 600. In 9 years, the population is expected to be 1000. What is the annual rate of population growth?

18. Find the derivative of the function $f(x) = \ln(x^2+1)$.

19. Find the derivative of the function $f(x) = \sqrt{3}\left(e^{x+1}\right)$.

20. Use logarithmic differentiation to find the derivative of the function $y = 12^x$.

Exam 5D

Name:
Instructor:
Section:

Write your work as neatly as possible.

1. Solve the equation $7^{3x+2} = \frac{1}{49}^{-2}$ for x.

2. Sketch the graph of $f(x) = \left(\frac{1}{2}\right)^x$.

3. Sketch the graph of $g(x) = 2 - \frac{1}{3}e^x$.

4. Express in logarithmic form: $\left(\frac{1}{5}\right)^{-4} = 625$.

5. Use the fact that $\log_c b = 0.9922$ and $\log_c a = 3.2211$ to find $\log_c ab$.

6. Use the fact that $\log_c a = 1.15$ and $\log_c b = 2.46$ to find $\log_c \frac{b}{a}$.

7. Use the laws of logarithms to expand and simplify the expression: $\log\left(\frac{\sqrt[3]{x}}{x^2+1}\right)$.

8. Use the laws of logarithms to expand and simplify the expression: $\ln\left(x^3 e^{2x}\right)$.

9. Use the laws of logarithms to solve the equation $\log_{1/2} 8 = x$.

10. Use the laws of logarithms to solve the equation $\log_x 1000 = -3$.

11. Sketch the graph of $h(x) = \ln(xe)$.

12. What is the interest from $2 million, invested at 12% per year for 4 years, and compounded annually?

13. Use the laws of logarithms to solve the equation $e^{x/3} = 4$.

14. A quantity $Q(t)$ is described by the exponential growth function $Q(t) = 170e^{0.15t}$, where t is measured in years.
(a) What quantity is initially present?

(b) What quantity is present after 4 years?

15. A radioactive element has a half-life of 9.7 minutes. What is the decay constant?

16. The population of rabbits in a park is initially 800 and is expected to increase at an annual rate of 12%. Find the expected population in 14 years.

17. A radioactive substance has a half-life of 10 years. If 50 g of the substance are present initially, find
(a) the amount present after 8 years.
(b) the rate at which the substance will be decaying 8 years later.

18. Find the derivative of the function $f(x) = \ln\sqrt{x}$.

19. Find the derivative of the function $f(x) = \dfrac{x}{e^x + 1}$.

20. Use logarithmic differentiation to find the derivative of the function $y = x^{1/2}(x^2 + 1)^{5/2}$.

Answers to Chapter 5 Exams

Exam 5A

1. (a) 2

   (b) $27x^6y^{18}$

2.

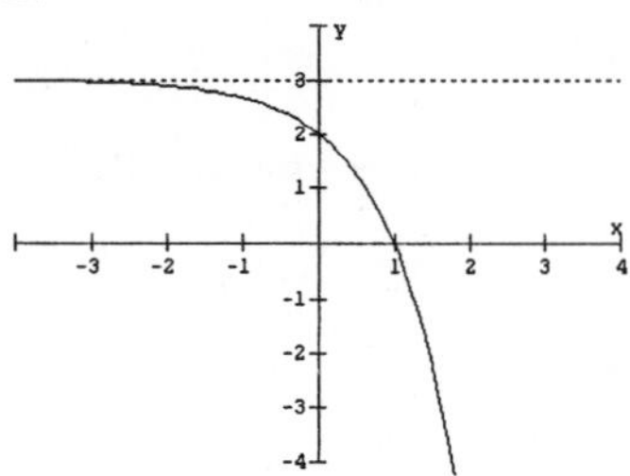

3.

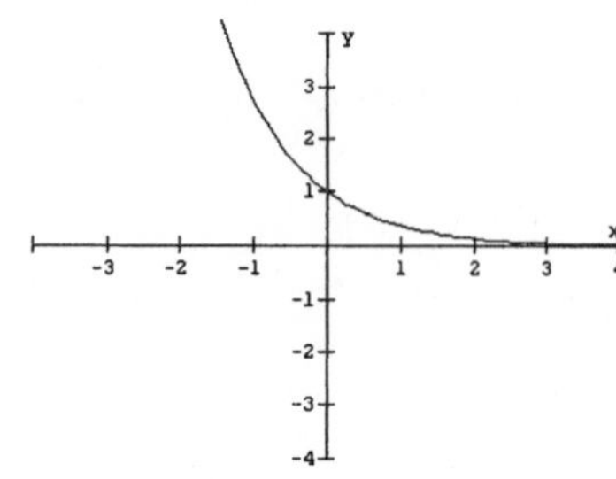

4. $\log_{49}\frac{1}{7} = -\frac{1}{2}$

5. \$10207.43

6. \$11.51

7. $\log x + \frac{1}{2}\log(x+2)$

8. $2\ln x + 2x$

9. $x = 2$

10. $x = \frac{1}{9}$

Exam 5B

1. (a) $18x^4$

   (b) $a^2/9$

2.

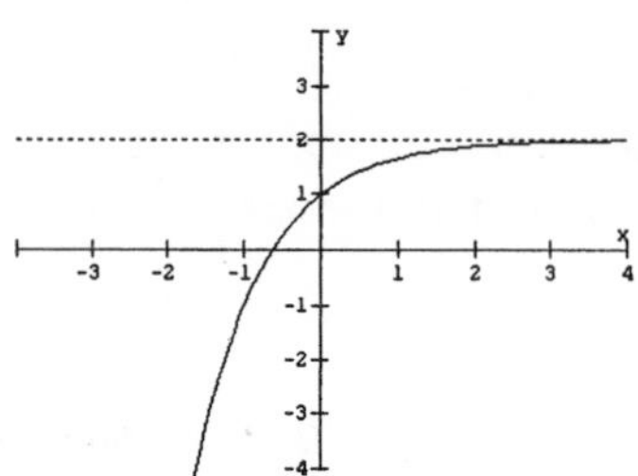

3.

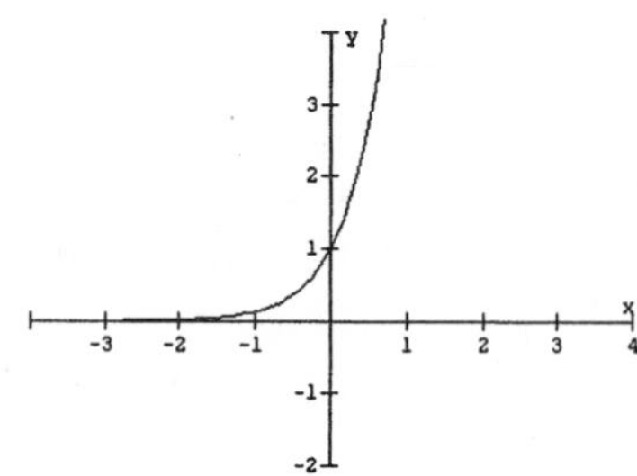

4. $\log_{1/4}\frac{1}{2} = \frac{1}{2}$

5. 2.4505

6. 2.1526

7. $\log x - \log(3x+1)$

8. $\frac{1}{2}x$

9. $x = -2$

10. $x = 4$

11.

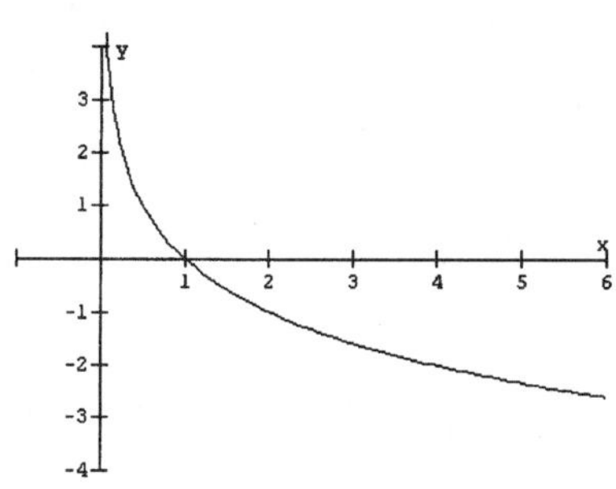

12. $x = \dfrac{\ln 18 - 1}{3}$

13. $7e^{7x}$

14. $1 + \ln x$

15. Absolute maximum $g(e) = \dfrac{1}{e}$;
absolute minimum $g(1) = 0$

16. $(9x-1)(x+7)^3(x-9)^4$

17. (a) 0.08
(b) 220

18. 0.00042

19. 154

20. ≈ 13 years

11.

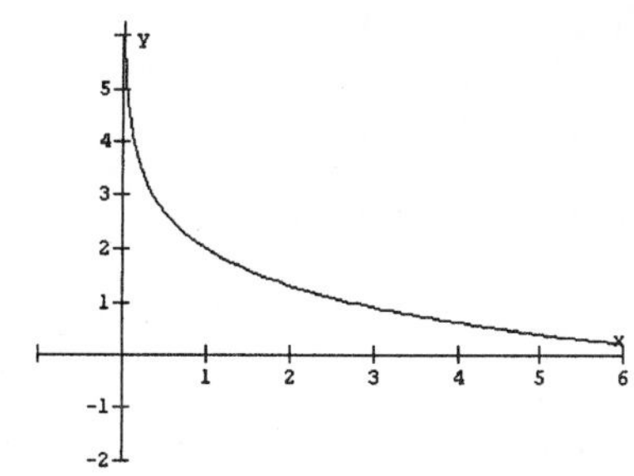

12. $x = \dfrac{1}{4} + \dfrac{1}{4}\ln 6$

13. (a) 410
(b) about 488

14. 0.01333

15. 1131

16. 0.048 or 4.8%

17. 5.79%

18. $\dfrac{3x^2 - 2}{x^3 - 2x}$

19. $\dfrac{e^3}{2\sqrt{x+1}}$

20. $\dfrac{e^x x^{2\ln x}\left(x + 4\ln x\right)}{x}$

Exam 5C

1. $x = 1/2$
2.

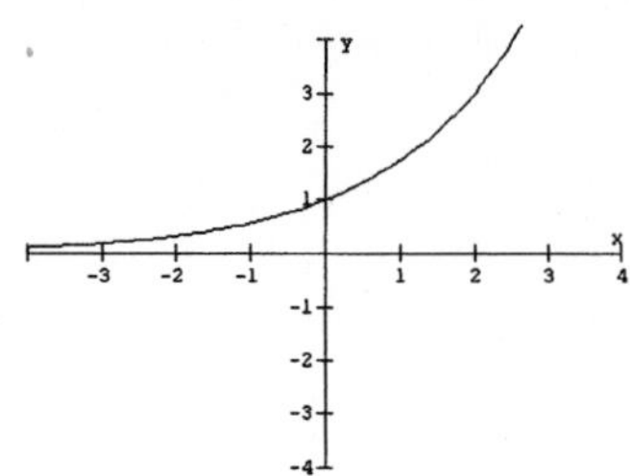

3.

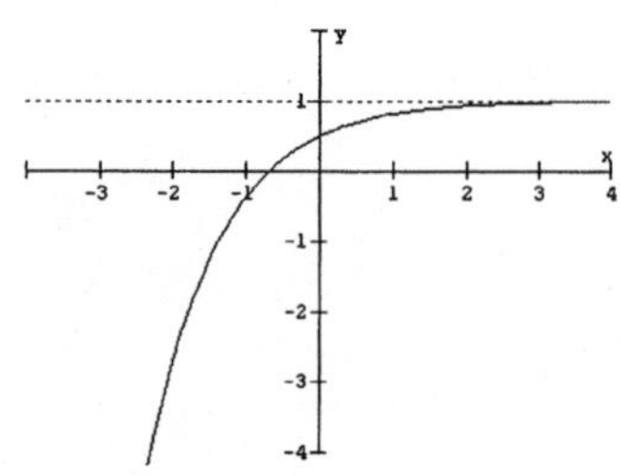

4. $\log_{64} \frac{1}{16} = -\frac{2}{3}$

5. 1.173

6. 0.478

7. $\frac{1}{2}\log x - \log(x+1)$

8. $x - \ln x$

9. $x = 0$

10. $x = 2$

Exam 5D

1. $x = 2/3$
2.

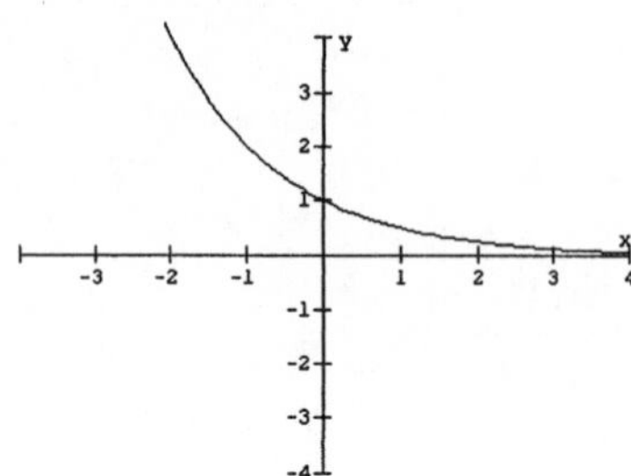

3.

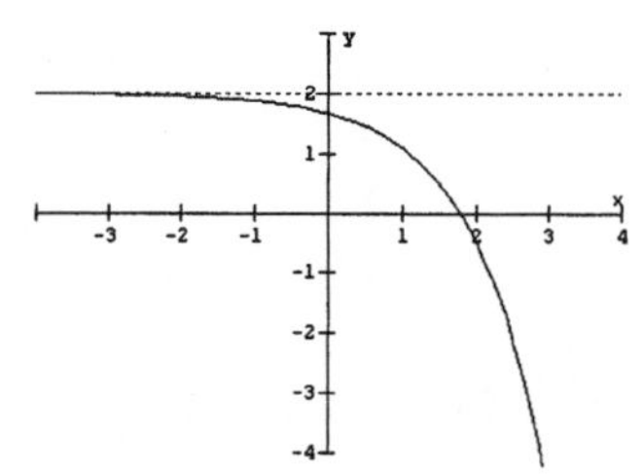

4. $\log_{1/5} 625 = -4$

5. 4.2133

6. 1.31

7. $\frac{1}{3}\log x - \log(x^2+1)$

8. $3\ln x + 2x$

9. $x = -3$

10. $x = \frac{1}{10}$

11.

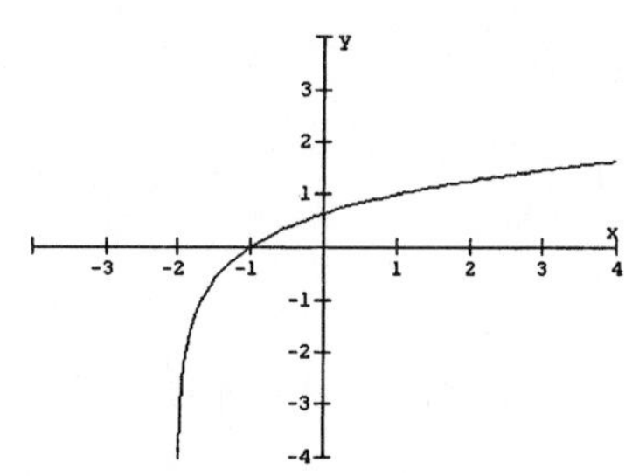

12. \$269.39

13. $x = \dfrac{1 - \ln 9}{3}$

14. (a) 1000
(b) 1036

15. 0.0007702

16. 875

17. 0.057 or 5.7%

18. $\dfrac{2x}{x^2 + 1}$

19. $\sqrt{3}\left(e^{x+1}\right)$

20. $12^x \ln 12$

11.

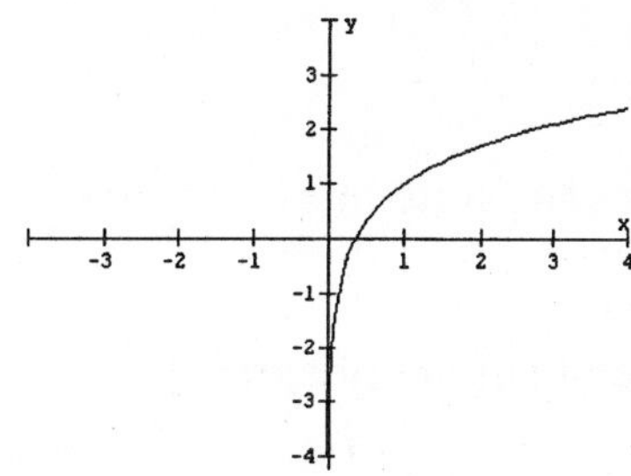

12. \$1.147 million

13. $x = 3\ln 4$

14. (a) 170
(b) 310

15. 0.07146

16. 4292

17. (a) 28.72g (b) -2 g/yr

18. $\dfrac{1}{2x}$

19. $\dfrac{e^x + 1 - xe^x}{\left(e^x + 1\right)^2}$

20. $\dfrac{(11x^2 + 1)(x^2 + 1)^{3/2}}{2x^{1/2}}$

Chapter 6 ■ Integration

Section 6.1

1. Find the indefinite integral $\int 3dx$. Answer: $3x+C$

2. Find the indefinite integral $\int \sqrt{5}dx$. Answer: $\sqrt{5}x+C$

3. Find the indefinite integral $\int 2x^3 dx$. Answer: $\frac{1}{2}x^4+C$

4. Find the indefinite integral $\int 4t^{-6}dt$. Answer: $-\frac{4}{5}t^{-5}+C$

5. Find the indefinite integral $\int x^{5/3}dx$. Answer: $\frac{3}{8}x^{8/3}+C$

6. Find the indefinite integral $\int 2x^{-2/3}dx$. Answer: $6x^{1/3}+C$

7. Find the indefinite integral $\int e\sqrt{t}dt$. Answer: $\frac{2}{3}et^{3/2}+C$

8. Find the indefinite integral $\int (1+2x+4x^2)dx$. Answer: $x+x^2+\frac{4}{3}x^3+C$

9. Find the indefinite integral $\int (0.4t^3-0.3t^2+1.5)dt$.

   Answer: $0.1t^4-0.1t^3+1.5t+C$

10. Find the indefinite integral $\int 3e^x dx$. Answer: $3e^x+C$

11. Find the indefinite integral $\int (2+\sqrt{x}+2x+e^x)dx$.

    Answer: $2x+\frac{2}{3}x^{3/2}+x^2+e^x+C$

12. Find the indefinite integral $\int (u^{7/2}+2u^{5/2}-u)du$.

    Answer: $\frac{2}{9}u^{9/2}+\frac{4}{7}u^{7/2}-\frac{1}{2}u^2+C$

13. Find the indefinite integral $\int\left(\sqrt[5]{x^2}-\frac{1}{x^3}\right)dx$.

Answer: $\frac{5}{7}x^{7/5}+\frac{1}{2}x^{-2}+C$

14. Find the indefinite integral $\int(2y+3)(3y-2)dy$.

Answer: $2y^3+\frac{5}{2}y^2-6y+C$

15. Find the indefinite integral $\int\sqrt{y}\left(y^2-y+1\right)dy$.

Answer: $\frac{2}{7}y^{7/2}-\frac{2}{5}y^{5/2}+\frac{2}{3}y^{3/2}+C$

16. Find the indefinite integral $\int\left(2e^x+x^{2e}\right)dx$.

Answer: $2e^x+\frac{1}{2e+1}x^{2e+1}+C$

17. Find the indefinite integral $\int\frac{x^5+\sqrt[5]{x}}{x^2}dx$.

Answer: $\frac{1}{4}x^4-\frac{5}{4}x^{-4/5}+C$

18. Find the indefinite integral $\int\frac{y^3-5y^2-y}{y}dy$.

Answer: $\frac{y^3}{3}-\frac{5}{2}y^2-y+C$

19. Find the indefinite integral $\int\frac{\left(\sqrt{x}+1\right)^2}{x^3}dx$.

Answer: $-x^{-1}-\frac{4}{3}x^{-3/2}-\frac{1}{2}x^{-2}+C$

20. Find the indefinite integral $\int\left(e^t+t^\pi\right)dx$.

Answer: $e^t+\frac{1}{\pi+1}t^{\pi+1}+C$

21. Find the function $f(x)$ if $f'(x)=6x^2-4x+7$ and $f(1)=3$.

Answer: $2x^3-2x^2+7x-4$

22. Find the function $f(x)$ if $f'(x)=3x^2+e^x$ and $f(0)=3$.

Answer: $x^3 + e^x + 2$

23. Find the function $f(x)$ if $f'(x) = 4x - 2$ and $f(1) = 1$.
Answer: $f = 2x^2 - 2x + 1$

24. Find the function $f(x)$ if $f'(x) = \sqrt[5]{x^2} - \frac{1}{x^3}$ and $f(1) = 2$
Answer: $\frac{5}{7}x^{7/5} + \frac{1}{2}x^{-2} + \frac{11}{14}$

25. Find the function $f(x)$ if $f'(x) = \frac{x-3}{x}$ and $f(1) = 2$.
Answer: $f = x - 3\ln x + 1$

26. A ball is thrown straight up into the air. Its velocity t seconds after being thrown is given by the function $f(t) = 64 - 32t$. Find the ball's position $s(t)$ at any time t, assuming its position is 0 when $t = 0$.
Answer: $s(t) = 64t - 16t^2$

27. A study conducted by Mega-Byte Ltd. estimates that the number of online service subscribers will grow at a rate of $250 + 200t^{5/6}$ new subscribers per month t months from the start date of the service. If 4000 customers signed up for the service initially, how many subscribers will there be 18 months later?
Answer: 30,333

28. The rate of growth of a particular type of pest can be approximated by the function $20 + 20t^{2/3}$ pests/month. If there are initially 20 pests present, how many will there be 8 months from beginning?
Answer: 564

29. A ball is thrown straight up into the air. Its velocity t seconds after being thrown is given by the function $f(t) = 64 - 32t$. Find the ball's position $s(t)$ at any time t, assuming its position is 100 when $t = 0$.
Answer: $s(t) = 64t - 16t^2 + 100$

30. A ball is thrown straight up into the air. Its velocity t seconds after being thrown is given by the function $f(t) = 64 - 32t$. Find the ball's position $s(t)$ at any time t, assuming its position is -50 when $t = 0$.
Answer: $s(t) = 64t - 16t^2 - 50$

Section 6.1 Multiple Choice Questions

1. Which function is an antiderivative of $f(x)=x^3-6x+7$?

   a. x^4-3x^2+7x

   b. $\frac{1}{4}x^4-3x^2+7x+e$

   c. $\frac{1}{4}x^4-6x^2+7x$

   d. $\frac{1}{4}x^4-3x^2+7$

   Answer: b.

2. Which function is an antiderivative of $f(x)=3x^2-2e^x$?

   a. $3x^3-2e^x$

   b. $3x^3-2e^x+C$

   c. $3x^3+2e^x$

   d. x^3-2e^x

   Answer: d.

3. Which function is an antiderivative function $f(x)=3x^2-4x+\frac{1}{x}+12$?

   a. $x^3-2x^2+\ln x+12x+100$

   b. $x^3-x^2+\ln x+12x+C$

   c. $x^3-2x^2+\ln x+12+C$

   d. $x^3-2x^2+\ln x-\frac{1}{x^2}+C$

   Answer: a.

4. Find the indefinite integral $f(x)=\int\left(x^2-4x+\frac{2}{x}\right)dx$.

   a. $\frac{1}{3}x^3+4x^2+2\ln x+C$

   b. $\frac{1}{3}x^3-2x^2+2\ln x$

   c. $\frac{1}{3}x^3-2x^2+2\ln x+C$

   d. $\frac{1}{3}x^3-2x^2+\ln x+C$

   Answer: c.

5. Find the indefinite integral $f(x)=\int\left(3e^x+\sqrt{5}\right)dx$.

a. $3e^x + \sqrt{5}x + C$
b. $3e^x + \sqrt{5} + C$
c. $3e^x + C$
d. $\frac{1}{3}e^x + \sqrt{5}x + C$

Answer: a.

6. Find the indefinite integral $f(x) = \int\left(3 - \sqrt{x}\right)dx$.

a. $3x^2 - \frac{2}{3}x^{3/2} + C$
b. $3x - \frac{2}{3}x^{3/2}$
c. $3x - \frac{3}{2}x^{3/2} + C$
d. $3x - \frac{2}{3}x^{3/2} + C$

Answer: d.

7. Find the indefinite integral $f(x) = \int(3 - x)(3 + x)\,dx$.

a. $6x - \frac{1}{3}x^3 + C$
b. $9x - \frac{1}{3}x^2 + C$
c. $9x - \frac{1}{3}x^3 + C$
d. $9x - x^3 + C$

Answer: c.

8. Find the indefinite integral $f(x) = \int\frac{x^4 + 3x^3 - 14x^2 + 5}{x}dx$.

a. $\frac{1}{4}x^4 + x^3 - 7x^2 + 5\ln x + C$
b. $\frac{1}{4}x^4 + x^3 + 7x^2 + 5\ln x + C$
c. $x^4 + x^3 - 7x^2 + 5\ln x + C$
d. $\frac{1}{4}x^4 + x^3 - 14x^2 + 5\ln x + C$

Answer: a

9. Find the indefinite integral $f(x) = \int\left(x^{-3} + x^{-1}\right)dx$.

a. $2x^{-2} + \ln x + C$

b. $\frac{1}{2}x^{-2} + \ln x + C$

c. $-\frac{1}{2}x^{-2} + \ln x + C$

d. $-\frac{1}{2}x^{-2} - \frac{1}{x} + C$

Answer: c

10. Given $f'(x) = 3x^2 + 8x - 9$. Find the function $f(x)$ passing through (1, 6).

a. $x^3 + 4x^2 - 9x + 15$

b. $x^3 + 4x^2 - 9x + 10$

c. $x^3 + 4x^2 - 9x + 20$

d. $x^3 + 4x^2 - 9x - 10$

Answer: b

11. The velocity of a truck (in feet/second) *t* seconds after starting from rest is given by the function $v(t) = 12\sqrt[3]{t}$, $(0 \le t \le 10)$. Find $S(t)$, the function that gives the position of the truck at any time *t*.

a. $3t^{4/3}$

b. $9t^{4/3}$

c. $4t^{-1/3}$

d. $16t^{4/3}$

Answer: b.

12. The velocity of a car (in feet/second) *t* seconds after starting from the station is given by the function $v(t) = 0.2t + 15$, $(0 \le t \le 30)$. Find $S(t)$, the function that gives the position of the car at any time *t*.

a. $0.1t^2 - 15t$

b. $0.1t^2 + 15t + 10$

c. $0.1t^2 + 15t$

d. $0.4t^2 + 15t$

Answer: c.

13. The management of Lorimar Watch Company has determined that the daily marginal revenue function associated with producing and selling their travel clocks is given by $R'(x) = -0.08x + 24$, where *x* denotes the number of units produced and sold and $R'(x)$ is measured in dollars/unit. Determine the revenue function $R(x)$ associated with producing and selling these clocks.

a. $-0.04x^2 - 24x$

b. $-0.02x^2 + 24x$

c. $0.04x^2 + 24x$

d. $-0.04x^2 + 24x$

Answer: d.

14. A publisher estimates the marginal cost function for printing a book is $\frac{dC}{dx} = 2x - 6$, where x is the number of books produced. It costs $50 to print 10 books. Find the total cost function.

a. $C(x) = x^2 - 6x + 110$

b. $C(x) = x^2 - 6x + 10$

c. $C(x) = x^2 - 6x + 60$

d. $C(x) = x^2 - 6x + 50$

Answer: b.

15. If $\frac{dy}{dx} = 3x^2 - 2x + 4$ and $y = 6$ when $x = 2$, then

a. $y = 6$

b. $y = x^3 - x^2 + 4x + 6$

c. $y = x^3 - x^2 + 4x - 6$

d. $y = x^3 + x^2 + 4x - 6$

Answer: c.

16. A study conducted by TeleCable estimates the number of cable TV subscribers will grow at the rate of $120 + 280t^{3/4}$ new subscribers/month, t months from the start date of the service. If 4000 subscribers signed up for the service before the starting date, how many subscribers will there be 16 months after the starting date?

a. 26000

b. 26400

c. 22400

d. 30400

Answer: b.

Section 6.2

1. Find the indefinite integral $\int 2x\sqrt{x^2+3}dx$. Answer: $\frac{2}{3}\left(x^2+3\right)^{3/2}+C$

2. Find the indefinite integral $\int 6(6x+4)^3\,dx$. Answer: $\frac{1}{4}(6x+4)^4+C$

3. Find the indefinite integral $\int\left(x^3+7x\right)^4\left(3x^2+7\right)dx$.

   Answer: $\frac{1}{5}\left(x^3+7x\right)^5+C$

4. Find the indefinite integral $\int\frac{3x^2}{\left(x^3+3\right)^4}dx$. Answer: $\frac{-1}{3\left(x^3+3\right)^3}+C$

5. Find the indefinite integral $\int\frac{3x}{3x^2+5}dx$. Answer: $\frac{1}{2}\ln\left(3x^2+5\right)+C$

6. Find the indefinite integral $\int\frac{3x^2+3}{\left(x^3+3x\right)^4}dx$. Answer: $\frac{-1}{3\left(x^3+3\right)^3}+C$

7. Find the indefinite integral $\int 4x\left(x^2-4\right)^{12}dx$. Answer: $\frac{2}{13}\left(x^2-4\right)^{13}+C$

8. Find the indefinite integral $\int\frac{x^3}{\sqrt{x^4+4}}dx$. Answer: $\frac{1}{2}\sqrt{x^4+4}+C$

9. Find the indefinite integral $\int\frac{2x+2}{x^2+2x+3}dx$. Answer: $\ln\left|x^2+2x+3\right|+C$

10. Find the indefinite integral $\int\frac{x^3+2x}{x^4+4x^2+2}dx$.

    Answer: $\frac{1}{4}\ln\left|x^4+4x^2+2\right|+C$

11. Find the indefinite integral $\int e^{3x}dx$. Answer: $\frac{1}{3}e^{3x}+C$

12. Find the indefinite integral $\int\left(2e^x+3e^{-x}\right)dx$. Answer: $2e^x-3e^{-x}+C$

13. Find the indefinite integral $\int\left(x+\frac{1}{2}\right)e^{x^2+x}dx$. Answer: $\frac{1}{2}e^{x^2+x}+C$

14. Find the indefinite integral $\int x^4 e^{x^5-2}dx$. Answer: $\frac{1}{5}e^{x^5-2}+C$

15. Find the indefinite integral $\int\frac{\ln x}{5x}dx$. Answer: $\frac{1}{10}(\ln x)^2+C$

16. Find the indefinite integral $\int\frac{e^{-2/x}}{x^2}dx$. Answer: $\frac{1}{2}e^{-2/x}+C$

17. Find the indefinite integral $\int\frac{4e^x}{2+e^x}dx$. Answer: $4\ln(2+e^x)+C$

18. Find the indefinite integral $\int\frac{1}{x(\ln x)^2}dx$. Answer: $\frac{-1}{\ln x}+C$

19. Find the indefinite integral $\int\frac{2}{t(\ln t)}dt$. Answer: $2\ln(\ln t)+C$

20. Find the indefinite integral $\int\frac{(\ln x)^4}{x}dx$. Answer: $\frac{1}{5}(\ln x)^5+C$

21. Find the function $f(x)$ if $f'(x)=4(3x-2)^5$ and f passes through the point (1,1).

Answer: $f=\frac{2}{9}(3x-2)^6+\frac{7}{9}$

Section 6.2 Multiple Choice Questions

1. $\int 7x\left(x^2+120\right)dx=$

   a. $\frac{1}{42}e^{3x^2}+C$

   b. $\frac{6}{7}e^{3x^2}+C$

   c. $\frac{7}{4}\left(x^2+120\right)^2+C$

   d. $7e^{3x^2}+C$

   Answer: c.

2. $\int(2x+3)\left(x^2+3x-70\right)dx=$

   a. $\frac{1}{42}e^{3x^2}+C$

   b. $\frac{1}{2}\left(x^2+3x-70\right)^2+C$

   c. $\frac{7}{4}\left(x^2+120\right)^2+C$

   d. $7e^{3x^2}+C$

   Answer: b.

3. $\int\frac{x^6}{1+x^7}dx=$

   a. $\frac{1}{7}\ln\left|1+x^7\right|+C$

   b. $\frac{1}{2}\left(x^2+3x-70\right)^2+C$

   c. $\frac{7}{4}\left(x^2+120\right)^2+C$

   d. $7e^{3x^2}+C$

   Answer: a.

4. $\int\frac{2+x^2}{\left(1+6x+x^3\right)^2}dx=$

   a. $\frac{-3}{\left(1+6x+x^3\right)}$

   b. $-\frac{1}{3\left(1+6x+x^3\right)}$

c. $\dfrac{1}{3\left(1+6x+x^3\right)}$

d. $\dfrac{3}{\left(1+6x+x^3\right)}$

Answer: b.

5. $\int \frac{\ln(5x)}{x} dx =$

a. $\ln(\ln 5x) + C$

b. $\ln 5 \ln x + C$

c. $(\ln 5x)^2 + C$

d. $\frac{1}{2}(\ln 5x)^2 + C$

Answer: d.

6. $\int 7xe^{3x^2} dx =$

a. $\frac{1}{42}e^{3x^2} + C$

b. $\frac{6}{7}e^{3x^2} + C$

c. $\frac{7}{6}e^{3x^2} + C$

d. $7e^{3x^2} + C$

Answer: c.

7. $\int e^x \left(e^{3x}\right) dx =$

a. $\frac{1}{3}e^{3x} + C$

b. $\frac{1}{4}e^{4x} + C$

c. $\frac{1}{5}e^{5x} + C$

d. $4e^{4x} + C$

Answer: b.

8. $\int \frac{\ln x}{3x} dx =$

a. $6\ln^2|x| + C$

b. $\frac{1}{6}\ln(\ln x)+C$

c. $\frac{1}{3}\ln^2|x|+C$

d. $\frac{1}{6}\ln^2|x|+C$

Answer: d.

9. $\int \frac{1}{x(\ln x)^5}dx =$

a. $\frac{1}{6(\ln x)^6}+C$

b. $-\frac{1}{6(\ln x)^6}+C$

c. $-\frac{1}{4(\ln x)^4}+C$

d. $\frac{1}{4(\ln x)^4}+C$

Answer: c.

10. Find the function $f(x)$ passing through (1, 3) with derivative $f'(x)=\frac{3x^2}{2\sqrt{x^3-1}}$.

a. $f(x)=2\sqrt{x^3-1}+3$

b. $f(x)=\sqrt{x^3-1}+3$

c. $f(x)=\frac{1}{3}\sqrt{x^3-1}+3$

d. $f(x)=\sqrt{x^3-1}-3$

Answer: b.

11. Find the function $f(x)$ passing through (0, 1) and $f'(x)=(2x+5)e^{x^2+5x}$.

a. $f(x)=5e^{x^2+5x}$

b. $f(x)=e^{x^2+5x}+1$

c. $f(x)=\frac{1}{2}e^{x^2+5x}$

d. $f(x)=e^{x^2+5x}$

Answer: d.

12. If the marginal cost function is given by $C'(x) = (2x+7)(x^2+7x+3)^3$, then a general expression for the total cost function is

a. $C(x) = \frac{1}{4}(x^2+7x+3)^4 + C$

b. $C(x) = (x^2+7x+3)^4 + C$

c. $C(x) = 4(x^2+7x+3)^4 + C$

d. $C(x) = (x^2+7x+3)^2 + C$

Answer: a.

13. The current deer population in a state park is estimated to be 9,600. It is increasing at the rate of $\frac{2t}{5t^2+1}$ deer per year. Find a function that gives the deer population in the state park at any time t.

a. $D(t) = \frac{t}{5t^2+1} + 9,600$

b. $D(t) = 5\ln(5t^2+1) + 9,600$

c. $D(t) = \frac{1}{5}\ln(5t^2+1)$

d. $D(t) = \frac{1}{5}\ln(5t^2+1) + 9,600$

Answer: d.

14. The population of a certain city is projected to grow at the rate of $r(t) = 300\left(1 + \frac{2t}{t^2+25}\right)$ $(0 \le t \le 5)$ people per year, t years from now. The current population is 60,000. What will be the population 4 years from now?

a. 65896
b. 54982
c. 61348
d. 71239

Answer: c.

15. The rate of change of the unit price p (in dollars) of Apex women's boots is given by $p'(x) = \frac{250}{(6-x)^2}$, $(0 \le x \le 5)$, where x is the number of hundred pairs that the supplier will make available in the market daily when the unit price is \$$p$ per pair. Find the supply equation for these boots if the quantity the supplier is willing to make available is 200 pairs daily ($x = 2$) when the unit price is \$50 per pair.

a. $-\frac{250}{(6-x)}+12.5$

b. $\frac{250}{(6-x)}-12.5$

c. $\frac{250}{(6-x)}+12.5$

d. $\frac{250}{(6-x)^2}-12.5$

Answer: b.

Section 6.3

1. Let $f(x)=x^2$ and compute the Riemann sum of f over the interval $[1,3]$ using four subintervals of equal length ($n = 4$). Choose the representative point in each subinterval to be the midpoint of the subinterval.
Answer: 8.625

2. Let $f(x)=x^2$ and compute the Riemann sum of f over the interval $[1,3]$ using four subintervals of equal length ($n = 4$). Choose the representative point in each subinterval to be the left endpoint of the subinterval.
Answer: 6.75

3. Let $f(x)=4x+1$ and compute the Riemann sum of f over the interval $[0,3]$ using six subintervals of equal length ($n = 6$). Choose the representative point in each subinterval to be the left endpoint of the subinterval.
Answer: 18

4. Let $f(x)=4x+1$ and compute the Riemann sum of f over the interval $[0,3]$ using six subintervals of equal length ($n = 6$). Choose the representative point in each subinterval to be the right endpoint of the subinterval.
Answer: 24

5. Let $f(x)=x^2$ and compute the Riemann sum of f over the interval $[1,3]$ using four subintervals of equal length ($n = 4$). Choose the representative point in each subinterval to be the right endpoint of the subinterval.
Answer: 10.75

6. Let $f(x)=x^4$ and compute the Riemann sum of f over the interval $[2,4]$ using four subintervals of equal length ($n = 4$). Choose the representative point in each subinterval to be the midpoint of the subinterval.
Answer: 196.0703125

7. Let $f(x)=x^4$ and compute the Riemann sum of f over the interval $[1,3]$ using four subintervals of equal length ($n = 4$). Choose the representative point in each subinterval to be the left endpoint of the subinterval.
Answer: 30.5625

8. Let $f(x)=x^4$ and compute the Riemann sum of f over the interval $[1,3]$ using four subintervals of equal length ($n = 4$). Choose the representative point in each subinterval to be the right endpoint of the subinterval.
Answer: 70.5625

9. Let $f(x) = 2x^2 + 2$ and compute the Riemann sum of f over the interval $[0,1]$ using four subintervals of equal length ($n = 4$). Choose the representative point in each subinterval to be the midpoint of the subinterval.
Answer: 2.65625

10. Let $f(x) = \frac{e^x}{x}$ and compute the Riemann sum of f over the interval $[0,1]$ using four subintervals of equal length ($n = 4$). Choose the representative point in each subinterval to be the midpoint of the subinterval.
Answer: about 4.669

11. Find the area of the region under the graph of the function $f(x) = 4x + 5$ on the interval $[-1,2]$.
Answer: 21

Section 6.3 Multiple Choice Questions

1. Let R be the region under the graph $f(x) = x^2 + 12$ on the interval [0, 2]. Find an approximation of the area A of R using four subintervals of [0, 2] of equal length and picking the left end point of each subinterval to evaluate $f(x)$ to obtain the height of the approximating rectangle.
a. 26.1875
b. 26.0370
c. 25
d. 25.75
Answer: d.

2. Let R be the region under the graph $f(x) = 3x^2 + 2$ on the interval [0, 2]. Find an approximation of the area A of R using five subintervals of [0, 2] of equal length and picking the left end point of each subinterval to evaluate $f(x)$ to obtain the height of the approximating rectangle.
a. 9.76
b. 8.45
c. 10.11
d. 11
Answer: a.

3. Let R be the region under the graph $f(x) = 5x^2 - 4$ on the interval [1, 3]. Find an approximation of the area A of R using three subintervals of [1, 3] of equal length and picking the left end point of each subinterval to evaluate $f(x)$ to obtain the height of the approximating rectangle.
a. 22.741
b. 25.75o

c. 26.471
d. 29.762
Answer: a.

4. Let R be the region under the graph $f(x) = x^2 + 12$ on the interval [0, 2]. Find an approximation of the area A of R using four subintervals of [0, 2] of equal length and picking the right end point of each subinterval to evaluate $f(x)$ to obtain the height of the approximating rectangle.
a. 29
b. 27.75
c. 27.3704
d. 27.1875
Answer: b.

5. Let R be the region under the graph $f(x) = 3x^2 + 2$ on the interval [0, 2]. Find an approximation of the area A of R using five subintervals of [0, 2] of equal length and picking the right end point of each subinterval to evaluate $f(x)$ to obtain the height of the approximating rectangle.
a. 14.11
b. 16.44
c. 14.56
d. 15.25
Answer: c.

6. Let R be the region under the graph $f(x) = 5x^2 - 4$ on the interval [1, 3]. Find an approximation of the area A of R using three subintervals of [1, 3] of equal length and picking the right end point of each subinterval to evaluate $f(x)$ to obtain the height of the approximating rectangle.
a. 49.407
b. 45.75
c. 57
d. 42.185
Answer: a.

7. Let R be the region under the graph $f(x) = x^2 + 12$ on the interval [0, 2]. Find an approximation of the area A of R using six subintervals of [0, 2] of equal length and picking the middle point of each subinterval to evaluate $f(x)$ to obtain the height of the approximating rectangle.
a. 26
b. 27.1875
c. 26.6482
d. 26.5
Answer: c.

8. Let R be the region under the graph $f(x)=5x^2-4$ on the interval [1, 3]. Find an approximation of the area A of R using three subintervals of [1, 3] of equal length and picking the middle point of each subinterval to evaluate $f(x)$ to obtain the height of the approximating rectangle.
   a. 36.963
   b. 35.125
   c. 35.265
   d. 35.316
   Answer: a.

9. Let R be the region under the graph $f(x)=x^3+1$ on the interval [1, 5]. Find an approximation of the area A of R using four subintervals of [1, 5] of equal length and picking the middle point of each subinterval to evaluate $f(x)$ to obtain the height of the approximating rectangle.
   a. 158.667
   b. 148
   c. 157
   d. 159.25
   Answer: c.

10. Let R be the region under the graph $f(x)=x^2+2x+1$ on the interval [0, 4]. Find an approximation of the area A of R using four subintervals of [0, 4] of equal length and picking the left end point of each subinterval to evaluate $f(x)$ to obtain the height of the approximating rectangle.
   a. 20
   b. 35.5
   c. 38.375
   d. 30
   Answer: d.

11. Let R be the region under the graph $f(x)=x^2+4$ on the interval [0, 2]. Find an approximation of the area A of R using four subintervals of [0, 2] of equal length and picking the left end point of each subinterval to evaluate $f(x)$ to obtain the height of the approximating rectangle.
   a. 9.00
   b. 9.75
   c. 11.75
   d. 10.65
   Answer: b.

12. Let R be the region under the graph $f(x)=\dfrac{1}{x+1}$ on the interval [1, 3]. Find an approximation of the area A of R using ten subintervals of [1, 3] of equal length and picking the left end point of each subinterval to evaluate $f(x)$ to obtain the height of the approximating rectangle.

a. 0.7254
b. 0.7595
c. 0.7188
d. 0.7144
Answer: c.

13. Let R be the region under the graph $f(x)=\ln(x+3)$ on the interval [5, 9]. Find an approximation of the area A of R using four subintervals of [5, 9] of equal length and picking the right end point of each subinterval to evaluate $f(x)$ to obtain the height of the approximating rectangle.
a. 9.3826
b. 9.2838
c. 9.5750
d. 9.2639
Answer: a.

14. Let R be the region under the graph $f(x)=e^{x+1}$ on the interval [0, 2]. Find an approximation of the area A of R using eight subintervals of [0, 2] of equal length and picking the right end point of each subinterval to evaluate $f(x)$ to obtain the height of the approximating rectangle.
a. 22.069
b. 27.475
c. 20.422
d. 19.629
Answer: d.

15. Let R be the region under the graph $f(x)=2x+5$ on the interval [4, 6]. Find an approximation of the area A of R using six subintervals of [4, 6] of equal length and picking the middle point of each subinterval to evaluate $f(x)$ to obtain the height of the approximating rectangle.
a. 10
b. 20
c. 30
d. 40
Answer: c.

16. Let R be the region under the graph $f(x)=25-x^2$ on the interval [0, 5]. Find an approximation of the area A of R using four subintervals of [0, 5] of equal length and picking the middle point of each subinterval to evaluate $f(x)$ to obtain the height of the approximating rectangle.
a. 83.623
b. 85.936
c. 83.496
d. 83.984
Answer: d.

Section 6.4

1. Evaluate the definite integral $\int_1^2 4dx$. Answer: 4

2. Evaluate the definite integral $\int_1^2 2xdx$. Answer: 3

3. Evaluate the definite integral $\int_{-2}^3 (4x+3)dx$. Answer: 25

4. Evaluate the definite integral $\int_1^5 \frac{1}{x}dx$. Answer: ln(5)

5. Evaluate the definite integral $\int_4^9 \frac{3}{\sqrt{x}}dx$. Answer: 6

6. Evaluate the definite integral $\int_{-1}^1 (3-2x)dx$. Answer: 6

7. Evaluate the definite integral $\int_0^1 \left(t-t^2\right)^2 dt$. Answer: $\frac{1}{30}$

8. Evaluate the definite integral $\int_5^7 \frac{3}{x-4}dx$. Answer: $3\ln 3$

9. Evaluate the definite integral $\int_1^4 \frac{3}{x^4}dx$. Answer: $\frac{63}{64}$

10. Evaluate the definite integral $\int_1^4 \left(1+\frac{1}{x^2}+\frac{1}{x^4}\right)dx$. Answer: $\frac{261}{64}$

11. Evaluate the definite integral $\int_1^8 \left(\sqrt[3]{x}-\frac{1}{\sqrt[3]{x}}\right)dx$. Answer: $\frac{27}{4}$

12. Find the area of the region R under the graph of $y=x^2+1$ and above x-axis from x = -1 to x = 2.
    Answer: 6.

13. Find the area of the region bounded by $y=x$ and $y=x^3$ from $x=0$ to $x=1$.

Answer: 0.25.

14. Find the area of the region bounded by $y = x$ and $y = \sqrt{x}$ from $x = 0$ to $x = 1$.

Answer: $\frac{1}{6} = 0.1\overline{6}$

15. Find the area of the region R under the graph of $y = x^2$ on the interval [0, 1].

Answer: $\frac{1}{3}$

16. Find the area of the region bounded by $y = x^2$ and $y = -x^2 + 18$ from $x = -3$ to $x = 3$.

Answer: 72.

17. Find the area of the region under the graph of the function $f(x) = 11$ on the interval $[-2, 4]$.

Answer: 66

18. Find the area of the region under the graph of the function $f(x) = x^2$ on the interval $[-1, 2]$.

Answer: 3

19. Find the area of the region under the graph of the function $f(x) = 4x^3$ on the interval $[1, 3]$.

Answer: 80

20. Find the area of the region under the graph of the function $f(x) = \frac{1}{x}$ on the interval $[2, 8]$.

Answer: 2 (ln2)

21. Find the area of the region under the graph of the function $f(x) = 2 + \sqrt[3]{x}$ on the interval $[0, 8]$.

Answer: 28

Section 6.4 Multiple Choice Questions

1. Evaluate $\int_1^3 2x\,dx$.

   a. 2
   b. 4
   c. 8
   d. 9
   Answer: c.

2. Evaluate $\int_0^1 e^x\,dx$.

   a. $e-1$
   b. 1
   c. 0
   d. $e+1$
   Answer: a.

3. Evaluate $\int_0^1 (x-1)(x+1)\,dx$.

   a. $\frac{2}{3}$
   b. $-\frac{2}{3}$
   c. $-\frac{1}{3}$
   d. $\frac{1}{3}$
   Answer: b.

4. Evaluate $\int_1^3 \frac{8}{x^3}\,dx$.

   a. $\frac{32}{9}$
   b. $\frac{40}{9}$
   c. 0
   d. $-\frac{32}{9}$
   Answer: a.

5. If $\int_{3}^{10} f(x)\,dx = A$ and $\int_{5}^{10} f(x)\,dx = B$, then $\int_{3}^{5} f(x)\,dx =$

a. $A + B$
b. $A - B$
c. 0
d. 20
Answer: b.

6. Evaluate $\int_{0}^{1} (t-1)(t+2)\,dt$.

a. $\frac{17}{6}$
b. $-\frac{17}{6}$
c. $-\frac{7}{6}$
d. $\frac{13}{6}$
Answer: c.

7. Find the area of the region under the graph of the function $f(x) = 3x^2 + 4$ on the interval [0, 2].
a. 8
b. 4
c. 8
d. 16
Answer: d.

8. Find the area of the region under the graph of the function $f(x) = 16 - x^2$ on the interval $[-4, 4]$.
a. $\frac{11}{3}$
b. $\frac{176}{3}$
c. $\frac{256}{3}$
d. $\frac{44}{3}$
Answer: c.

9. Find the area of the region under the graph of the function $f(x) = e^x$ on the interval [0, 4].

a. e^4+1
b. e^4-1
c. 1
d. e^4
Answer: b.

10. Evaluate $\int_{-3}^{3} 2x\,dx$?
a. 18
b. 9
c. 27
d. 0
Answer: d.

11. The daily marginal revenue function associated with selling x units of a certain product is given by $R'(x) = -0.2x + 74$, where R is measured in dollars/unit. Find the additional revenue realized when the production (and sales) level is increased from 100 to 200 units.
a. \$6400
b. \$4400
c. \$10,800
d. \$5400
Answer: b.

12. Annual sales (in millions of units) of hand-held computers are expected to grow in accordance with the function $f(t) = 0.21t^2 + 0.14t + 2.31,\ (0 \le t \le 6)$, where t is measured t years, with $t = 0$ corresponding to 1997. How many hand-held computers will be sold over the 6-year period between the beginning of 1997 and the end of 2002?
a. 31.5 million
b. 30.4 million
c. 29.2 million
d. 32.3 million
Answer: a.

Section 6.5

1. Evaluate the definite integral $\int_0^4 2x\sqrt{x^2+9}dx$. Answer: $\frac{196}{3}$

2. Evaluate the definite integral $\int_0^1 \frac{3e^x}{e^x+2}dx$. Answer: $3\ln(e+2)-3\ln 3$

3. Evaluate the definite integral $\int_0^3 e^{3x}dx$. Answer: $\frac{1}{3}e^9-\frac{1}{3}$

4. Evaluate the definite integral $\int_0^2 xe^{x^2+2}dx$. Answer: $\frac{1}{2}e^6-\frac{1}{2}e^2$

5. Evaluate the definite integral $\int_2^3 x^4e^{x^5-2}dx$. Answer: $\frac{1}{5}e^{241}-\frac{1}{5}e^{30}$

6. Evaluate the definite integral $\int_2^4 \frac{\ln x}{5x}dx$. Answer: $\frac{3}{10}(\ln 2)^2$

7. Evaluate the definite integral $\int_{-4}^{-2} \frac{e^{-2/x}}{x^2}dx$. Answer: $\frac{1}{2}e-\frac{1}{2}\sqrt{e}$

8. Evaluate the definite integral $\int_{12}^{16} \frac{1}{x(\ln x)^2}dx$. Answer: $\frac{1}{\ln 12}-\frac{1}{\ln 16}$

9. Evaluate the definite integral $\int_1^{32} x^{-2/5}dx$. Answer: $\frac{35}{3}$

10. Evaluate the definite integral $\int_1^2 \frac{6x^4+4x^3+2}{x^2}dx$. Answer: 21

11. Evaluate the definite integral $\int_e^{e^2} \frac{(\ln x)^4}{x}dx$. Answer: $\frac{31}{5}$

12. Evaluate the definite integral $\int_0^1 2x^2\left(x^3+2\right)^2dx$. Answer: $4\frac{2}{9}$

13. Evaluate the definite integral $\int_0^2 \frac{x}{\sqrt{4x^2+9}}dx$. Answer: $\frac{1}{2}$

14. Evaluate the definite integral $\int_0^3 \left(e^{-x}+1\right)dx$. Answer: $4-e^{-3}$

15. Find the average value of the function $f(x)=x^2+3$ over the interval $[1,5]$.

Answer: $\frac{40}{3}$

16. Find the average value of the function $f(x) = 10 - 2x$ over the interval $[1,3]$.

Answer: 6

17. Find the average value of the function $f(x) = \sqrt{x}$ over the interval $[1,9]$.

Answer: $\frac{13}{6}$

18. Find the average value of the function $f(x) = e^x$ over the interval $[0,10]$.

Answer: $\frac{1}{10}e^{10} - \frac{1}{10}$

19. Find the average value of the function $f(x) = \frac{1}{x+2}$ over the interval $[-1,3]$.

Answer: $\frac{1}{4}\ln 5$

Section 6.5 Multiple Choice Questions

1. Evaluate $\int_1^e \frac{\ln ex}{x}\,dx$.

   a. 1
   b. 2.47
   c. $\frac{3}{2}$
   d. $\frac{3-2e}{2}$

   Answer: c.

2. Evaluate $\int_2^{e+1} \left(\frac{4}{x-1}\right) dx$.

   a. $-4e$
   b. 0
   c. $4e$
   d. 4

   Answer: d.

3. Evaluate $\int_1^2 \frac{\ln x}{x}\,dx$.

   a. $\frac{(\ln 2)^2}{2}$
   b. $\ln 4$
   c. $\ln(\ln 2 - \ln 1)$
   d. $(\ln 2)^2$

   Answer: a.

4. Evaluate $\int_0^2 \frac{3x}{1+2x^2}\,dx$.

   a. 1.591
   b. 1.648
   c. 2.356
   d. 1.032

   Answer: b.

5. Evaluate $\int_0^1 \frac{e^x}{4+e^x}\,dx$.

   a. 0.561
   b. 2.371

c. 0.295
d. 1.231
Answer: c.

6. Evaluate $\int_1^2 \left(1+\frac{1}{x}+\frac{1}{x+1}\right)dx$.
a. 4.129
b. 3.458
c. 1.940
d. 2.099
Answer: d.

7. The average value of the function $f(x)=\ln^2 x$ on the interval [2, 4] is
a. 2.159
b. 1.204
c. 2.408
d. 8.636
Answer: b.

8. Find the distance traveled (to three decimal places) in the first four seconds, for a particle whose velocity in ft/sec is given by $v(t)=6te^{-t^2}$, where t is measured in seconds.
a. 3.000 ft
b. 3.523 ft
c. 2.951 ft
d. 2.875 ft
Answer: a.

9. Find the distance traveled (to three decimal places) in the first five seconds, for a particle whose velocity in ft/sec is given by $v(t)=\frac{20}{1+t}$, where t is measured in seconds.
a. 39.156 ft
b. 32.458 ft
c. 35.835 ft
d. 30.782 ft
Answer: c.

10. The concentration of a certain drug in a patient's blood stream t hours after injection is $C(t)=\frac{0.3t}{t^2+1}$ mg/cm^3. Determine the average concentration of the drug in the patient's bloodstream over the first 4 hours after the drug is injected. where t stands for time.
a. 0.424 mg/cm^3

b. 0.212 mg/cm^3
c. 0.106 mg/cm^3
d. 0.846 mg/cm^3
Answer: c.

11. The concentration of a certain drug in a patient's blood stream t hours after injection is $C(t) = \frac{0.2t}{t^2+5}$ mg/cm^3. Determine the average concentration of the drug in the patient's bloodstream over the first 3 hours after the drug is injected. where t stands for time.
a. 0.034 mg/cm^3
b. 0.342 mg/cm^3
c. 0.065 mg/cm^3
d. 0.625 mg/cm^3
Answer: a.

12. The manager of TeleStar Cable Service estimates hat the total number of subscribers to the service in a certain city t years from now will be $-\frac{20,000}{\sqrt{1+0.3t}} + 40,000$. Find the average number of cable television subscribers over the next 5 years if this prediction holds true.
a. 29,457
b. 24,503
c. 28,129
d. 23,108
Answer: b.

13. The sales of Universal Instruments in the first t years of its operation are approximated by the function $S(t) = t\sqrt{0.35t^2+9}$, where $S(t)$ is measured in millions of dollars. What were Universal's average yearly sales over its first 5 years of operation?
a. \$10.959 million
b. \$9.101 million
c. \$8.125 million
d. \$7.561 million
Answer: b.

Section 6.6

1. Find the area of the region bounded by the graphs of the functions $f(x) = x^2$ and $g(x) = 10$ and the vertical lines $x = 0$ and $x = 2$.

   Answer: $\dfrac{52}{3}$

2. Find the area of the shaded region below where $y = f(x) = x^3 - 4x^2$.

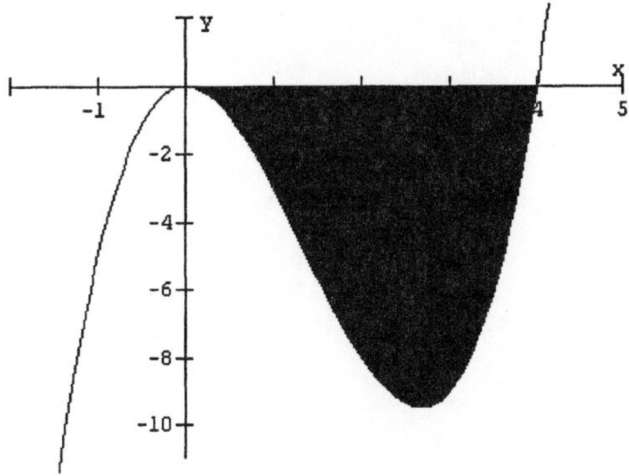

   Answer: $\dfrac{64}{3}$

3. Find the area of the region bounded by the graphs of the functions $f(x) = x^3$ and $g(x) = x^{2/3}$.

   Answer: $\dfrac{7}{20}$

4. Find the area of the region bounded by the graphs of the functions $f(x) = 2 + x^2$ and $g(x) = 1$ and the vertical lines $x = 1$ and $x = 3$.

   Answer: $\dfrac{32}{3}$

5. Find the area of the region bounded by the graphs of the functions $f(x) = e^{x-2}$ and $g(x) = 0$ and the vertical lines $x = -2$ and $x = 2$.

   Answer: $1 - e^{-4}$

6. Find the area of the region bounded by the graphs of the functions $f(x) = -x^2 + 4x$ and $g(x) = 2x - 8$.

Answer: 36

7. Find the area of the region completely enclosed by the graphs of the functions $f(x) = x^3$ and $g(x) = x$.

Answer: $\frac{1}{2}$

8. Find the area of the region completely enclosed by the graphs of the functions $f(x) = x$ and $g(x) = x^2 - 2x$.

Answer: $\frac{9}{2}$

9. Find the area of the region completely enclosed by the graphs of the functions $f(x) = 4x$ and $g(x) = x^2 - 2x$.

Answer: 36

10. Find the area of the region completely enclosed by the graph of the function $f(x) = x(x^2 - 9)$ and x-axis.

Answer: 40.5.

11. Find the area of the region completely enclosed by the graph of the function $f(x) = x^3 - 25x$ and x-axis.

Answer: 312.50.

Section 6.6 Multiple Choice Questions

1. Find the area of the region bounded by the graph of the function $f(x) = -x^2$ and x-axis from $x = 2$ to $x = 5$.
   a. -39
   b. $\frac{39}{2}$
   c. 78
   d. 39
   Answer: d.

2. Find the area of the region bounded by the graph of the function $f(x) = -e^{2x}$ and x-axis from $x = 0$ to $x = 1$.
   a. 3.8646
   b. 3.1945
   c. 3.2162
   d. -3.1945
   Answer: b.

3. Find the area of the region bounded by the graph of the function $f(x) = -\frac{1}{x+4}$ and x-axis from $x = 0$ to $x = 3$.
   a. 0.5423
   b. 1.5912
   c. 0.6932
   d. 0.5596
   Answer: d.

4. Find the area of the region bounded by the graph of the function $f(x) = \frac{\ln x}{x}$ and x-axis from $x = 3$ to $x = 9$.
   a. 2.3478
   b. 0.9052
   c. 1.8104
   d. -1.8104
   Answer: c.

5. Find the area of the region bounded by the graph of the function $f(x) = x(x-3)(x+3)$ and x-axis from $x = -3$ to $x = 3$.
   a. $\frac{81}{4}$
   b. $\frac{81}{2}$

c. $-\dfrac{81}{2}$

d. 0

Answer: b.

6. Find the area of the region bounded by the graph of the function $f(x) = 16 - x^2$ and x-axis from $x = -4$ to $x = 4$.

a. $\dfrac{128}{3}$

b. $-\dfrac{256}{3}$

c. $\dfrac{256}{3}$

d. 64

Answer: c.

7. Find the area of the region completely enclosed by $f(x) = x^2$ and $g(x) = x^{1/3}$

a. $\dfrac{5}{12}$

b. $-\dfrac{5}{12}$

c. $\dfrac{5}{6}$

d. $\dfrac{5}{3}$

Answer: a.

8. Find the area of the region completely enclosed by $f(x) = x + 7$ and $g(x) = x^2 - 5$

a. $-\dfrac{343}{6}$

b. $\dfrac{343}{6}$

c. $\dfrac{343}{2}$

d. $\dfrac{343}{3}$

Answer: b.

9. Find the area of the region completely enclosed by $f(x) = x^2 - 4x$ and $g(x) = x - 4$.

a. $\frac{9}{2}$

b. $\frac{23}{6}$

c. $\frac{8}{3}$

d. $-\frac{9}{2}$

Answer: a.

10. Find the area of the region completely enclosed by $f(x) = 2x$ and $g(x) = x\sqrt{x+1}$

a. $\frac{1}{3}$

b. $\frac{15}{19}$

c. $-\frac{19}{15}$

d. $\frac{19}{15}$

Answer: d.

11. Which of the following integrals correctly gives the area of the region consisting of all points above the x-axis and below the curve $g(x) = 8 + 2x - x^2$?

a. $\int_{-4}^{4} (8 + 2x - x^2)\,dx$

b. $\int_{-4}^{2} (8 + 2x - x^2)\,dx$

c. $\int_{-2}^{4} (8 + 2x - x^2)\,dx$

d. $\int_{-2}^{4} (x^2 - 2x - 8)\,dx$

Answer: c.

12. Find the area of the region bounded by the parabolas $y = 6x - x^2$ and $y = x^2$.

a. 9

b. 27

c. 6

d. 18

Answer: a.

13. Find the area of the region completely bounded by the parabola $y=(x-4)^2-25$ and the line $y=0$.

a. $\frac{500}{9}$

b. $-\frac{500}{3}$

c. $\frac{500}{3}$

d. $\frac{250}{3}$

Answer: c.

14. In tests conducted by *Auto Test Magazine* on two identical models of the Phoenix Elite–one equipped with a standard engine and the other with a turbo-charger- it was found that the acceleration of the former is given by $a(t)=f(t)=5+0.7t$ $(0 \le t \le 12)$ ft/sec/sec, *t* second after staring from rest at full throttle, whereas the acceleration of the latter is given by $a(t)=f(t)=3+1.5t+0.04t^2$ $(0 \le t \le 12)$ ft/sec/sec. How much faster is the turbo-charged model moving than the model with the standard engine at the end of a 10-sec test run at full throttle?

a. 33.33 ft/sec

b. −33.33 ft/sec

c. −28.32 ft/sec

d. 28.32 ft/sec

Answer: a.

*Section 6.7**

1. Find the amount of an annuity if \$225/month is paid into it for a period of 15 years earning interest at the rate of 8%/year compounded continuously.
   Answer: \$78,303.95

2. Find the amount of an annuity if \$350/month is paid into it for a period of 35 years earning interest at the rate of 12%/year compounded continuously.
   Answer: \$2,299,021.59

3. Estimate the present value of an annuity if payments are \$600 monthly for 25 years and the account earns interest at the rate of 9%/year compounded continuously.
   Answer: \$71,568.06

4. Estimate the present value of an annuity if payments are \$1100 monthly for 12 years and the account earns interest at the rate of 6%/year compounded continuously.
   Answer: \$112,914.50

5. Suppose that for a certain product, the demand equation is $p = 500 - 10x$ and the supply equation is $p = 0.5x^2 + 100$. The price is set at the equilibrium price.
   (a) Find the consumer surplus.
   Answer: \$2000
   (b) Find the producer surplus.
   Answer: \$2667

6. A particular profession's income distribution is given by $f(x) = \frac{7}{8}x^2 + \frac{1}{8}x$.
   Compute the coefficient of inequality for the Lorentz curve.
   Answer: $\frac{7}{24}$

Section 6.7 Multiple Choice Questions

1. The demand function for a printer is given by $p = -0.02x^2 - 0.3x + 65$, where p is the unit price in dollars and x is the quantity demanded each week, measured in units of a thousand. Determine the consumer's surplus if the market price is set at $64.32 per printer.
   a. $2,132
   b. $707
   c. $2,089
   d. $591
   Answer: b.

2. The demand function for a computer disc is given by $p = -0.01x^2 - 0.5x + 4$, where p is the unit price in dollars and x is the quantity demanded each week, measured in units of a thousand. Determine the consumer's surplus if the market price is set at $3.49 per disc.
   a. $263.00
   b. $256.67
   c. $245.27
   d. $312.49
   Answer: b.

3. The supplier of the portable hair dryers will make x hundred units of hair dryers available in the market when the wholesale unit price is $p = \sqrt{25 + 15x}$ dollars. Determine the producers' surplus if the wholesale market price is set at $10 per unit.
   a. $1,111
   b. $1,046
   c. $1,202
   d. $1,197
   Answer: a.

4. Suppose an investment is expected to generate income at the rate of $r(t) = 250{,}000$ dollars per year for the next 10 years. Find the present value of this investment if the prevailing interest rate is 8% per year compounded continuously.
   a. $1,720,904.76
   b. $1,723,846.99
   c. $1,720,846.99
   d. $1,845,846.99
   Answer: c.

5. Terra plans to save for her retirement. Suppose her investment is expected to generate income at the rate of $r(t) = 2500$ dollars per year for the next 30 years.

Find the future value of this investment if the prevailing interest rate is 8% per year compounded continuously.

a. $313,224.26
b. $314,674.21
c. $313,894.22
d. $313,292.27

Answer: a.

6. Find the amount of an annuity if $300 per month is paid into it for a period of 25 years, earning interest at the rate of 6% per year compounded continuously.

a. $208578.21
b. $208901.34
c. $208911.35
d. $212563.76

Answer: b.

7. A state lottery commission pays the winner of the "Million Dollar" lottery 20 annual installments of $60,000 each. If the prevailing interest rate is 5% per year compounded continuously, find the present value of the winning ticket.

a. $928,544.67
b. $786,544.67
c. $758,544.67
d. $778,544.67

Answer: c.

8. Kathy would like to establish a fund from which she can withdraw $1000 per month for the next 10 years. If the fund earns interest at the rate of 7% per year compounded continuously, how much money does she need to establish the fund?

a. $86,326.78
b. $68,299.66
c. $96,299.66
d. $86,299.66

Answer: d.

9. Nick would like to establish a fund from which he can withdraw $4,000 per month for the next 4 years. If the fund earns interest at the rate of 9% per year compounded continuously, how much money does he need to establish the fund?

a. $151,239.31
b. $161,239.29
c. $191,239.29
d. $161,240.30

Answer: b.

10. On January 1, 2000, Mike deposited $2500 into an IRA paying interest at the rate of 7% per year compounded continuously. Assuming that he deposits $2500

annually into the account, how much will he have in his IRA at the beginning of the year 2015?

a. $68,344.68

b. $66,984.68

c. $66,344.68

d. $69,344.68

Answer: c.

11. In order to save for her son's college tuition, Jessica deposited $3000 into an Education IRA paying interest at the rate of 5% per year compounded continuously starting from 1990. Assuming that she deposits $3000 annually into the account, how much will she have in her son's Education IRA at the beginning of the year 2006?

a. $73,532.46

b. $37,532.46

c. $73,352.46

d. $83,532.46

Answer: a.

12. A certain country's income distribution is described by the function $f(x) = \frac{14}{17}x^2 + \frac{3}{17}x$. Find the coefficient of inequality of the Lorentz curve.

a. 2

b. $\frac{51}{7}$

c. $\frac{14}{51}$

d. $\frac{7}{51}$

Answer: c.

Exam 6A

Name:
Instructor:
Section:

Write your work as neatly as possible.

1. Find the indefinite integral $\int \sqrt{7}\,dx$.

2. Find the indefinite integral $\int \left(x^{3/2}+2\right)dx$.

3. Find the indefinite integral $\int \left(x^{-2}+x^{2}\right)dx$.

4. Find the function $f(x)$ if $f'(x)=x^2-x+1$ and $f(0)=2$.

5. Find the indefinite integral $\int 12xe^{x^2}\,dx$.

6. Find the indefinite integral $\int \frac{x+2}{x^2+4x+3}\,dx$.

7. Find the indefinite integral $\int 5x\sqrt{3x^2+1}\,dx$.

8. Let $f(x)=x^2$ and compute the Riemann sum of f over the interval $[1,3]$ using four subintervals of equal length ($n = 4$). Choose the representative point in each subinterval to be the midpoint of the subinterval.

9. Find the area of the region under the graph of the function $f(x)=x^3$ on the interval $[0,2]$.

10. Evaluate the definite integral $\int_{-1}^{2}\left(2x^3-2\right)dx$.

11. Evaluate the definite integral $\int_1^e \frac{(\ln x)^2}{x} dx$.

12. Evaluate the definite integral $\int_{\sqrt{2}}^{\sqrt{7}} 3x\sqrt{x^2+2}dx$.

13. Find the average value of the function $f(x) = 2 - x^2$ over the interval $[1,5]$.

14. Find the area of the region bounded by the graphs of the functions $f(x) = x^2 + 16$ and $g(x) = x$ and the vertical lines $x = 0$ and $x = 2$.

15. The demand function for a certain product is given by $p = -0.01x^2 - 0.3x + 6$, where p represents the unit price in dollars and x is the quantity demanded measured in units of a thousand. Determine the consumer surplus if the price is set at \$2.

16. Find the amount of an annuity if \$375/month is paid into it for a period of 10 years earning interest at the rate of 11%/year compounded continuously.

Exam 6B

Name:
Instructor:
Section:

Write your work as neatly as possible.

1. Find the indefinite integral $\int\left(25x^4+4x-3\right)dx$.

2. Find the indefinite integral $\int\frac{x^3-2x^2}{2x}\,dx$.

3. Find the indefinite integral $\int\left(x^{1/4}+\frac{1}{x^{1/4}}\right)dx$.

4. Find the function $f(x)$ if $f'(x)=8x-3$ and $f(1)=2$.

5. Find the indefinite integral $\int\frac{1}{x\ln x}\,dx$.

6. Find the indefinite integral $\int\frac{2x+1}{x^2+x-1}\,dx$.

7. Find the indefinite integral $\int\frac{6x^5-4}{\sqrt{x^6-4x}}\,dx$.

8. Let $f(x)=x^3$ and compute the Riemann sum of f over the interval $[1,3]$ using four subintervals of equal length ($n = 4$). Choose the representative point in each subinterval to be the midpoint of the subinterval.

9. Find the area of the region under the graph of the function $f(x)=10+x^3$ on the interval $[0,4]$.

10. Evaluate the definite integral $\int_{-1}^{4}(6x)\,dx$.

11. Evaluate the definite integral $\int_{0}^{1} e^{4x+1}dx$.

12. Evaluate the definite integral $\int_{0}^{1}(2x+1)\sqrt{x^2+x}dx$.

13. Find the average value of the function $f(x)=4-x^2$ over the interval $[0,2]$.

14. Find the area of the region bounded by the graphs of the functions $f(x)=16-x^2$ and $g(x)=7$.

15. The demand function for a certain product is given by $p=-0.01x^2-0.2x+10$, where p represents the unit price in dollars and x is the quantity demanded measured in units of a thousand. Determine the consumer surplus if the price is set at \$2.

16. Find the amount of an annuity if \$800/month is paid into it for a period of 20 years earning interest at the rate of 7%/year compounded continuously.

Exam 6C

Name:
Instructor:
Section:

Write your work as neatly as possible.

1. Find the indefinite integral $\int \pi^2 dx$.

2. Find the indefinite integral $\int \left(x - \frac{3}{\sqrt{x}} \right) dx$.

3. Find the indefinite integral $\int \left(x^{-3} + x + 1 \right) dx$.

4. Find the function $f(x)$ if $f'(x) = 2x + 3$ and $f(0) = 2$

5. Find the indefinite integral $\int \frac{(\ln x + 2)^2}{x} dx$.

6. Find the indefinite integral $\int \frac{8x}{1 - x^2} dx$.

7. Find the indefinite integral $\int x^2 \sqrt{x^3 + 1} dx$.

8. Let $f(x) = x^3 + 1$ and compute the Riemann sum of f over the interval $[0,2]$ using four subintervals of equal length ($n = 4$). Choose the representative point in each subinterval to be the midpoint of the subinterval.

9. Find the area of the region under the graph of the function $f(x) = 4 - x^2$ on the interval $[0,2]$.

10. Evaluate the definite integral $\int_{-1}^{4} (3x - 2) dx$.

11. Evaluate the definite integral $\int_0^1 \frac{e^x}{1+e^x} dx$.

12. Evaluate the definite integral $\int_0^{\sqrt{2}} x\sqrt{x^2+2}dx$.

13. Find the average value of the function $f(x)=3x^2-1$ over the interval $[0,2]$.

14. Find the area of the region bounded by the graphs of the functions $f(x)=9-x^2$ and $g(x)=x$ and the vertical lines $x=0$ and $x=2$.

15. The demand function for a certain product is given by $p=-0.01x^2-0.2x+12$, where p represents the unit price in dollars and x is the quantity demanded measured in units of a thousand. Determine the consumer surplus if the price is set at \$4.

16. Estimate the present value of an annuity if payments are \$300 monthly for 35 years and the account earns interest at the rate of 9%/year compounded continuously.

Exam 6D

Name:
Instructor:
Section:

Write your work as neatly as possible.

1. Find the indefinite integral $\int(5x^4 - x + 7)\,dx$.

2. Find the indefinite integral $\int\left(\sqrt[4]{t} + t^{-2}\right)dx$.

3. Find the indefinite integral $\int\left(\frac{4}{x^3} + \frac{x^3}{4}\right)dx$.

4. Find the function $f(x)$ if $f'(x) = 3x^2 + 2$ and $f(1) = -1$

5. Find the indefinite integral $\int \frac{e^x}{e^x - 3}\,dx$.

6. Find the indefinite integral $\int(3x^2 + 5x)^6(6x + 5)\,dx$.

7. Find the indefinite integral $\int \frac{x}{\sqrt{x^2 - 1}}\,dx$.

8. Let $f(x) = x^3$ and compute the Riemann sum of f over the interval $[0,2]$ using four subintervals of equal length ($n = 4$). Choose the representative point in each subinterval to be the midpoint of the subinterval.

9. Find the area of the region under the graph of the function $f(x) = 4x^2 - 2x^3$ on the interval $[0,2]$.

10. Evaluate the definite integral $\int_1^3(3x^2 - 2x)\,dx$.

11. Evaluate the definite integral $\int_0^{e-1} \frac{1}{x+1} dx$.

12. Evaluate the definite integral $\int_0^1 2x\sqrt{3x^2+1}dx$.

13. Find the average value of the function $f(x) = e^x + 1$ over the interval $[0,3]$.

14. Find the area of the region bounded by the graphs of the functions $f(x) = x^2 - 2$ and $g(x) = x$ and the vertical lines $x = 0$ and $x = 2$.

15. The demand function for a certain product is given by $p = -0.01x^2 - 0.3x + 8$, where p represents the unit price in dollars and x is the quantity demanded measured in units of a thousand. Determine the consumer surplus if the price is set at \$4.

16. Estimate the present value of an annuity if payments are \$2000 monthly for 6 years and the account earns interest at the rate of 10%/year compounded continuously.

Answers to Chapter 6 Exams

Exam 6A

1. $\sqrt{7}x+C$
2. $\frac{2}{5}x^{5/2}+2x+C$
3. $-\frac{1}{x}+\frac{1}{3}x^3+C$
4. $\frac{x^3}{3}-\frac{x^2}{2}+x+2$
5. $6e^{x^2}+C$
6. $\frac{1}{2}\ln\left|x^2+4x+3\right|+C$
7. $\frac{5}{9}\left(3x^2+1\right)^{3/2}+C$
8. 8.625
9. 4
10. 1.5
11. $\frac{1}{3}$
12. 19
13. $-\frac{25}{3}$
14. $\frac{98}{3}$
15. \$21,667
16. \$81988.61

Exam 6B

1. $5x^5+2x^2-3x+C$
2. $\frac{1}{6}x^3-\frac{1}{2}x^2+C$
3. $\frac{4}{5}x^{5/4}+\frac{4}{3}x^{3/4}+C$
4. $4x^2-3x+1$
5. $\ln(\ln x)+C$
6. $\ln\left|x^2+x-1\right|+C$
7. $2\sqrt{x^6-4x}+C$
8. 19.75
9. 104
10. 45
11. $\frac{1}{4}\left(e^5-e\right)$
12. $\frac{4\sqrt{2}}{3}$
13. $\frac{8}{3}$
14. 36
15. \$93,333
16. \$418,998.85

Exam 6C

1. $\pi^2 x + C$
2. $\frac{1}{2}x^2 - 6x^{1/2} + C$
3. $-\frac{1}{2x^2} + \frac{1}{2}x^2 + x + C$
4. $x^2 + 3x + 2$
5. $\frac{1}{3}(\ln x + 2)^3 + C$
6. $-4\ln\left|1 - x^2\right| + C$
7. $\frac{2}{9}\left(x^3 + 1\right)^{3/2} + C$
8. 5.875
9. $\frac{16}{3}$
10. 12.5
11. $\ln\left(\frac{1+e}{2}\right)$
12. $\frac{1}{3}\left(8 - 2^{3/2}\right)$
13. 3
14. $\frac{40}{3}$
15. \$93,333
16. \$38,285.91

Exam 6D

1. $x^5 - \frac{x^2}{2} + 7x + C$
2. $\frac{4}{5}t^{5/4} - \frac{1}{t} + C$
3. $-\frac{2}{x^2} + \frac{x^4}{16} + C$
4. $x^3 + 2x - 4$
5. $\ln\left(e^x - 3\right) + C$
6. $\frac{\left(3x^2 + 5x\right)^7}{7} + C$
7. $\sqrt{x^2 - 1} + C$
8. 3.875
9. $\frac{8}{3}$
10. 18
11. 1
12. $\frac{14}{9}$
13. $\frac{e^3 + 2}{3}$
14. 4.5
15. \$21,667
16. \$108,285.21

Chapter 7 ■ Additional Topics in Integration

Section 7.1

1. Find the indefinite integral $\int xe^{3x}\,dx$. Answer: $\frac{1}{3}xe^{3x} - \frac{1}{9}e^{3x} + C$

2. Find the indefinite integral $\int x\ln x dx$. Answer: $\frac{1}{2}x^2\ln x - \frac{1}{4}x^2 + C$

3. Find the indefinite integral $\int 12xe^{4x}\,dx$. Answer: $3xe^{4x} - \frac{3}{4}e^{4x} + C$

4. Find the indefinite integral $\int \left(e^{-x} + 2x\right)^2 dx$.

   Answer: $-\frac{1}{2}e^{-2x} - 4xe^{-x} - 4e^{-x} + \frac{4}{3}x^3 + C$

5. Find the indefinite integral $\int \ln x dx$. Answer: $x\ln x - x + C$

6. Find the indefinite integral $\int (t+2)e^t\,dt$. Answer: $e^t(t+1) + C$

7. Find the indefinite integral $\int t^2 \ln t dt$. Answer: $\frac{1}{9}t^3(3\ln t - 1) + C$

8. Find the indefinite integral $\int t(t-2)^{-3}\,dt$. Answer: $-\frac{1}{t-2} - \frac{1}{(t-2)^2} + C$

9. Find the indefinite integral $\int t^3 e^t\,dt$. Answer: $\left(t^3 - 3t^2 + 6t - 6\right)e^t + C$

10. Find the indefinite integral $\int x\sqrt{x-11}\,dx$.

    Answer: $\frac{2}{5}(x-11)^{5/2} + \frac{22}{3}(x-11)^{3/2} + C$

11. Find the indefinite integral $\int x\ln 3x\,dx$. Answer: $\frac{1}{2}x^2\ln 3x - \frac{1}{4}x^2 + C$

12. Find the indefinite integral $\int \ln(8x)\,dx$. Answer: $x\ln(8x) - x + C$

13. Find the indefinite integral $\int x^2 \ln 4x\, dx$. Answer: $\frac{1}{3}x^3 \ln 4x - \frac{1}{9}x^3 + C$

14. Find the indefinite integral $\int x^3 e^{x^2}\, dx$. Answer: $\frac{1}{2}e^{x^2}\left(x^2 - 1\right) + C$

15. Find the indefinite integral $\int \sqrt[3]{x} \ln x\, dx$. Answer: $\frac{3}{4}x^{4/3} \ln x - \frac{9}{16}x^{4/3} + C$

16. Find the indefinite integral $\int (2x+3)e^x dx$. Answer: $(2x+1)e^x + C$

17. Find the indefinite integral $\int \frac{\ln x}{x^{5/2}}\, dx$. Answer: $\frac{-2\ln x}{3x^{3/2}} - \frac{4}{9x^{3/2}} + C$

18. Evaluate the definite integral $\int_0^1 te^{-t} dt$. Answer: $1 - \frac{2}{e}$

19. Evaluate the definite integral $\int_0^3 2te^{-t} dt$. Answer: $2 - \frac{8}{e^3}$

20. Evaluate the definite integral $\int_1^4 \sqrt{t} \ln t dt$. Answer: $\frac{32}{3}\ln 2 - \frac{28}{9}$

21. Evaluate the definite integral $\int_0^1 x^2 e^{-x} dx$. Answer: $2 - \frac{5}{e}$

22. Evaluate the definite integral $\int_1^4 \ln \sqrt{x} dx$. Answer: $4\ln 2 - \frac{3}{2}$

Section 7.1 Multiple Choice Questions

1. Evaluate $\int 3xe^{3x}\,dx$.

   a. $\dfrac{e^{3x}(3x-1)}{4}+C$

   b. $\dfrac{e^{3x}(3x-1)}{3}+C$

   c. $\dfrac{e^{3x}(3x-1)}{9}+C$

   d. $\dfrac{e^{3x}(3x-1)}{3}+e^{3x}+C$

   Answer: b.

2. Evaluate $\int 18x^2e^{3x}\,dx$.

   a. $\dfrac{2e^{3x}\left(9x^2-6x-2\right)}{3}+C$

   b. $\dfrac{e^{3x}\left(9x^2-6x+2\right)}{3}+C$

   c. $\dfrac{2e^{3x}\left(9x^2-6x+2\right)}{3}+C$

   d. $\dfrac{2e^{3x}\left(9x^2-6x+2\right)}{9}+C$

   Answer: c.

3. Evaluate $\int (x+6)e^x\,dx$.

   a. $(x+5)e^x+C$

   b. $-(x+5)e^x+C$

   c. $(x+5)e^x+x+C$

   d. $(x+7)e^x+C$

   Answer: a.

4. Evaluate $\int \left(e^{-x}+3x\right)^2\,dx$.

   a. $-6e^{-x}(x+1)+\dfrac{e^{-2x}}{2}+3x^3+C$

   b. $-6e^{-x}(x+1)-\dfrac{e^{-2x}}{2}+9x^3+C$

c. $e^{-x}(x+1)-\frac{e^{-2x}}{2}+3x^3+C$

d. $-6e^{-x}(x+1)-\frac{e^{-2x}}{2}+3x^3+C$

Answer: d.

5. Evaluate $\int \frac{x}{\sqrt{4x+5}}\,dx$.

a. $\frac{(4x-5)\sqrt{4x+5}}{12}+C$

b. $\frac{(2x-5)\sqrt{4x+5}}{8}+C$

c. $\frac{(2x-5)\sqrt{4x+5}}{12}+C$

d. $\frac{(2x-5)\sqrt{4x+5}}{6}+C$

Answer: c.

6. Evaluate $\int \frac{\ln x}{x^2}\,dx$.

a. $-\frac{\ln x}{x}-\frac{1}{x}+C$

b. $-\frac{\ln x}{x}+\frac{1}{x}+C$

c. $+\frac{\ln x}{x}+\frac{1}{x}+C$

d. $-\frac{\ln x}{2x}+\frac{1}{x}+C$

Answer: a.

7. Evaluate $\int \frac{1}{5}\ln x\,dx$.

a. $(x\ln-x)+C$

b. $\frac{1}{5}(x\ln-x)+C$

c. $5(x\ln-x)+C$

d. $\frac{1}{25}(x\ln-x)+C$

Answer: b.

8. Evaluate $\int_0^1 xe^{-x}\,dx$.

a. $1-5e^{-1}$
b. $1-2e^{-1}$
c. $1+2e^{-1}$
d. $4-2e^{-1}$
Answer: b.

9. Evaluate $\int_1^e x\ln x\,dx$.

a. $\frac{e^2-1}{4}$
b. $\frac{e^4+1}{4}$
c. $\frac{e^2+1}{2}$
d. $\frac{e^2+1}{4}$
Answer: d.

10. Find the distance traveled in feet (to three decimal places) in the first four seconds, by a particle whose velocity (measured in ft/sec) is given by $v(t)=7e^{-t^2}$, where t is measured in seconds.
a. 7.000 ft
b. 12.720 ft
c. 0.976 ft
d. 6.204 ft
Answer: d.

11. Find the distance traveled in feet (to three decimal places) from $t = 1$ to $t = 5$, by a particle whose velocity (measured in ft/sec) is given by $v(t)=t+\ln t$, where t is measured in seconds.
a. 16.00 ft
b. 16.091 ft
c. 16.047 ft
d. 148.413 ft
Answer: c.

12. The price of a certain commodity in dollars/unit at time t (measured in weeks) is given by $p(t)=12+5e^{-3t}+te^{-3t}$. What is the average price of the commodity over the 4-week period from $t = 0$ to $t = 4$?
a. $49.78

b. $12.44
c. $16.34
d. $10.87
Answer: b.

13. Suppose an investment is expected to generate income at the rate $R(t) = 2000 + 400t$ dollars/year for the next 5 years. Find the present value of this investment if the prevailing interest rate is 8% per year compounded continuously. (Hint: $PV = \int_0^5 R(t)e^{-rt}\,dt$.)

a. $14,698
b. $13,781
c. $12,089
d. $11,098
Answer: c.

14. Mike purchased a 15-year franchise for a computer outlet store that is expected to generate income at the rate of $R(t) = 45,000 + 4000t$ dollars/year. If the prevailing interest rate is 10% per year compounded continuously, find the present value of the franchise. (Hint: $PV = \int_0^{15} R(t)e^{-rt}\,dt$.)

a. $546,461
b. $526,461
c. $516,461
d. $536,491
Answer: b.

*Section 7.2**

1. Use a table of integrals to find $\int \frac{3x}{2+5x} dx$.

   Answer: $\frac{3}{5}x - \frac{6}{25}\ln|2+5x| + C$

2. Use a table of integrals to find $\int \frac{4x^2}{2+5x} dx$.

   Answer: $\frac{2}{5}x^2 - \frac{8}{25}x + \frac{16}{125}\ln|2+5x| + C$

3. Use a table of integrals to find $\int x^2\sqrt{16+9x^2}\,dx$.

   Answer: $\frac{1}{36}(8+9x^2)\sqrt{16+9x^2} - \frac{32}{27}\ln\left|3x+\sqrt{16+9x^2}\right| + C$

4. Use a table of integrals to find $\int \frac{dx}{x\sqrt{1+9x}}$.

   Answer: $\ln\left|\frac{\sqrt{1+9x}-1}{\sqrt{1+9x}+1}\right| + C$

5. Use a table of integrals to find $\int \frac{xdx}{\sqrt{4+3x}}$.

   Answer: $\frac{2}{27}(3x-8)\sqrt{4+3x} + C$

6. Use a table of integrals to evaluate $\int_0^3 \frac{dx}{\sqrt{16+9x^2}}$.

   Answer: $\frac{1}{3}\ln\left(9+\sqrt{97}\right) - \frac{2}{3}\ln 2$

7. Use a table of integrals to find $\int \frac{dx}{\left(4-x^2\right)^{3/2}} dx$.

   Answer: $\frac{x}{4\sqrt{4-x^2}} + C$

8. Use a table of integrals to find $\int x^2\sqrt{x^2-9}dx$.

   Answer: $\frac{x}{8}\left(2x^2-9\right)\sqrt{x^2-9} - \frac{81}{8}\ln\left|x+\sqrt{x^2-9}\right| + C$

9. Use a table of integrals to find $\int x^2\sqrt{15+x^2}\,dx$.

Answer: $\frac{x}{8}\left(15+2x^2\right)\sqrt{15+x^2}-\frac{225}{8}\ln\left|x+\sqrt{15+x^2}\right|+C$

10. Use a table of integrals to find $\int xe^{5x}\,dx$.

Answer: $\frac{1}{5}xe^{5x}-\frac{1}{25}e^{5x}+C$

11. Use a table of integrals to find $\int\frac{xdx}{\left(x^2-1\right)\ln\left(x^2-1\right)}$.

Answer: $\frac{1}{2}\ln\left|\ln\left(x^2-1\right)\right|+C$

12. Use a table of integrals to find $\int\frac{e^{2x}dx}{\sqrt{16+e^{4x}}}$.

Answer: $\frac{1}{2}\ln\left(e^{2x}+\sqrt{16+e^{4x}}\right)+C$

13. Use a table of integrals to find $\int\frac{\ln x}{x(1+4\ln x)}dx$.

Answer: $\frac{1}{16}[4\ln x-\ln|1+4\ln x|]+C$

14. Use a table of integrals to find $\int\frac{\ln x}{x(3+2\ln x)}dx$.

Answer: $\frac{1}{4}\left[3+2x-3\ln|3+2\ln x|\right]+C$

15. Use a table of integrals to find $\int\frac{2x}{\left(x^2+1\right)\ln\left(x^2+1\right)}dx$.

Answer: $\ln\left|\ln(x^2+1)\right|+C$

16. Use a table of integrals to find $\int x^4e^x\,dx$.

Answer: $e^x\left(x^4-4x^3+12x^2-24x+24\right)+C$

17. Use a table of integrals to find $\int x^4\ln x\,dx$.

Answer: $\frac{1}{5}x^5 \ln x - \frac{1}{25}x^5 + C$

18. Use a table of integrals to find $\int (\ln x)^2\,dx$.

Answer: $x\left[(\ln x)^2 - 2\ln x + 2\right] + C$

19. Find $\int \frac{dx}{x^{1/3} + x^{1/2}}$.

Answer: $2x^{1/2} - 3x^{1/3} + 6x^{1/6} - 6\ln(1 + x^{1/6}) + C$

20. Find $\int \frac{6u^3}{1+u}du$.

Answer: $2u^3 - 3u^2 + 6u - 6\ln|1+u| + C$

21. Find $\int \frac{dx}{1+e^x}$.

Answer: $-\ln(1+e^{-x}) + C$

22. Find $\int 5x^2\sqrt{3x^2+1}dx$.

Answer: $-\frac{5\sqrt{3}\ln\left|\sqrt{3x^2+1}+\sqrt{3}x\right|}{72} - \frac{5x\sqrt{3x^2+1}(6x^2+1)}{24} + C$

Section 7.2 Multiple Choice Questions

1. Evaluate $\int \frac{x}{3+5x}\,dx$.

   a. $\frac{1}{5}\left[3+5x-3\ln|3+5x|\right]+C$

   b. $\frac{1}{25}\left[3+5x-3\ln|3+5x|\right]+C$

   c. $\frac{1}{25}\left[3+25x-3\ln|3+5x|\right]+C$

   d. $\frac{1}{25}\left[3+5x+3\ln|3+5x|\right]+C$

   Answer: b.

2. Evaluate $\int \frac{x^2}{7+2x}\,dx$.

   a. $\frac{1}{4}\left[(7+2x)^2-28(7+2x)+49\ln|7+2x|\right]+C$

   b. $\frac{1}{4}\left[(7+2x)^2-28(7+2x)+98\ln|7+2x|\right]+C$

   c. $\frac{1}{16}\left[(7+2x)^2-28(7+2x)+98\ln|7+2x|\right]+C$

   d. $\frac{1}{4}\left[(7+2x)^2-7(7+2x)+98\ln|7+2x|\right]+C$

   Answer: c.

3. Evaluate $\int x^2\sqrt{25+x^2}\,dx$.

   a. $\frac{x}{8}(25+2x^2)\sqrt{25+x^2}-\frac{25}{8}\ln\left|x+\sqrt{25+x^2}\right|+C$

   b. $\frac{x}{8}(5+2x^2)\sqrt{25+x^2}-\frac{625}{8}\ln\left|x+\sqrt{25+x^2}\right|+C$

   c. $\frac{x}{8}(25+2x^2)\sqrt{25+x^2}-\frac{625}{8}\ln\left|x+\sqrt{25+x^2}\right|+C$

   d. $\frac{x}{16}(25+2x^2)\sqrt{25+x^2}-\frac{625}{8}\ln\left|x+\sqrt{25+x^2}\right|+C$

   Answer: c.

4. Evaluate $\int \frac{1}{\sqrt{x^2-121}}\,dx$.

   a. $\ln\left|x+\sqrt{x^2-121}\right|+C$

b. $\ln\left|x+\sqrt{x^2-11}\right|+C$

c. $\ln\left|x+\sqrt{x^2-121}\right|+11x+C$

d. $\ln\left|x^2+\sqrt{x^2-121}\right|+C$

Answer: a.

5. Evaluate $\int \frac{1}{\left(x^2-49\right)^{3/2}}\,dx$.

a. $-\frac{2x}{49\sqrt{x^2-49}}+C$

b. $-\frac{x}{7\sqrt{x^2-49}}+C$

c. $\frac{x}{49\sqrt{x^2-49}}+C$

d. $-\frac{x}{49\sqrt{x^2-49}}+C$

Answer: d.

6. Evaluate $\int \frac{1}{x^2\left(x^2+4\right)^{1/2}}\,dx$.

a. $-\frac{\sqrt{x^2+4}}{2x}+C$

b. $\frac{\sqrt{x^2+4}}{4x}+C$

c. $-\frac{\sqrt{x^2+4}}{4x}+C$

d. $-\frac{\sqrt{x^2+4}}{4x}+2x+C$

Answer: c.

7. Evaluate $\int \frac{1}{\left(x^2+16\right)^{1/2}}\,dx$.

a. $\ln\left|x+\sqrt{x^2+16}\right|+C$

b. $-\ln\left|x+\sqrt{x^2+16}\right|+C$

c. $\ln\left|2x+\sqrt{x^2+16}\right|+C$

d. $\ln\left|x+\sqrt{x^2+4}\right|+C$

Answer: a.

8. Evaluate $\int xe^{5x}\,dx$.

a. $25(5x-1)e^{5x}+C$

b. $\frac{1}{25}(5x-1)e^{5x}+C$

c. $\frac{1}{5}(5x-1)e^{5x}+C$

d. $\frac{1}{25}(5x-1)e^{-5x}+C$

Answer: b.

9. Evaluate $\int x^2 \ln x\,dx$.

a. $\frac{x^2}{4}(2\ln x-1)+C$

b. $\frac{x^3}{9}(3\ln x-1)+C$

c. $\frac{x^3}{9}(2\ln x-1)+C$

d. $\frac{x^3}{9}(9\ln x-1)+C$

Answer: b.

10. Evaluate $\int \frac{2}{t\ln t}\,dt$.

a. $\left(\ln\left|\ln t\right|\right)^2+C$

b. $\ln\left|\ln t\right|+\ln\left|t\right|+C$

c. $2\ln\left|\ln t\right|+C$

d. $\ln\left|\ln t\right|+t+C$

Answer: c.

11. The number of voters in a certain district of a city is expected to grow at the rate of $\frac{2000}{\sqrt{16+t^2}}$ people/yr t years from now. If the number of voters at present is 10,000, how many voters will be in the district 4 years from now?

a. 12,000

b. 11,763

c. 13,000

d. 11,899
Answer: b.

12. The population of a certain town of a city is expected to grow at the rate of $\frac{12,000}{1+5e^{3x}}$ people/yr t years from now. If the population at present is 25,000, how many voters will be in the town 7 years from now?
a. 28,109
b. 25,142
c. 27,729
d. 25,729
Answer: d.

13. The percent of households that own VCRs is given by $\frac{600}{1+29e^{-0.02t}}$, where t is measured in years, with $t = 0$ corresponding to the beginning of 1981. Find the average percent of households owning VCRs from the beginning of 1981 to the beginning of 1993.
a. 25%
b. 23%
c. 30%
d. 31%
Answer: b.

Section 7.3

1. Use the Trapezoidal Rule to approximate $\int_0^1 te^{-t}\,dt$ with $n = 4$.

   Answer: 0.2590

2. Use the Trapezoidal Rule to approximate $\int_1^4 \sqrt{t}\ln t\,dt$ with $n = 6$.

   Answer: 4.2792

3. Use the Trapezoidal Rule to approximate $\int_0^1 x^2e^{-x}\,dx$ with $n = 8$.

   Answer: 0.1611

4. Use the Trapezoidal Rule to approximate $\int_1^4 \left(x^2+1\right)dx$ with $n = 6$.

   Answer: 22.375

5. Use Simpson's Rule to approximate $\int_1^4 \left(x^2+1\right)dx$ with $n = 6$.

   Answer: 24

6. Use the Trapezoidal Rule to approximate $\int_1^4 \ln\sqrt{x}\,dx$ with $n = 6$.

   Answer: 1.2649

7. Use the Trapezoidal Rule to approximate $\int_0^1 \sqrt{1+t^4}\,dt$ with $n = 4$.

   Answer: 1.0968

8. Use the Trapezoidal Rule to approximate $\int_1^2 \sqrt{2+t^2}\,dt$ with $n = 4$.

   Answer: 2.0724

9. Use the Trapezoidal Rule to approximate $\int_0^2 \frac{dx}{\sqrt{x^4+1}}$ with $n = 6$.

   Answer: 1.3550

10. Use the Trapezoidal Rule to approximate $\int_2^3 \frac{2dx}{x^2}$ with $n = 4$.

    Answer: 0.3352

11. Use the Trapezoidal Rule to approximate $\int_0^3 e^{-x^2}\,dx$ with $n = 8$.

    Answer: 0.8862

12. Use the Trapezoidal Rule to approximate $\int_1^4 x^{-3/2}e^x dx$ with $n = 4$.
Answer: 11.0558

13. Use Simpson's Rule to approximate $\int_0^1 te^{-t} dt$ with $n = 4$.
Answer: 0.2642

14. Use Simpson's Rule to approximate $\int_2^3 \frac{2dx}{x^2}$ with $n = 4$.
Answer: 0.3334

15. Use Simpson's Rule to approximate $\int_1^2 \sqrt{2+t^2}\, dt$ with $n = 4$.
Answer: 2.0712

16. Use Simpson's Rule to approximate $\int_1^4 \sqrt{t} \ln t dt$ with $n = 6$.
Answer: 4.2825

17. Use Simpson's Rule to approximate $\int_0^1 x^2 e^{-x} dx$ with $n = 8$.
Answer: 0.1606

18. Use Simpson's Rule to approximate $\int_1^4 \ln \sqrt{x} dx$ with $n = 6$.
Answer: 1.2723

19. Use Simpson's Rule to approximate $\int_0^1 \sqrt{1+t^4}\, dt$ with $n = 4$.
Answer: 1.0894

20. Use Simpson's Rule to approximate $\int_0^2 \frac{dx}{\sqrt{x^4+1}}$ with $n = 6$.
Answer: 1.3566

21. Use the Simpson's Rule to approximate $\int_0^3 e^{-x^2} dx$ with $n = 8$.
Answer: 0.8862

22. Use the Simpson's Rule to approximate $\int_1^4 x^{-3/2}e^x dx$ with $n = 4$.
Answer: 10.8143

23. Find a bound on the error in approximating $\int_1^3 (2x^5 - 4)\,dx$ using the trapezoidal rule with $n = 8$.
Answer: 11.25

24. Find a bound on the error in approximating $\int_1^3 (2x^5 - 4)\,dx$ using Simpson's rule with $n = 8$.
Answer: 0.3125

25. Find a bound on the error in approximating $\int_0^2 \frac{e^{-2x}}{4}\,dx$ using the trapezoidal rule with $n = 6$.
Answer: 0.01852

26. Find a bound on the error in approximating $\int_0^2 \frac{e^{-2x}}{4}\,dx$ using Simpson's rule with $n = 6$.
Answer: 0.0005487

Section 7.3 Multiple Choice Questions

1. Approximate the value of $\int_1^5 \frac{x}{3+5x}\,dx$ using the trapezoidal rule with $n = 4$.

a. 0.6491
b. 0.6462
c. 0.6489
d. 0.6481
Answer: b.

2. Approximate the value of $\int_0^1 xe^{x^2}\,dx$ using the trapezoidal rule with $n = 4$.

a. 0.8959
b. 0.8756
c. 0.8684
d. 0.8912
Answer: a.

3. Approximate the value of $\int_1^2 \frac{1}{1+\ln x}\,dx$ using the trapezoidal rule with $n = 6$.

a. 0.7414
b. 0.7382
c. 0.7391

d. 0.7378

Answer: c.

4. Approximate the value of $\int_0^1 e^{x^2}\,dx$ using the trapezoidal rule with $n = 4$.

a. 1.4672
b. 1.4697
c. 1.4752
d. 1.4907

Answer: d.

5. Approximate the value of $\int_1^5 \frac{x}{3+5x}\,dx$ using the Simpson's rule with $n = 4$.

a. 0.6493
b. 0.6496
c. 0.6497
d. 0.6491

Answer: a.

6. Approximate the value of $\int_1^2 \frac{1}{1+\ln x}\,dx$ using the Simpson's rule with $n = 4$.

a. 0.7370
b. 0.7371
c. 0.7374
d. 0.7372

Answer: c.

7. Approximate the value of $\int_1^3 \frac{1}{1+x}\,dx$ using the Simpson's rule with $n = 6$.

a. 0.6930
b. 0.6934
c. 0.6935
d. 0.6932

Answer: d.

8. Approximate the value of $\int_0^1 e^{x^2}\,dx$ using the Simpson's rule with $n = 4$.

a. 1.4637
b. 1.4623
c. 1.4611
d. 1.4627

Answer: a.

9. Approximate the value of $\int_0^1 \frac{1}{1+x^2}dx$ using the Simpson's rule with $n = 4$.

a. 0.7854
b. 0.7812
c. 0.7862
d. 0.7824
Answer: a.

10. Approximate the value of $\int_0^1 \frac{1}{\sqrt{1+x^2}}dx$ using the Simpson's rule with $n = 6$.

a. 0.8815
b. 0.8814
c. 0.8813
d. 0.8819
Answer: b.

11. The demand equation for the Sicard wristwatch is given by $p = D(x) = \frac{60}{0.02x^2+1}$, $(0 \le x \le 20)$, where x (measured in units of a thousand) is the quantity demanded per week and p is the unit price in dollars. Use Simpson's rule with $n = 4$ to estimate the consumer's surplus if the market price is \$20/watch.
a. \$205.23
b. \$405.23
c. \$205.54
d. \$412.24
Answer: a.

12. The amount of nitrogen dioxide, a brown gas that impairs breathing, present in the atmosphere on a certain May day in the city of Boston has been approximated by $A(t) = \frac{138}{1+0.29(t-4.7)^2} + 21$, $(0 \le t \le 10)$, where $A(t)$ is measured in pollutant standard index (PSI), and t is measured in hours, with $t = 0$ corresponding to 7 A.M. Use the trapezoidal rule with $n = 4$ to estimate the average PSI between 7 A.M. and 1 P.M..
a. 97.350 PSI
b. 96.470 PSI
c. 97.917 PSI
d. 97.682 PSI
Answer: b.

Section 7.4

1. Find the area of the region under the curve $y = \dfrac{3}{x^2}$ for $x \geq 4$.

   Answer: $\dfrac{3}{4}$

2. Find the area of the region under the curve $y = \dfrac{1}{(x-3)^2}$ for $x \geq 4$.

   Answer: 1

3. Find the area of the region under the curve $y = \dfrac{1}{x^{5/2}}$ for $x \geq 3$.

   Answer: $\dfrac{2\sqrt{3}}{27}$

4. Find the area of the region under the curve $y = \dfrac{1}{(x-1)^{3/2}}$ for $x \geq 2$.

   Answer: 2

5. Find the area of the region under the curve $y = e^{3x}$ for $x \leq 0$.

   Answer: $\dfrac{1}{3}$

6. Evaluate the improper integral $\int_2^\infty \dfrac{2}{x^5}\,dx$ if it is convergent.

   Answer: $\dfrac{1}{32}$

7. Evaluate the improper integral $\int_4^\infty \dfrac{3}{x^{5/2}}\,dx$ if it is convergent.

   Answer: $\dfrac{1}{4}$

8. Evaluate the improper integral $\int_1^\infty \dfrac{3}{\sqrt[3]{x}}\,dx$ if it is convergent.

   Answer: Not convergent.

9. Evaluate the improper integral $\int_5^\infty \dfrac{6}{x}\,dx$ if it is convergent.

   Answer: Not convergent.

10. Evaluate the improper integral $\int_{-\infty}^{1} \frac{2}{(x-3)^3}dx$ if it is convergent.

Answer: $-\frac{1}{4}$

11. Evaluate the improper integral $\int_{2}^{\infty} \frac{1}{(3x-1)^{3/2}}dx$ if it is convergent.

Answer: $\frac{2\sqrt{5}}{15}$

12. Evaluate the improper integral $\int_{1}^{\infty} e^{-x}dx$ if it is convergent.

Answer: $\frac{1}{e}$

13. Evaluate the improper integral $\int_{0}^{\infty} e^{-x/5}dx$ if it is convergent.

Answer: 5

14. Evaluate the improper integral $\int_{-\infty}^{1} e^{3x}dx$ if it is convergent.

Answer: $\frac{1}{3}e^3$

15. Evaluate the improper integral $\int_{2}^{\infty} \frac{e^{\sqrt{x}}}{\sqrt{x}}dx$ if it is convergent.

Answer: Not convergent.

16. Evaluate the improper integral $\int_{0}^{\infty} xe^{-3x}dx$ if it is convergent.

Answer: $\frac{1}{9}$

17. Evaluate the improper integral $\int_{-\infty}^{\infty} 2x^5dx$ if it is convergent.

Answer: Not convergent.

18. Evaluate the improper integral $\int_{0}^{\infty} x^3\left(1+x^4\right)^{-2} dx$ if it is convergent.

Answer: $1/4$

19. Evaluate the improper integral $\int_{0}^{\infty} x\left(x^2+9\right)^{-3/2} dx$ if it is convergent.

Answer: 1/3

20. Evaluate the improper integral $\int_{-\infty}^{\infty} x^3\left(1+x^4\right)^{-2} dx$ if it is convergent.
Answer: 0

21. Evaluate the improper integral $\int_{-\infty}^{\infty} x\left(x^2+3\right)^{-3/2} dx$ if it is convergent.
Answer: 0

22. Evaluate the improper integral $\int_0^{\infty} xe^{2-x^2} dx$ if it is convergent.
Answer: $\frac{1}{2}e^2$

23. Evaluate the improper integral $\int_0^{\infty}\left(x-\frac{1}{2}\right)e^{-x^2+x+1}dx$ if it is convergent.
Answer: $\frac{1}{2}e$

24. Evaluate the improper integral $\int_0^{\infty}\frac{e^{-x}}{1+e^{-x}}dx$ if it is convergent.
Answer: $\ln 2$

25. Evaluate the improper integral $\int_{-\infty}^{0}\frac{e^{-x}}{1+e^{-x}}dx$ if it is convergent.
Answer: Not convergent.

26. Evaluate the improper integral $\int_0^{\infty}\frac{xe^{-x^2}}{1+e^{-x^2}}dx$ if it is convergent.
Answer: $\frac{1}{2}\ln 2$

27. The Robinson family wishes to create a scholarship fund at a college. If a scholarship in the amount of \$2500 is awarded annually beginning 1 year from now, find the amount of the endowment they are required to make now. Assume that this fund will earn interest at a rate of 8% per year compounded continuously.
Answer: \$31,250.

28. A university alumni group wishes to provide an annual scholarship in the amount of \$8000 beginning next year. If the scholarship fund will earn an interest rate of 8% per year compounded continuously, find the amount of the endowment the alumni are required to make now.
Answer: \$80,000

29. Mel Thompson wishes to establish a fund to provide a university medical center with an annual research grant of \$100,000 beginning next year. If the fund will earn an interest rate of 5% per year compounded continuously, find the amount of the endowment he is required to make now.
Answer: \$2,000,000

30. The Simpson family wishes to create a scholarship fund at a college. If a scholarship in the amount of \$6000 is awarded annually beginning 1 year from now, find the amount of the endowment they are required to make now. Assume that this fund will earn interest at a rate of 8% per year compounded continuously.
Answer: \$75,000.

31. The Robinson family wishes to create a scholarship fund at a college. If a scholarship in the amount of \$2500 is awarded annually beginning 2 years from now, find the amount of the endowment they are required to make now. Assume that this fund will earn interest at a rate of 8% per year compounded continuously.
Answer: \$62,500.

Section 7.4 Multiple Choice Questions

1. Find the area of the region under the curve $\frac{4}{x^3}$, above the x-axis, and over the interval $x \geq 2$.
   a. 2
   b. $\frac{1}{4}$
   c. $\frac{1}{2}$
   d. 4
   Answer: c.

2. Find the area of the region under the curve $\frac{5}{(2x+3)^{5/2}}$, above the x-axis, and over the interval $x \geq 1$.
   a. $-\frac{\sqrt{5}}{15}$
   b. $\frac{\sqrt{5}}{15}$
   c. $\frac{\sqrt{5}}{5}$

d. $\frac{\sqrt{5}}{3}$

Answer: b.

3. Find the area of the region under the curve xe^{-x^2}, above the x-axis, and over the interval $x \geq 0$.

a. $\frac{1}{2}$

b. $\frac{2}{5}$

c. $\frac{1}{4}$

d. 2

Answer: a.

4. Find the area of the region between the curve $\frac{1}{\sqrt{2\pi}}e^{-x^2/2}$ and the x-axis.

a. 0.5

b. 0.49

c. 1.2

d. 1

Answer: d.

5. Find the area of the region between the curve $\frac{x}{\left(1+x^2\right)^2}$ and the x-axis for $x \geq 0$.

a. $\frac{1}{2}$

b. $\frac{1}{4}$

c. $\frac{1}{8}$

d. 2

Answer: a.

6. Evaluate the improper integral $\int_0^{\infty} e^{-3x}dx$, if it exists.

a. $\frac{1}{6}$

b. -3

c. $\frac{1}{3}$

d. 3

Answer: c.

7. Evaluate the improper integral $\int_{-\infty}^{\infty} \frac{1}{\left(x^2+1\right)^3} dx$, if it exists.

a. 2.1262
b. 1.1781
c. 1.2451
d. 1.9824

Answer: b.

8. Evaluate the improper integral $\int_{-\infty}^{\infty} \frac{x^3}{\left(x^2+1\right)^5} dx$, if it exists.

a. $-\frac{1}{24}$
b. 0
c. $\frac{1}{24}$
d. $\frac{1}{12}$

Answer: b.

9. Evaluate the improper integral $\int_{0}^{\infty} \frac{e^x}{2+e^x} dx$, if it exists.

a. 2
b. 8
c. $\frac{1}{3}$
d. Does not exist.

Answer: d.

10. Evaluate the improper integral $\int_{e^2}^{\infty} \frac{1}{x \ln x} dx$, if it exists.

a. $\frac{1}{3}$
b. 12
c. Does not exist.
d. $\frac{1}{12}$

Answer: c.

11. Evaluate the improper integral $\int_{e}^{\infty} \frac{1}{x \ln^5 x} dx$, if it exists.

a. $\frac{1}{3}$
b. $\frac{1}{4}$
c. $\frac{1}{2}$
d. 4
Answer: b.

12. Evaluate the improper integral $\int_1^\infty \frac{e^{\sqrt{x+2}}}{\sqrt{x+2}}dx$, if it exists.

a. $\frac{1}{4}$
b. $\frac{1}{3}$
c. Does not exist.
d. $\frac{1}{2}$
Answer: c.

13. Evaluate the improper integral $\int_1^\infty \frac{1}{\sqrt{x+2}}dx$, if it exists.

a. $\frac{1}{\sqrt{3}}$
b. $\frac{1}{5}$
c. $\frac{1}{4}$
d. Does not exist.
Answer: d.

14. Evaluate the improper integral $\int_1^\infty \frac{1}{(x+2)\sqrt{x+2}}dx$, if it exists.

a. 1.1547 or $\frac{2\sqrt{3}}{3}$
b. 1.2653
c. 1.0095
d. 1.3254
Answer: a.

Section 7.5

1. Is the function $\frac{1}{100}e^{-100x}$ a probability density function on the interval $(0,\infty)$?

   Answer: No

2. Is the function $\frac{1}{3}x^3$ a probability density function on the interval $(0,1)$?

   Answer: No

3. Is the function $\frac{3}{4}x^3$ a probability density function on the interval $\left(0,\frac{1}{4}\right)$?

   Answer: No

4. Determine the value of the constant k so that the function $\frac{1}{k}e^{-50x}$ is a probability density function on the interval $(0,\infty)$.

   Answer: $\frac{1}{50}$

5. Determine the value of the constant k so that the function $4e^{kx}$ is a probability density function on the interval $(0,\infty)$.

   Answer: -4

6. Determine the value of the constant k so that the function $k(3-x)$ is a probability density function on the interval $[1, 9]$.

   Answer: $-\frac{1}{16}$

7. Determine the value of the constant k so that the function $\frac{3k}{x^4}$ is a probability density function on the interval $x \ge 1$.

   Answer: 1

8. Determine the value of the constant k so that the function kxe^{-9x^2} is a probability density function on the interval $x \ge 0$.

   Answer: 18

9. Determine the value of the constant k so that the function $kx(7-x)$ is a probability density function on the interval $[0, 7]$.

   Answer: $\frac{6}{343}$

10. The life span of a certain plant species (in days) is described by the probability density function $f(t) = \frac{1}{80}e^{-t/80}$ $(0 \le t \le \infty)$. Find the probability that a plant of this species will live for 70 days or less?
Answer: 0.583

11. The life span of a certain plant species (in days) is described by the probability density function $f(t) = \frac{1}{120}e^{-t/120}$ $(0 \le t \le \infty)$. Find the probability that a plant of this species will live for more than 50 days?
Answer: 0.659

12. The amount of gas (in thousands of gallons) Budget Gas station sells on a typical Tuesday is a continuous random variable with probability density $f(x) = 3(x-3)^2$ $(3 \le x \le 4)$. How much gas can the gas station expect to sell each Tuesday?
Answer: $\frac{15}{4}$

13. The amount of time t (in minutes) a shopper spends browsing in the magazine section of a supermarket is a continuous random variable with probability density function $f(t) = \frac{1}{18}t$ $(0 \le t \le 6)$. How much time is a shopper chosen at a random expected to spend in the magazine section?
Answer: 4

14. The number of chocolate chips in each cookie of a certain brand has a distribution described by the probability density function $f(x) = \frac{1}{36}(6x - x^2)$ $(0 \le x \le 6)$. Find the expected number of chips in each cookie.
Answer: 3

Section 7.5 Multiple Choice Questions

1. Which function is a probability density function on the indicated interval?

   a. $f(x) = \frac{1}{4}x^3$; $[1, 5]$

   b. $\frac{1}{24}e^{-24x}$; $(0, \infty)$

   c. $\frac{1}{24}e^{-\frac{24}{x}}$; $(0, \infty)$

d. $\dfrac{x\left(x^2+3\right)}{88}$; $(0,4)$

Answer: d.

2. Determine the value of the constant k so that the function $\dfrac{4k}{x^3}$ is a probability density function on the interval $[1,\ 5]$.

a. $\dfrac{16}{5}$

b. $-\dfrac{25}{48}$

c. $\dfrac{25}{48}$

d. $\dfrac{8}{5}$

Answer: c.

3. Determine the value of the constant k so that the function $k(2-x)$ is a probability density function on the interval $[1,\ 9]$.

a. -24

b. $\dfrac{1}{24}$

c. 24

d. $-\dfrac{1}{24}$

Answer: d.

4. Determine the value of the constant k so that the function $\dfrac{4k}{x^3}$ is a probability density function on the interval $x \geq 2$.

a. 2

b. 1

c. 4

d. 8

Answer: a.

5. Determine the value of the constant k so that the function kxe^{-4x^2} is a probability density function on the interval $x \geq 0$.

a. 2

b. 8

c. 4

d. 16

Answer: b.

6. Determine the value of the constant k so that the function $kx(5-x)$ is a probability density function on the interval $[0,\ 5]$.
   a. $-\frac{6}{125}$
   b. $\frac{6}{125}$
   c. $\frac{125}{6}$
   d. $\frac{6}{25}$

   Answer: b.

7. The life span of a certain plant species (in days) is described by the probability density function $f(t)=\frac{1}{80}e^{-t/80}\ (0 \le t \le \infty)$. Find the probability that a plant of this species will live for 50 days or less?
   a. 23.12%
   b. 53.53%
   c. 46.47%
   d. 33.45%

   Answer: c.

8. The life span of a certain plant species (in days) is described by the probability density function $f(t)=\frac{1}{120}e^{-t/120}\ (0 \le t \le \infty)$. Find the probability that a plant of this species will live for more than 30 days?
   a. 80.12%
   b. 45.23%
   c. 22.12%
   d. 77.88%

   Answer: d.

9. The amount of gas (in thousands of gallons) Budget Gas station sells on a typical Monday is a continuous random variable with probability density function $f(x)=3(x-3)^2\ (3 \le x \le 4)$. How many gallons can the gas station expect to sell each Monday?
   a. 2.75 thousands of gallons
   b. 4.75 thousands of gallons
   c. 3 thousands of gallons
   d. 3.75 thousands of gallons

   Answer: d.

10. The amount of time t (in minutes) a shopper spends browsing in the magazine section of a supermarket is a continuous random variable with probability density function $f(t) = \frac{6}{147}t \ (0 \le t \le 7)$. Find the time that a shopper, chosen randomly, is expected to spend in the magazine section?
a. 4.7 minutes
b. 4 minutes
c. 3 minutes
d. 5.2 minutes
Answer: a.

11. The number of chocolate chips in each cookie of a certain brand has a distribution described by the probability density function $f(x) = \frac{6}{125}(5x - x^2) \ (0 \le x \le 5)$. Find the expected number of chocolate chips in each cookie.
a. 1 chocolate chip
b. 2 chocolate chips
c. 3 chocolate chips
d. 4 chocolate chips
Answer: c.

12. The life span (in years) of a certain brand of color television tube is a continuous random variable with probability density function $f(t) = 16(16 + t^2)^{-3/2}$, $(0 \le t \le \infty)$. How long is one of these color television tubes expected to last?
a. 6 years
b. 3 years
c. 5 years
d. 4 years
Answer: d.

13. The amount of snowfall in feet in a remote region of Alaska in the month of January is a continuous random variable with probability density function $f(x) = \frac{3}{32}x(4 - x)$, $(0 \le x \le 4)$. Find the amount of snowfall that one can expect in any given January in Alaska.
a. 4 ft
b. 5 ft
c. 3 ft
d. 2 ft
Answer: d.

Exam 7A

Name:
Instructor:
Section:

Write your work as neatly as possible.

1. Find the indefinite integral $\int 2xe^{x+1}\,dx$.

2. Find the indefinite integral $\int t^3 \ln\left(t^2\right)dt$.

3. Find the indefinite integral $\int x(x-3)^{-3/2}\,dx$.

4. Evaluate the definite integral $\int_1^4 t^{3/2} \ln t\,dt$.

5. Use a table of integrals to find $\int x^2\sqrt{16+9x^2}\,dx$.

6. Use a table of integrals to find $\int \frac{1}{1+5e^{3x}}\,dx$.

7. Use a table of integrals to find $\int x^5 \ln x\,dx$.

8. Use the Trapezoidal Rule to approximate $\int_2^4 \left(x^2-2\right)dx$ with $n=4$.

9. Use Simpson's Rule to approximate $\int_0^2 \frac{dx}{\sqrt{x^5+1}}dx$ with $n=6$.

10. Find the area of the region under the curve $y=\frac{1}{(x-1)^{3/2}}$ for $x \geq 3$.

11. A scholarship fund being set up in the name of a deceased math teacher. If the scholarship is to award \$2200/year and the fund earns interest at a rate of 7% per year compounded continuously, find the required amount for the endowment.

12. Evaluate the improper integral $\int_1^{\infty} \frac{1}{2x+1}\,dx$ if it is convergent.

13. Evaluate the improper integral $\int_{-\infty}^{\infty} x\left(x^2+3\right)^{-2} dx$ if it is convergent.

14. Evaluate the improper integral $\int_{-\infty}^{0} \frac{e^x}{1+e^{-x}}\,dx$ if it is convergent.

15. Use the table of integrals to evaluate the integral $\int \frac{x^2\,dx}{(3+2x)^2}$.

Exam 7B

Name:
Instructor:
Section:

Write your work as neatly as possible.

1. Find the indefinite integral $\int x \ln x^2 dx$.

2. Find the indefinite integral $\int t(t+2)^{-6} dt$.

3. Find the indefinite integral $\int \sqrt[5]{x} \ln x \, dx$.

4. Evaluate the definite integral $\int_0^1 xe^{x/3} dx$.

5. Use a table of integrals to find $\int \frac{dx}{x\sqrt{1+16x}}$.

6. Use a table of integrals to find $\int \frac{dx}{x \ln x \sqrt{4+(\ln x)^2}}$.

7. Use a table of integrals to find $\int \frac{(\ln x)^2}{4} dx$.

8. Use the Trapezoidal Rule to approximate $\int_0^1 \frac{dx}{\sqrt{x^6+1}}$ with $n = 6$.

9. Find a bound on the error in approximating $\int_0^2 \sqrt{4x+1} dx$ using Simpson's rule with $n = 8$.

10. Use Simpson's Rule to approximate $\int_0^4 e^{-x^2} dx$ with $n = 8$.

11. Find the area of the region under the curve $y = e^{4x}$ for $x \leq 0$.

12. Evaluate the improper integral $\int_{-\infty}^{1} \frac{2}{(x-4)^3} dx$ if it is convergent.

13. Evaluate the improper integral $\int_{0}^{\infty} e^{-x} dx$ if it is convergent.

14. Evaluate the improper integral $\int_{0}^{\infty} xe^{4-x^2} dx$ if it is convergent.

15. A scholarship fund being set up in the name of a famous biologist. If the scholarship is to award \$1000/year and the fund earns interest at a rate of 7.5% per year compounded continuously, find the required amount for the endowment.

16. Use the table of integrals to evaluate the integral $\int \frac{dx}{(x^2 - 25)^{3/2}}$.

Exam 7C

Name:
Instructor:
Section:

Write your work as neatly as possible.

1. Find the indefinite integral $\int \frac{xe^{4x}}{8} dx$.

2. Find the indefinite integral $\int t^4 e^t \, dt$.

3. Find the indefinite integral $\int x^2 \ln(6x) dx$.

4. Evaluate the definite integral $\int_4^9 \ln \sqrt{x} dx$.

5. Use a table of integrals to evaluate $\int_0^2 \frac{dx}{\sqrt{4+x^2}}$.

6. Use a table of integrals to find $\int \frac{dx}{2+8e^{6x}}$.

7. Use the Trapezoidal Rule to approximate $\int_2^3 te^{-t} dt$ with $n = 4$.

8. Use Simpson's Rule to approximate $\int_2^4 \sqrt{t} (\ln t)^2 \, dt$ with $n = 6$.

9. Find a bound on the error in approximating $\int_1^5 \frac{1}{6x} dx$ using the trapezoidal rule with $n = 8$.

10. Find a bound on the error in approximating $\int_0^2 e^{-x/2} dx$ using Simpson's rule with $n = 6$.

11. Find the area of the region under the curve $y = \frac{2}{x^2}$ for $x \geq 2$.

12. Find the area of the region bounded by the x-axis and the graph of the function $f(x) = \frac{e^x}{\left(1+e^x\right)^2}$.

13. Evaluate the improper integral $\int_2^{\infty} \frac{1}{(3x-2)^{3/2}}\,dx$ if it is convergent.

14. Evaluate the improper integral $\int_{-\infty}^{\infty} x^8\,dx$ if it is convergent.

15. Evaluate the improper integral $\int_0^{\infty} (x-2)e^{-x^2+4x+3}\,dx$ if it is convergent.

16. The Robinson family wishes to create a scholarship fund at a college. If a scholarship in the amount of \$2500 is awarded annually beginning 1 year from now, find the amount of the endowment they are required to make now. Assume that this fund will earn interest at a rate of 10% per year compounded continuously.

17. If a continuous random variable x is exponentially distributed with probability density function $f(x) = 0.005e^{-0.005x}$ $(0 \leq x < \infty)$ find the expected value of x.

(The expected value of $x = E(x) = \int_0^{\infty} 0.005xe^{-0.005x}\,dx$.)

Exam 7D

Name:
Instructor:
Section:

Write your work as neatly as possible.

1. Find the indefinite integral $\int (e^x + 2x)^2 \, dx$.

2. Find the indefinite integral $\int x \ln 2x \, dx$.

3. Find the indefinite integral $\int \frac{\ln x}{x^{5/3}} dx$.

4. Use a table of integrals to find $\int \frac{dx}{x\sqrt{49 - x^2}}$.

5. Use a table of integrals to find $\int \frac{\ln x}{x(1 + 2\ln x)} dx$.

6. Use the Trapezoidal Rule to approximate $\int_2^3 te^{-t} dt$ with $n = 4$.

7. Use Simpson's Rule to approximate $\int_4^9 \sqrt{t} \ln t \, dt$ with $n = 6$.

8. Find a bound on the error in approximating $\int_0^1 xe^x dx$ using the trapezoidal rule with $n = 6$.

9. Find a bound on the error in approximating $\int_1^4 \left(x^{7/2} + 5x^2\right) dx$ using Simpson's rule with $n = 4$.

10. Find the area of the region under the curve $y = \dfrac{1}{(x-4)^2}$ for $x \geq 6$.

11. Evaluate the improper integral $\int_2^{\infty} \frac{7}{x^6}\,dx$ if it is convergent.

12. Evaluate the improper integral $\int_1^{\infty} e^{-3x}\,dx$ if it is convergent.

13. Evaluate the improper integral $\int_0^{\infty} x^4\left(1+x^5\right)^{-2}\,dx$ if it is convergent.

14. Evaluate the improper integral $\int_0^{\infty} \frac{e^{-2x}}{1+e^{-2x}}\,dx$ if it is convergent.

15. The Robinson family wishes to create a scholarship fund at a college. If a scholarship in the amount of \$5000 is awarded annually beginning 1 year from now, find the amount of the endowment they are required to make now. Assume that this fund will earn interest at a rate of 10% per year compounded continuously.

16. If a continuous random variable *x* is exponentially distributed with probability density function $f(x) = 0.1e^{-0.1x}$ $(0 \leq x < \infty)$ find the probability that *x* is between 10 and 50. (The probability that *x* is between 10 and 50 is $= \int_{10}^{50} 0.1e^{-0.1x}$.)

Answers to Chapter 7 Exams

Exam 7A

1. $2e^{x+1}(x-1)+C$
2. $\frac{1}{4}t^4\ln(t^2)-\frac{1}{8}t^4+C$
3. $2(x-3)^{1/2}-6(x-3)^{-1/2}+C$
4. $\frac{128}{5}\ln 2-\frac{124}{25}$
5. $\frac{1}{27}\left[\frac{3x}{8}(16+18x^2)\sqrt{16+9x^2}-32\ln\left|3x+\sqrt{16+9x^2}\right|\right]+C$
6. $x-\frac{1}{3}\ln(1+5e^{3x})+C$
7. $\frac{1}{6}x^6\ln|x|-\frac{1}{36}x^6+C$
8. 14.75
9. 1.3138496
10. $\sqrt{2}$
11. \$31,428.57
12. Not convergent
13. 0
14. $1-\ln 2$
15. $\frac{1}{8}\left[3+2x-\frac{9}{3+2x}-6\ln|3+2x|\right]+C$

Exam 7B

1. $\frac{1}{2}x^2\ln(x^2)-\frac{1}{2}x^2+C$
2. $-\frac{1}{4(t+2)^4}+\frac{2}{5(t+2)^5}+C$
3. $\frac{5}{6}x^{6/5}\ln x-\frac{25}{36}x^{6/5}+C$
4. $9-6e^{1/3}$
5. $\ln\left|\frac{\sqrt{1+16x}-1}{\sqrt{1+16x}+1}\right|+C$
6. $-\frac{1}{2}\ln\left|\frac{\sqrt{4+(\ln x)^2}+2}{\ln x}\right|+C$
7. $\frac{x(\ln x)^2}{4}-\frac{x\ln x-x}{2}+C$
8. 0.9449085
9. 0.010417
10. 0.886196
11. $\frac{1}{4}$
12. $-\frac{1}{9}$
13. 1
14. $\frac{1}{2}e^4$
15. \$13,333.33
16. $-\frac{x}{25\sqrt{x^2-25}}+C$

Exam 7C

1. $\left(\frac{x}{32}-\frac{1}{128}\right)e^{4x}+C$
2. $\left(t^4-4t^3+12t^2-24t+24\right)e^t+C$
3. $\frac{x^3}{3}\ln(6x)-\frac{x^3}{9}+C$
4. $9\ln 3-4\ln 2-\frac{5}{2}$
5. $\ln\left(\sqrt{2}+1\right)$
6. $\frac{1}{2}\left[x-\frac{1}{6}\ln\left(1+4e^{6x}\right)\right]+C$
7. 0.2070446
8. 4.2929681
9. 0.02778
10. 0.000008573
11. 1
12. 1
13. $\frac{1}{3}$
14. Not Convergent
15. $\frac{e^3}{2}$
16. $25,000.
17. 200

Exam 7D

1. $\frac{e^{2x}}{2}+4xe^x-4e^x+\frac{4}{3}x^3+C$
2. $\frac{1}{2}x^2\ln 2x-\frac{1}{4}x^2+C$
3. $-\frac{3}{2x^{2/3}}\ln x-\frac{9}{4x^{2/3}}+C$
4. $-\frac{1}{7}\ln\left|\frac{7+\sqrt{49-x^2}}{x}\right|+C$
5. $\frac{1}{2}\ln x-\frac{1}{4}\ln\left|1+2\ln x\right|+C$
6. 0.222208
7. 23.7120118
8. 0.01062
9. 0.03461
10. $\frac{1}{2}$
11. $\frac{7}{160}$
12. $\frac{1}{3e^3}$
13. $\frac{1}{5}$
14. $\frac{\ln 2}{2}$
15. $50,000
16. 0.36114

Chapter 8 ■ Calculus of Several Variables

Section 8.1

1. Let $f(x, y) = xy^2 + 4x$. Compute $f(2, 4)$.
   Answer: 40

2. Let $f(x, y) = 3x + y^2$. Compute $f(2, 3), f(3, 2)$, and $f(1, 1)$.
   Answer: 15, 13, 4

3. Let $f(x, y) = x^2 y^3 + 3x$. Compute $f(-1, 2)$.
   Answer: 5

4. Let $f(x, y) = x^2 y^2 - 3x$. Compute $f(-1, 3)$.
   Answer: 12

5. Let $f(x, y) = 2x + 5y - 7$. Compute $f(1,3)$ and $f(0,5)$.
   Answer: 10; 18

6. Let $h(p, r) = \dfrac{3p + 3r}{p^2 - r^2}$. Compute $h(3, 2), h(2, 3)$, and $h(0, 1)$.
   Answer: $3, -3, -3$

7. Let $f(r, t) = \dfrac{3 + r}{t - r}$. Compute $f(3, 2)$ and $f(7, 5)$.
   Answer: $-6; -5$

8. Let $f(x, y) = 3x\sqrt{y} - y\sqrt{x}$. Compute $f(0, 0), f(1, 4)$, and $f(4, 1)$.
   Answer: 0, 2, 10

9. Let $h(x, y) = \dfrac{x}{y} e^{x/y}$. Compute $h(1, 1)$, $h(2, 1)$, and $h(1, 2)$.
   Answer: $e, 2e^2, \dfrac{1}{2}\sqrt{e}$

10. Let $g(u, v, w) = \dfrac{ue^v + ve^w + we^u}{uvw}$. Compute $g(1, 2, 3)$ and $g(3, 2, 1)$.
    Answer: $\dfrac{1}{6}\left(2e^3 + e^2 + 3e\right), \dfrac{1}{6}\left(e^3 + 3e^2 + 2e\right)$

11. Find the domain of the function $f(x, y) = 2x - y$.
Answer: The set of all points (x, y) in the xy-plane.

12. Find the domain of the function $f(x, y) = e^{7x-y}$.
Answer: The set of all points (x, y) in the xy-plane.

13. Find the domain of the function $f(x, y, z) = x^2 + y^2 + \dfrac{1}{z^2}$.
Answer: The set of all points (x, y, z) in the xyz-space except those lying on the xy-plane.

14. Find the domain of the function $f(x, y) = e^{-x^2/y}$.
Answer: The set of all points (x, y) in the xy-plane except those lying on the x-axis.

15. Find the domain of the function $f(x, y) = x^3 - y^3$.
Answer: The set of all points (x, y) in the xy-plane.

16. Find the domain of the function $f(x, y) = \dfrac{3}{x+y}$.
Answer: The set of all points (x, y) in the xy-plane except those lying on the line $y = -x$.

17. Find the domain of the function $f(x, y) = \sqrt{4 - x^2 - y^2}$.
Answer: The set of all points (x, y) in the xy-plane lying on and inside the circle $x^2 + y^2 = 4$.

18. Find the domain of the function $g(x, y) = \ln(3x + y - 4)$.
Answer: The set of all points (x, y) in the xy-plane that satisfy $y > -3x + 4$.

19. Find the domain of the function $f(x, y) = x^2 + 2y^2$.
Answer: The set of all points (x, y) in the xy-plane

20. Find the domain of the function $f(x, y) = \dfrac{4}{x-y}$.
Answer: The set of all points (x, y) in the xy-plane except those lying on the line $y = x$.

21. Find the domain of the function $f(x, y) = 3x^2y^2 - 4x^3$.
Answer: The set of all points (x, y) in the xy-plane.

22. Sketch the level curves of the function $f(x, y) = x + y$ corresponding to the values $z = -2,\ 0,\ 2$.
Answer:

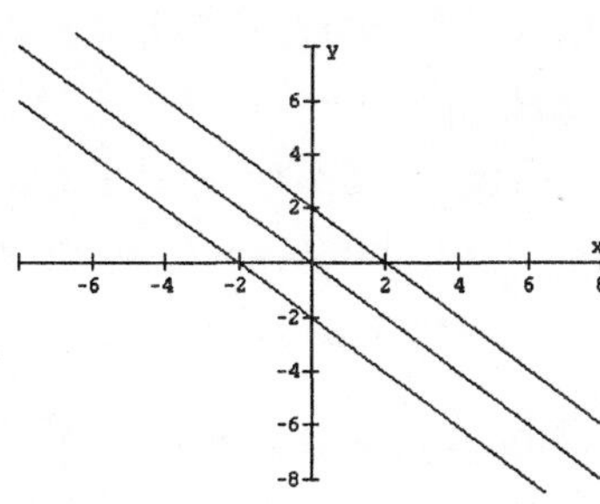

23. Sketch the level curves of the function $f(x, y) = e^{-x} - y$ corresponding to the values $z = -2,\ 0,\ 2$.
Answer:

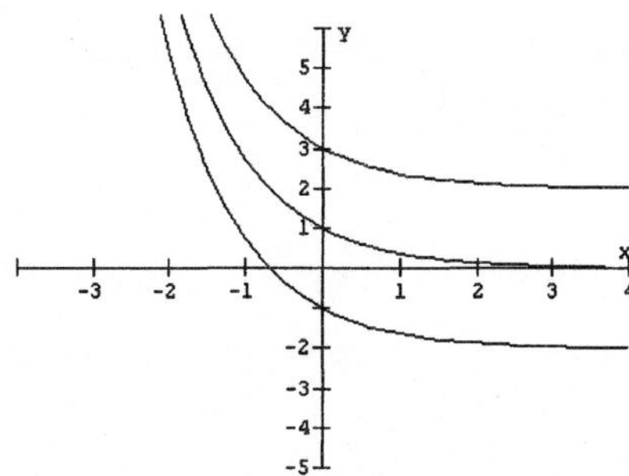

24. Sketch the level curves of the function $f(x, y) = x - y^2$ corresponding to the values $z = -2,\ 0,\ 2$.
Answer:

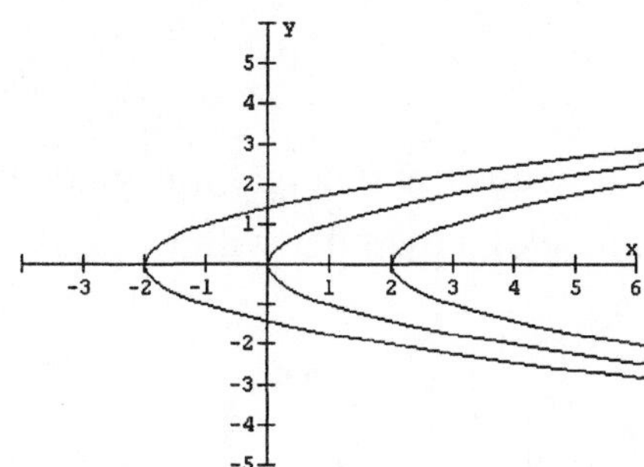

25. The IQ (intelligence quotient) of a person whose mental age is m years and whose chronological age is c years is defined as $f(m, c) = \dfrac{100m}{c}$. What is the IQ of a ten-year old child who has a mental age of 12.5 years?
Answer: 125

26. If a principal of P dollars is deposited in an account earning interest at the rate of r per year compounded continuously, then the accumulated amount at the end of t years is given by $A = f(P, r, t) = Pe^{rt}$ dollars. Find the accumulated amount at the end of three years if a sum of $5000 is deposited in an account bearing interest at the rate of 8% per year compounded continuously.
Answer: $6356.25

27. The monthly payment P that amortizes a loan of A dollars in t years at an interest rate of r per year is given by $P(A, r, t) = \dfrac{A\left(\dfrac{r}{12}\right)}{1-\left(1+\dfrac{r}{12}\right)^{-12t}}$.
Find the monthly payment for a loan of $75,000 that will be amortized over 15 years at 5% per year, compounded monthly.
Answer: $593.10

28. The volume of a cylinder with radius r and height h is given by the function $V(r, h) = \pi r^2 h$. Find the volume of a cylinder with a radius of 3 inches and a height of 2 inches.
Answer: 18π cubic inches

29. The volume of a cylinder with radius r and height h is given by the function $V(r, h) = \pi r^2 h$. Find the volume of a cylinder with a radius of 2 inches and a height of 3 inches.
Answer: 12π cubic inches

30. The volume of a cylinder with radius r and height h is given by the function $V(r, h) = \pi r^2 h$. Find the volume of a cylinder with a radius of 3 inches and a height of 4 inches.
Answer: 36π cubic inches

31. The volume of a cylinder with radius r and height h is given by the function $V(r, h) = \pi r^2 h$. Find the volume of a cylinder with a radius of 2 inches and a height of 1 inch.
Answer: 4π cubic inches

Section 8.1 Multiple Choice Questions

1. Let $f(x, y) = 3x - 4y + 6$. Compute $f(0, 1)$.
   a. 0
   b. −2
   c. 2
   d. 6
   Answer: c.

2. Let $f(x, y) = e^{x+y-2} + 3$. Compute $f(1, 1)$.
   a. 4
   b. $e + 3$
   c. 3
   d. $e^2 + 3$
   Answer: a.

3. Let $f(x, y) = \dfrac{x+y}{1-xy}$. Compute $f(-1, 1)$.
   a. $\dfrac{1}{2}$
   b. 1
   c. 2
   d. 0
   Answer: d.

4. Let $f(x, y) = \left(x^2 - y^3\right) \ln|x + y| + 3x$. Compute $f(-1, 0)$.
   a. $\dfrac{1}{3}$
   b. −3
   c. 3
   d. 0
   Answer: b.

5. Let $f(x, y, z) = \left(x^2 + y^3\right) \ln|x + y| + 3z$. Compute $f(-1, 0, 4)$.
   a. $\ln 2 + 12$
   b. −12
   c. 12
   d. 0
   Answer: c.

6. Find the domain of the function $f(x, y) = \sqrt{x^2 + y^2} \ln\left|x^2 + y^8\right| + 3xe^y$.
   a. All values satisfying $x \geq y \geq 0$
   b. All real values except (0, 0).

c. All values satisfying $x \geq 0,\ y \geq 0$

d. All values satisfying $x > 0,\ y > 0$

Answer: b.

7. Find the domain of the function $f(x, y) = \dfrac{xy}{x+y}$.

a. All values satisfying $x \geq y \geq 1$

b. All real values of x and y

c. All values satisfying $x \neq 0,\ y \neq 0$

d. All values satisfying $x \neq -y$

Answer: d.

8. Let $f(x, y) = 4 - \sqrt{x^2 + y^2}$, the level curve for $z = -2$ is:

a. $x^2 - y^2 = 36$

b. $x^2 + y^2 = 36$

c. $y = x^2 - 2x + 36$

d. $x^2 + y^2 = 4$

Answer: b.

9. Let $f(x, y) = 6 + \sqrt{x^2 + y^2}$, the level curve for $z = 9$ is:

a. $x^2 + y^2 = 36$

b. $x^2 + y^2 = 9$

c. $y = x^2 - 2x + 6$

d. $x^2 + y^2 = 3$

Answer: b.

10. The volume of a cylindrical tank of radius r and height h is given by $V = f(r, h) = \pi r^2 h$. Find the volume of a cylindrical tank of radius 2 feet and height 4 feet.

a. 16π ft^3

b. 8π ft^3

c. 32π ft^3

d. 4π ft^3

Answer: a.

11. The IQ of a person whose mental age is m years and whose chronological age is c years is defined as $f(m, c) = \dfrac{102m}{c}$. What is the IQ of a 9 years old child who has a mental age of 15 years?

a. 204

b. 102
c. 170
d. 136
Answer: c.

12. The distance a car travels is given by $f(v_0, s_0, t) = 3t^2 + v_0 t + s_0$, where v_0 is the initial velocity, s_0 is the initial position, and t (measured in seconds) is the time. Find the distance the car travels in 3 seconds given that s_0 is 10 feet and v_0 is 4 ft/sec.
a. 37 feet
b. 27 feet
c. 22 feet
d. 49 feet
Answer: d.

13. A study conducted by TeleCable estimates the number of cable TV subscribers, t days after the start of service, is given by $f(t, P_0) = 280t^{3/4} + P_0$, where P_0 is the number of subscribers signed up for the service before the starting date. How many subscribers will there be 16 months after the start of service when 4000 subscribers signed up before the starting date?
a. 6240
b. 2240
c. 5240
d. 4000
Answer: a.

Section 8.2

1. Let $f(x, y) = 3x^2y - 2y$. Find $\dfrac{\partial f}{\partial y}$. Answer: $3x^2 - 2$

2. Find the first partial derivatives of $f(x, y) = 3xy$. Answer: $f_x = 3y;\ f_y = 3x$

3. Find the first partial derivatives of $f(x, y) = 10x - 7y$.
Answer: $f_x = 10;\ f_y = -7$

4. Find the first partial derivatives of $g(m,n) = \dfrac{m}{n+2}$.

   Answer: $g_m = \dfrac{1}{n+2};\ g_n = \dfrac{-m}{(n+2)^2}$

5. Find the first partial derivatives of $f(x, y) = e^{2xy}$.
Answer: $f_x = 2ye^{2xy};\ f_y = 2xe^{2xy}$

6. Let $f(x, y) = 4xy^2 + 3x$. Find $\dfrac{\partial f}{\partial x}$. Answer: $4y^2 + 3$

7. Let $f(x, y) = 8x^3y^2 + 2xy$. Find $\dfrac{\partial f}{\partial y}$. Answer: $16x^3y + 2x$

8. Let $f(x, y) = \dfrac{3x}{y} - e^{xy}$. Find f_x. Answer: $\dfrac{3}{y} - ye^{xy}$

9. Let $f(x, y) = \dfrac{4y}{x} - \ln(xy)$. Find f_y. Answer: $\dfrac{4}{x} - \dfrac{1}{y}$

10. Let $f(x, y) = 2y\ln(xy)$. Find f_y. Answer: $2 + 2\ln(xy)$

11. Let $f(x, y) = \dfrac{\ln y}{2xy^2}$. Find f_x. Answer: $-\dfrac{\ln y}{2x^2y^2}$

12. Evaluate the first partial derivatives of $f(x, y) = 2x^2y + 4x$ at the point (1, 2).
Answer: $f_x(1,2) = 12;\ f_y(1,2) = 2$

13. Evaluate the first partial derivatives of $f(x, y, z) = y + 4xz^3$ at the point (1, 0, 3).
Answer: $f_x(1,0,3) = 108;\ f_y(1,0,3) = 1;\ f_z(1,0,3) = 108$

14. Let $f(x, y, z) = 4x^2yz^3 + 3xz$. Find f_{xz}. Answer: $24xyz^2 + 3$

15. Let $f(x, y, z) = 3xyz + 2x^2yz^3$. Find f_{zx}. Answer: $3y + 12xyz^2$

16. Let $f(x, y, z) = 3xyz + 2x^2yz^3$. Find f_{zy}. Answer: $3x + 6x^2z^2$

17. Let $f(x, y, z) = 4x^2yz^3 + 3xz$. Find f_{xy}. Answer: $8xz^3$

18. Let $f(x, y) = e^{xy}$. Find $f_{yy}(2,0)$. Answer: 4

19. Let $f(x, y) = xe^{xy}$. Find $f_{xx}(0,3)$. Answer: 6

20. Let $f(x, y) = x^2e^{2y}$. Find $f_{yy}(2,0)$. Answer: 16

21. Let $f(x, y) = e^{x^2y}$. Find $f_{xx}(2,2)$. Answer: $68\,e^8$

22. Let $f(x, y) = 2x^2 + 3y$. Find $\dfrac{\partial f}{\partial x}$. Answer: $4x$

23. Let $f(x, y) = 2x^2 + 3y$. Find $\dfrac{\partial f}{\partial y}$ Answer: 3

24. Let $g(a,b,c) = ab^2 + bc^3 - abc$.

(a) Find $\dfrac{\partial g}{\partial a}$. Answer: $b^2 - bc$

(b) Find $\dfrac{\partial g}{\partial c}$. Answer: $3bc^2 - ab$

25. Let $f(x, y) = 3x^2y^3 + xy^2$. Find $f_x(2, 1)$. Answer: 13

26. Let $f(x, y) = e^{xy} - \ln(xy)$. Find $f_y(1, 1)$. Answer: $e - 1$

27. Let $f(x, y, z) = e^{xz} + xyz^2$. Find $\dfrac{\partial^2 f}{\partial z^2}$. Answer: $x^2e^{xz} + 2xy$

28. Let $f(x, y) = 3x^2y^3$. Find $\dfrac{\partial^2 f}{\partial y^2}$. Answer: $18x^2y$

29. Let $f(x, y) = 3x^6 y^8$. Find $\dfrac{\partial^2 f}{\partial x \partial y}$. Answer: $144x^5 y^7$

30. Let $f(x, y) = 4x^2 y^5$. Find $\dfrac{\partial^2 f}{\partial y^2}$. Answer: $80x^2 y^3$

31. Let $g(a, b) = a^2 b^5$. Find g_{ab}. Answer: $10ab^4$

Section 8.2 Multiple Choice Questions

1. Let $f(x, y) = 3x - 4y + 6$. Compute $f_x(x, y)$.
   a. 0
   b. −2
   c. 3
   d. 6
   Answer: c.

2. Let $f(x, y, z) = 3x - 4y + 6z + 12$. Compute $f_z(x, y, z)$.
   a. 12
   b. −4
   c. 3
   d. 6
   Answer: d.

3. Let $f(x, y, z) = \ln\left|x^2 + 10y - 6z + 100\right|$. Compute $f_y(x, y, z)$.
   a. $f_y(x, y, z) = \dfrac{-10}{x^2 + 10y - 6z + 100}$
   b. $f_y(x, y, z) = \dfrac{10}{x^2 + 10y - 6z + 100}$
   c. $f_y(x, y, z) = \dfrac{6}{x^2 + 10y - 6z + 100}$
   d. $f_y(x, y, z) = \dfrac{2x}{x^2 + 10y - 6z + 100}$
   Answer: b.

4. Let $f(x, y) = e^{xy} + \ln|x + y|$. Compute $f_y(x, y)$.
   a. $f_y(x, y) = e^{xy} + \dfrac{x}{x + y}$

b. $f_y(x, y) = xe^{xy} + \dfrac{1}{x+y}$

c. $f_y(x, y) = xe^{xy} + \dfrac{y}{x+y}$

d. $f_y(x, y) = xe^{xy} + \dfrac{1}{y}$

Answer: b.

5. Let $f(x, y) = \sqrt{x^2 + y^2}$. Compute $f_y(x, y)$.

a. $f_y(x, y) = \dfrac{y}{2\sqrt{x^2 + y^2}}$

b. $f_y(x, y) = \dfrac{2y}{\sqrt{x^2 + y^2}}$

c. $f_y(x, y) = \dfrac{y}{\sqrt{x^2 + y^2}}$

d. $f_y(x, y) = \dfrac{x+y}{\sqrt{x^2 + y^2}}$

Answer: c.

6. Let $f(x, y) = e^{xy^3} + 1 - y$. Compute $f_y(x, y)$.

a. $f_y(x, y) = 3xy^2e^{xy^3} - 1$

b. $f_y(x, y) = xy^2e^{xy^3} - 1$

c. $f_y(x, y) = 3xy^2e^{xy^3} + 1$

d. $f_y(x, y) = 3xy^2e^{xy^3} + 1 - y$

Answer: a.

7. Let $f(x, y) = xy^3 + x^2 + y^3 - xy$. Compute $f_{xy}(x, y)$.

a. $f_{xy}(x, y) = 3y^3 + 2x - 1$

b. $f_{xy}(x, y) = 3y^2 - 1$

c. $f_{xy}(x, y) = 3y^3 - x$

d. $f_{xy}(x, y) = 3y^3 + 2y - 1$

Answer: b.

8. Let $f(x, y) = xy^3 + x^2 + y^3 - xy$. Compute $f_{xx}(x, y)$.

a. $f_{xx}(x, y) = 2$

b. $f_{xx}(x, y) = -1$

c. $f_{xx}(x, y) = 3y^3 - 2$

d. $f_{xx}(x, y) = 3y^3 + 2$

Answer: a.

9. Let $f(x, y) = xy^2 + e^{x^2}$. Compute $f_x(0, 1)$.

a. -1

b. $1 + e$

c. 1

d. $1 + 2e$

Answer: c.

10. Let $f(x, y) = \sqrt{x^2 + y^4}$. Compute $f_x(\sqrt{3}, 1)$.

a. $\dfrac{\sqrt{3}}{4}$

b. $\dfrac{\sqrt{3}}{5}$

c. $\dfrac{2\sqrt{3}}{3}$

d. $\dfrac{\sqrt{3}}{2}$

Answer: d.

11. The productivity of a country in Western Europe is given by the function $f(x, y) = 44x^{4/5}y^{1/5}$, when x units of labor and y units of capital are used. Find the marginal productivity of labor when the amount expended on labor is 32 units and the amount on capital is 243 units?

a. 88

b. 52.8

c. 35.2

d. 33

Answer: b.

12. The productivity of a country in Western Europe is given by the function $f(x, y) = 55x^{3/4}y^{1/4}$, when x units of labor and y units of capital are used. Find the marginal productivity of capital when the amount expended on labor is 16 units and the amount of capital is 81 units?

a. $\dfrac{110}{27}$

b. $\dfrac{55}{27}$

c. $\frac{44}{81}$

d. $\frac{88}{9}$

Answer: a.

13. A study conducted by TeleCable estimates the number of cable TV subscribers, t days after the start of service, is given by $f(t, P_0) = 280t^{3/4} + P_0$, where P_0 is the number of subscribers signed up for the service before the starting date. Find the rate of the change of the number of subscribers after the start of service with respect to time.

a. $f_t(t, P_0) = 260t^{-1/4}$

b. $f_t(t, P_0) = 210t^{-1/4} + 1$

c. $f_t(t, P_0) = 210t^{-1/4} + P_0$

d. $f_t(t, P_0) = 210t^{-1/4}$

Answer: d.

Section 8.3

1. The productivity of a country is given by the function $f(x, y) = 30x^{2/5}y^{3/5}$, where x units of labor and y units of capital are used. Find the marginal productivity of capital when $x = 32$ and $y = 243$.
Answer: 8

2. The productivity of a country is given by the function $f(x, y) = 60x^{1/3}y^{2/3}$, where x units of labor and y units of capital are used. Find the marginal productivity of labor when $x = 8$ and $y = 64$.
Answer: 80

3. The productivity of a country is given by the function $f(x, y) = 32x^{1/4}y^{3/4}$, where x units of labor and y units of capital are used. Find the marginal productivity of capital when $x = 16$ and $y = 81$.
Answer: 16

4. The productivity of a country is given by the function $f(x, y) = 30x^{2/5}y^{3/5}$, where x units of labor and y units of capital are used.
(a) Find the marginal productivity of labor when $x = 32$ and $y = 243$.
Answer: $\frac{81}{2}$
(b) Find the marginal productivity of capital when the amount expended on labor is 243 units and the amount expended on capital is 32 units.
Answer: $\frac{81}{2}$
(c) If the amounts actually expended on labor and capital are currently 243 units and 32 units, respectively, then should the government encourage increased expenditure on labor or on capital to increase productivity the most?
Answer: Capital

5. Find any critical points of the function $f(x, y) = x^2 - xy + y^2 + 1$.
Answer: (0, 0)

6. Find any critical points of the function $f(x, y) = 3x - 4yx$.
Answer: (0, 3/4)

7. Find any critical points of the function $f(x, y) = y^2 + xy - x^2 - 5y + 2$.
Answer: (1, 2)

8. Find any critical points of the function $f(x, y) = x^2 + xy - y^2 + 5x + 2$.
Answer: $(-2, -1)$

9. Find any critical points of the function $f(x, y) = 4x^2 + 3y^2 - 2$.
Answer: (0, 0)

10. Find any critical points of the function $f(x, y) = 3x^2 + xy - y^2 + 26x - 2$.
Answer: $(-4, -2)$

11. Find any critical points of the function $f(x, y) = 3x^2 + 6y^2 - 2$.
Answer: $(0,0)$

12. Find any critical points of the function $f(x, y) = e^{x^2+x+y^2}$.
Answer: $\left(-\frac{1}{2}, 0\right)$

13. Identify any relative extrema or saddle points of the function
$f(x, y) = x^2 + y^2 - 10$.
Answer: Relative minimum at (0, 0)

14. Identify any relative extrema or saddle points of the function
$f(x, y) = 2x^2 + 3xy - 5y^2 - 12x$.
Answer: Saddle point at $\left(\frac{120}{49}, \frac{36}{49}\right)$

15. Identify any relative extrema or saddle points of the function
$f(x, y) = -x^2 - 2y^2 + 8x + 12y - 3$.
Answer: Relative maximum at (4, 3)

16. Identify any relative extrema or saddle points of the function
$f(x, y) = 4y^3 + x^2 - 12y^2 - 36y - 4$.
Answer: Saddle point at $(0, -1)$; relative minimum at (0, 3)

17. Identify any relative extrema or saddle points of the function
$f(x, y) = 3x^2 + 3y^2 + 4xy - 8x + 4y + 2$.
Answer: Relative minimum at $\left(\frac{16}{5}, -\frac{14}{5}\right)$

18. Identify any relative extrema or saddle points of the function $f(x, y) = \frac{1}{e^{x^2+y^2}}$.
Answer: Relative maximum at (0, 0)

19. Identify any relative extrema or saddle points of the function $f(x, y) = x^2 + xy + y^3$.
Answer: Saddle point at (0, 0), Relative minimum at $\left(-\frac{1}{12}, \frac{1}{6}\right)$

20. Let $f(x, y) = x^2 + y^2 + 2x - 4y + 2$.
(a) Find any critical points of *f*.
Answer: $(-1,2)$

(b) For any critical points found in part (a), use the Second Derivative Test to classify the critical points as relative extrema, if possible.
Answer: $(-1,2)$: relative minimum

21. Let $f(x, y) = x^3 + y^2 - 12x - 6y + 2$.
(a) Find any critical points of *f*.
Answer: $(2,3), (-2,3)$

(b) For any critical points found in part (a), use the Second Derivative Test to classify the critical points as relative extrema, if possible.
Answer: $(2,3)$: relative minimum, $(-2,3)$: saddle point

22. Let $f(x, y) = 2y^3 - x^2 - 12y^2 + 4x - 30y + 15$.
(a) Find any critical points of *f*.
Answer: $(2, -1), (2, 5)$

(b) If there were any critical points found in part (a), use the Second Derivative Test to classify the critical points as relative extrema, if possible.
Answer: $(2, 5)$: saddle point, $(2, -1)$: relative maximum

23. A company has a revenue function of $R(x) = 2x^2 + 4y^2 + 6x + 12y + 300$ and a cost function of $C(x) = 3x^2 + 6y^2 + 100$, where *R* and *C* are measured in dollars and *x* and *y* represent the number of units of two types of products which are produced and sold.
(a) Find the profit function $P(x)$.
Answer: $P(x) = -x^2 - 2y^2 + 6x + 12y + 200$

(b) Find the values of *x* and *y* which result in a maximum profit.
Answer: $x = 3, y = 3$

(c) What is the maximum profit?
Answer: $227

24. A company produces two products. Its revenue R in hundreds of dollars from selling x hundred units of product A and y hundred units of product B is given by the function of $R(x, y) = -2x^2 - 20y^2 + 68x + 73y - 2xy$. Determine how many of each product should be sold to maximize the revenue. What is the maximum revenue?
Answer: 1650 of A, 100 of B, and the revenue is $59,750

25. A furniture company has found that the labor cost, L, for the production of its finished furniture pieces is given by the following function of construction time, c, and finishing time, f: $L(c, f) = c^2 + 6cf + 10f^2 - 16c - 52f + 110$. Determine how many hours of each type of time should be used to minimize the labor cost. What is the minimum labor cost?
Answer: 2 hours of construction time, 2 hours of finishing time, for a cost of $42.

Section 8.3 Multiple Choice Questions

1. If $f(x, y)$ is a function and (a,b) is a critical point, then which of the following is/are true statement(s)?
   a. $f_x(a,b) = f_y(a,b) = 0$
   b. $f_{xx}(a,b) < 0$ and $D(a,b) > 0$ implies (a,b) is a relative minimum
   c. $f_{xx}(a,b) > 0$ and $D(a,b) > 0$ implies (a,b) is a relative minimum
   d. Both choices a and c are correct.
   Answer: d.

2. If $f(x, y) = x^2 - y^2 - 2x - 4y - 6$, then which of the following is/are true statement(s)?
   a. $(1, -2)$ is a relative maximum.
   b. $(1, -2)$ is a saddle point.
   c. $(1, -2)$ is a relative minimum.
   d. There is no critical point.
   Answer: b.

3. If $f(x, y) = x^4 + y^4 - 4xy$, then which of the following is/are true statement(s)?
   a. $(0,0)$ is a saddle point.
   b. $(1,1)$ is a relative maximum.
   c. $(1,1)$ and $(-1,-1)$ are relative minima.
   d. Both choices of a and c are correct.
   Answer: d.

4. An automobile manufacturer produces x thousand pickup trucks and y thousand sport vehicles per year and has a profit equation of $P(x, y) = 120x + 120y - xy - x^2 - y^2$. How many of each type of vehicle should be produced to maximize the profit?
   a. 20,000 pickups and 60,000 sport vehicles
   b. 60,000 pickups and 20,000 sport vehicles
   c. 40,000 pickups and 40,000 sport vehicles
   d. None of the above.
   Answer: c.

5. Find the three positive integers that satisfy the sum of the three numbers is 21 and the sum of the squares of the numbers is as small as possible.
   a. 5, 6, and 10
   b. 7, 7, and 7
   c. 3, 7, and 11
   d. None of the above.
   Answer: b.

6. Find the minimum value of the function $f(x, y) = x^2 + y^2 - xy - 4$.
   a. 0
   b. 2
   c. −12
   d. −4
   Answer: d.

7. Classify all critical points of the function $f(x, y) = xy + \frac{8}{x} + \frac{1}{y}$.
   a. There is no critical point.
   b. $\left(4, \frac{1}{2}, 6\right)$ is a relative maximum.
   c. $\left(4, \frac{1}{2}, 6\right)$ is a relative minimum.
   d. $\left(4, \frac{1}{2}, 6\right)$ is a saddle point.
   Answer: c.

8. Find the saddle point for $f(x, y) = x^2 - y^2 - 2x - 6y - 3$.
   a. $(1, -3, 5)$
   b. $(-1, -3, 5)$
   c. $(1, -3, -5)$
   d. $(1, -3, 0)$
   Answer: a.

9. Use the Second Derivative Test to determine the nature of the function $f(x,y)$ at the point $(a,\ b)$ if $f_{xx}(a,b)=2$, $f_{yy}(a,b)=8$, and $f_{xy}(a,b)=4$. Assume $f_x(a,b)=f_y(a,b)=0$
   a. $(a,\ b)$ is a relative maximum.
   b. $(a,\ b)$ is a relative minimum.
   c. $(a,\ b)$ is a saddle point.
   d. Test is inconclusive.

   Answer: d.

10. Use the Second Derivative Test to determine the nature of the function $f(x,y)$ at the point $(a,\ b)$ if $f_{xx}(a,b)=13$, $f_{yy}(a,b)=8$, and $f_{xy}(a,b)=4$. Assume $f_x(a,b)=f_y(a,b)=0$
   a. $(a,\ b)$ is a relative maximum.
   b. $(a,\ b)$ is a relative minimum.
   c. $(a,\ b)$ is a saddle point.
   d. Test is inconclusive.

   Answer: b.

11. Use the Second Derivative Test to determine the nature of the function $f(x,y)$ at the point (a,b) if $f_{xx}(a,b)=-23$, $f_{yy}(a,b)=-8$, and $f_{xy}(a,b)=4$. Assume $f_x(a,b)=f_y(a,b)=0$
   a. $(a,\ b)$ is a relative maximum.
   b. $(a,\ b)$ is a relative minimum.
   c. $(a,\ b)$ is a saddle point.
   d. Test is inconclusive.

   Answer: a.

12. The total weekly profit (in dollars) of the Country Workshop realized in manufacturing and selling its desks is given by $f(x,y)=-0.4x^2-0.8y^2+16x+336y+120$, where x denotes the number of finished units and y denotes the number of unfinished units manufactured and sold each week. Determine how many finished units and how many unfinished units the company should manufacture and sold each week in order to maximize the profit.
   a. 210 finished units and 20 unfinished units
   b. 20 finished units and 210 unfinished units
   c. 20 finished units and 20 unfinished units
   d. 210 finished units and 210 unfinished units

Answer: b.

13. The total weekly cost (in dollars) of the Country Workshop realized in manufacturing desks is given by $f(x, y) = x^2 + y^2 - xy - 3x - 9y + 15$, where x denotes the number of finished units and y denotes the number of unfinished units manufactured each week. Determine how many finished units and how many unfinished units the company should manufacture each week in order to minimize the cost.
   a. 7 finished units and 7 unfinished units
   b. 5 finished units and 5 unfinished units
   c. 5 finished units and 7 unfinished units
   d. 7 finished units and 5 unfinished units
   Answer: c.

Section 8.4

1. Find the equation of the least-squares line for the following data:

x	1	2	3	4
y	3	4	9	6

Answer: $y = \frac{7}{5}x + 2$

2. Find the equation of the least-squares line for the following data:

x	1	3	4	6
y	2	2.7	3.5	4.2

Answer: $y = \frac{59}{130}x + \frac{393}{260}$

3. Find the equation of the least-squares line for the following data:

x	1	2	3	4
y	5	6	8	11

Answer: $y = 2x + \frac{5}{2}$

4. Find the equation of the least-squares line for the following data:

x	1	3	4	5	7
y	0	3	5	8	13

Answer: $y = \frac{11}{5}x - 3$

5. Find the equation of the least-squares line for the following data:

x	2	4	5	7	9
y	7	8	10	13	16

Answer: $y = \frac{197}{146}x + \frac{513}{146}$

Section 8.4 Multiple Choice Questions

1. Find the least squares regression line for the points (2, 2), (1, 2), (0, 1), (-1, 1), and (-2, -1).
   a. $y = 0.7x - 1$
   b. $y = 0.7x + 1$
   c. $y = 0.35x + 1$
   d. $y = x + 0.7$
   Answer: b.

2. Find the least squares regression line for the points (0, 2), (1, 4), (3, 5), (-1, 0), and (-2, -6).
   a. $y = 2.027x - 0.5946$
   b. $y = 20.27x + 0.5946$
   c. $y = 2.027x + 0.1258$
   d. $y = 2.027x + 0.5946$
   Answer: d.

3. Find the least squares regression line for the points

x	1	1	2	3	4	4
y	2	3	3	3.5	3.7	4

   a. $y = 0.4526x + 2.068$
   b. $y = -0.4526x + 2.068$
   c. $y = 0.4526x - 2.068$
   d. $y = -0.4526x - 2.068$
   Answer: a.

4. Find the least squares regression line for the points

x	-1	0	1	1	2	3
y	2	-1	-5	-2	-3	0

   a. $y = 0.6x - 0.9$
   b. $y = -0.6x + 0.9$
   c. $y = -0.6x - 0.9$
   d. $y = -0.9x + 0.6549$
   Answer: c.

5. Find the least squares regression line for the points

x	-2	-1	0	0	2	5
y	10	8	3	7	6	4

   a. $y = 0.681x - 0.935$
   b. $y = 6.787x + 0.681$
   c. $y = 0.681x + 6.787$
   d. $y = -0.681x + 6.787$

Answer: d.

6. According to company reports, the number of a certain fast-food franchise stores in North America between 1996 and 2000 are as follows ($x = 0$ corresponds to 1996.)

Year, x	0	1	2	3	4
Stores, y	929	1300	1499	2012	2503

Find an equation of the least-squares line for these data. (Round your answer to integers.)

a. $y = 877x + 386$

b. $y = 386x - 877$

c. $y = 386x + 877$

d. $y = -386x + 877$

Answer: c.

7. According to company reports, the number of a certain fast-food franchise stores in North America between 1996 and 2000 are as follows ($x = 0$ corresponds to 1996.)

Year, x	0	1	2	3	4
Stores, y	929	1300	1499	2012	2503

Use the least-squares line to estimate the number of stores in North America on 2005.

a. 4189

b. 4200

c. 4213

d. 4351

Answer: d.

8. The spending (in billions of dollars) on a government program in a certain state over the 5-year period from 1988 to 1992 is summarized in the following table. ($x = 0$ corresponds to 1988.)

Year, x	0	1	2	3	4
Spending, y	1.45	1.67	1.72	1.85	2.00

Find an equation of the least-squares line.

a. $y = 0.128x + 1.482$

b. $y = -0.128x + 1.482$

c. $y = 0.128x - 1.482$

d. $y = 1.482x + 0.128$

Answer: a.

9. The spending (in billions of dollars) on a government program in a certain state over the 5-year period from 1988 to 1992 is summarized in the following table. ($x = 0$ corresponds to 1988.)

Year, x	0	1	2	3	4
Spending, y	1.45	1.67	1.72	1.85	2.00

Use the least-squares line to estimate the spending for 2008.
a. 5.128 billion dollars
b. 4.042 billion dollars
c. 3.786 billion dollars
d. 4.561 billion dollars
Answer: b.

10. The tuition for a certain private college (in thousands of dollars) over the 5-year period from 1996 to 2000 is summarized in the following table. ($x = 0$ corresponds to 1996.)

Year, x	0	1	2	3	4
Spending, y	21	25	29	31	37

Find an equation of the least-squares line.
a. $y = -3.8x - 21$
b. $y = 21x + 3.8$
c. $y = -3.8x + 21$
d. $y = 3.8x + 21$
Answer: d.

11. The tuition for a certain private college (in thousands of dollars) over the 5-year period from 1996 to 2000 is summarized in the following table. ($x = 0$ corresponds to 1996.)

Year, x	0	1	2	3	4
Spending, y	21	25	29	31	37

Use the equation of the least-squares line to estimate the tuition for the year of 2005.
a. 48.2 thousand dollars
b. 52.2 thousand dollars
c. 55.2 thousand dollars
d. 58.2 thousand dollars
Answer: c.

12. The revenue of a certain travel agent (in thousands of dollars) over the 5-year period from 1999 to 2003 is summarized in the following table. ($x = 0$ corresponds to 1999.)

Year, x	0	1	2	3	4
Spending, y	61	73	85	91	102

Find an equation of the least-squares line.
a. $y = -10x + 62.4$
b. $y = 10x + 62.4$
c. $y = 15x + 62.3$
d. $y = 10x - 62.4$
Answer: b.

13. The revenue of a certain travel agent (in thousands of dollars) over the 5-year period from 1999 to 2003 is summarized in the following table. ($x = 0$ corresponds to 1999.)

Year, x	0	1	2	3	4
Spending, y	61	73	85	91	102

Use the equation of the least-squares line to estimate the revenue for the year of 2006.

a. 125.7 thousand dollars
b. 132.4 thousand dollars
c. 142.1 thousand dollars
d. 145.2 thousand dollars

Answer: b.

Section 8.5

1. Use the Method of Lagrange Multipliers to maximize the function $f(x, y) = 3x + 2y - x^2 - y^2$ subject to the constraint $x + 3y - 8 = 0$.

   Answer: $f\left(\dfrac{37}{20}, \dfrac{41}{20}\right) = \dfrac{81}{40}$

2. Use the Method of Lagrange Multipliers to maximize the function $f(x, y) = 3xy$ subject to the constraint $6x + 9y - 12 = 0$.

   Answer: $f\left(1, \dfrac{2}{3}\right) = 2$

3. Use the Method of Lagrange Multipliers to maximize the function $f(x, y, z) = xy + 2yz + 4xz$ subject to the constraint $xyz = 27$.

   Answer: $f(3, 6, 3/2) = 54$

4. Find the points of the rectangular hyperbola $xy = 1$ that are closest to the origin (0, 0).

   Answer: (1, 1) and (-1, -1).

5. The plane $x + y + z = 12$ intersects the paraboloid $z = x^2 + y^2$ in an ellipse. Find the highest and lowest points on this ellipse.

   Answer: (-3, -3, 18) and (2, 2, 8).

6. Find the maximum volume of a rectangular box inscribed in the ellipsoid $\dfrac{x^2}{a^2} + \dfrac{y^2}{b^2} + \dfrac{z^2}{c^2} = 1$ with its faces parallel to the coordinate planes.

   Answer: $V = \dfrac{8}{3\sqrt{3}} abc$

7. Use the Method of Lagrange Multipliers to minimize the function $f(x, y) = x^3 + 2y^2$ subject to the constraint $x + y - 1 = 0$.

   Answer: $f\left(\dfrac{2}{3}, \dfrac{1}{3}\right) = \dfrac{14}{27}$

Section 8.5 Multiple Choice Questions

1. Find the absolute maximum and minimum values of the function $f(x, y) = 2x^2 + 4y^2$ subject to the constraint $x^2 + y^2 = 1$
   a. absolute maximum at (0, 1) and absolute minimum at (1, 0)
   b. absolute maximum at (1, 0) and absolute minimum at (1, 0)
   c. absolute maximum at (0, 1) and absolute minimum at (0, 0)
   d. absolute maximum at (2, 2) and absolute minimum at (1, 0)
   Answer: a.

2. Use Lagrange multipliers to find the maximum of the function $f(x, y) = x^2 - y^2$ subject to the constraint $y - x^2 = 0$ where $x \geq 0$ and $y \geq 0$.
   a. Maximum is $\frac{1}{4}$ at $f\left(\frac{1}{2}, 0\right)$
   b. Maximum is 4 at $f(2, 0)$
   c. Maximum is $\frac{1}{4}$ at $f\left(\frac{\sqrt{2}}{2}, \frac{1}{2}\right)$
   d. None of the above
   Answer: c.

3. Use Lagrange multipliers to find the minimum distance from the point (2, 1, 1) to the function $z = f(x, y) = 1 - x - y$.
   a. $\sqrt{3}$
   b. 3
   c. $\frac{1}{3}$
   d. None of the above
   Answer: a.

4. Use Lagrange multipliers to find the maximum of the function $f(x, y, z) = 4x^2 + y^2 + z^2$ with the constraint $2x - y + z = 4$.
   a. $\frac{8}{3}$
   b. $\frac{16}{9}$
   c. $\frac{16}{3}$
   d. 36
   Answer: c.

5. Use Lagrange multipliers to find the point on the plane $2x + 3y - z = 1$ which is closest to the origin.

a. $(0, 0, -1)$

b. $\left(\frac{1}{7}, \frac{3}{14}, -\frac{1}{14}\right)$

c. $\left(-\frac{1}{7}, -\frac{3}{14}, -\frac{1}{14}\right)$

d. $(1, 1, 2)$

Answer: b.

6. Let $f(x, y, z) = 4x^2 + y^2 + 5z^2$. Use Lagrange multipliers to find the point on the plane $2x + 3y + 4z = 12$ at which $f(x, y, z)$ has a minumum value.

a. $(1, 2, 1)$.

b. $\left(\frac{5}{11}, \frac{30}{11}, \frac{8}{11}\right)$

c. $\frac{112}{3}$

d. None of the above

Answer: a.

7. Find three numbers whose sum is 100 such that their product is a maximum.

a. $(33, 33, 34)$

b. $\left(\frac{100}{3}, \frac{100}{3}, \frac{100}{3}\right)$

c. $(30, 30, 40)$

d. None of the above

Answer: b.

8. Find three numbers whose sum is 33 such that their product is a maximum.

a. $(11, 11, 11)$

b. $(0, 0, 33)$

c. $(10, 10, 13)$

d. None of the above

Answer: a.

9. Use Lagrange multipliers to find all points on the circle $x^2 + y^2 = 18$ at which the product xy is a maximum.

a. $(-3, -3)$ only

b. $(3, 3)$ and $(-3, -3)$

c. $(3, 3)$ only

d. None of the above

Answer: b.

10. Find the point(s) on the graph of the function $xy = 1$ that are closest to the origin.
    a. $(1,\ 1)$ only
    b. $(1,\ 1)$ and $(-1,\ -1)$
    c. $(-1,\ -1)$ only
    d. None of the above

Answer: b.

11. If x thousand dollars is spent on labor and y thousand dollars is spent on equipment, it is estimated that the output of a certain factory will be $Q(x, y) = 50x^{2/5}y^{3/5}$ units. If total of \$150,000 is available, how should this capital be allocated between labor and equipment to generate the largest possible output?
    a. (\$60,000, \$90,000)
    b. (\$90,000, \$60,000)
    c. (\$50,000, \$100,000)
    d. None of the above

Answer: a.

12. Find the point(s) on the graph of the function $x + y = 1$ that are closest to the origin.
    a. $(1,\ 0)$ only
    b. $(1,\ 0)$ and $(0,\ 1)$
    c. $\left(\frac{1}{2},\ \frac{1}{2}\right)$
    d. None of the above

Answer: c.

Section 8.6

1. Evaluate $\iint_R f(x, y)\, dA$ for $f(x, y) = 5 + 3y - x$, where R is the rectangle defined by $1 \le x \le 2$ and $0 \le y \le 2$.
   Answer: 13

2. Evaluate $\iint_R f(x, y)\, dA$ for $f(x, y) = x^2 y$, where R is the rectangle defined by $0 \le x \le 3$ and $0 \le y \le 2$.
   Answer: 18

3. Evaluate $\iint_R f(x, y)\, dA$ for $f(x, y) = e^x - y$, where R is the rectangle defined by $-1 \le x \le 1$ and $0 \le y \le 1$.
   Answer: $e - \frac{1}{e} - 1$

4. Evaluate $\iint_R f(x, y)\, dA$ for $f(x, y) = e^{x+y}$, where R is the rectangle defined by $-1 \le x \le 1$ and $0 \le y \le 1$.
   Answer: $e^2 - 1 - e + \frac{1}{e}$

5. Evaluate $\iint_R f(x, y)\, dA$ for $f(x, y) = 2xy$, where R is bounded by $x = 0, x = 1, y = 0$ and $y = x$.
   Answer: $\frac{1}{4}$

6. Evaluate $\iint_R f(x, y)\, dA$ for $f(x, y) = 3x - 4y$, where R is bounded by $x = 0, x = 2, y = 0$ and $y = x^2$.
   Answer: $-\frac{4}{5}$

7. Evaluate $\int_0^2 \int_{\sqrt{x}}^{x^2} (xy)\, dydx$.
   Answer: 4

8. Evaluate $\int_0^2 \int_2^5 10 \, dydx$.

Answer: 60

9. Evaluate $\int_0^1 \int_x^{x+2} \left(x^2 - 2y\right) dydx$.

Answer: -5

10. Evaluate $\int_0^3 \int_x^{x+1} \left(e^x\right) dydx$.

Answer: $e^3 - 1$

11. Find the volume of the solid bounded above by $z = f(x, y) = 2y + 2$ and below by $y = 9 - x^2, 0 \le x \le 3$.

Answer: $165\frac{3}{5}$

12. Find the volume of the solid bounded above by $z = f(x, y) = 2e^x + y$ and below by $y = x$, $y = 1$, and $0 \le x \le 1$.

Answer: $2e - \frac{11}{3}$

13. Find the volume of the solid bounded above by $z = f(x, y) = 2 - y - 2x$ and below by the triangle with vertices in the *xy*-plane at $(0,\ 0), (1,\ 0)$, and $(0,\ 2)$.

Answer: $\frac{2}{3}$

14. Find the average value of $z = f(x, y) = 2y + 2$ over the region bounded by $y = 9 - x^2, 0 \le x \le 3$.

Answer: 9.2

15. Find the average value of $z = f(x, y) = 2 - y - 2x$ over the region bounded by the triangle with vertices in the *xy*-plane at $(0,\ 0), (1,\ 0)$, and $(0,\ 2)$.

Answer: $\frac{2}{3}$

16. Find the average value of $z = f(x,\ y) = 2xy$, over the region bounded by $x = 0, x = 1, y = 0$ and $y = x$.

Answer: $\frac{1}{2}$

Section 8.6 Multiple Choice Questions

1. Evaluate the double integral $\int_0^3\int_0^4 y\,dxdy$.

   a. 4
   b. 36
   c. 9
   d. 18
   Answer: d.

2. Evaluate the double integral $\int_0^2\int_0^{10} x\,dxdy$.

   a. 100
   b. 50
   c. 25
   d. 20
   Answer: a.

3. Evaluate the double integral $\int_0^2\int_1^e y^2 \ln x\,dxdy$.

   a. 0
   b. $\frac{8}{3}$
   c. 2
   d. 8
   Answer: b.

4. Evaluate the integral: $\iint_R \left(x^2 + 4y\right)\,dA$ where R is the rectangle defined by $0 \le x \le 1$ and $0 \le y \le 1$.

   a. $\frac{2}{3}$
   b. $\frac{14}{3}$
   c. $\frac{7}{3}$
   d. 1
   Answer: c.

5. Evaluate the integral: $\iint_R \left(y^2 + 2xy\right)\,dA$ where R is a triangle with vertices $(0,0)$, (2, 0), and (1, 2).

   a. $\frac{5}{3}$

b. $\frac{10}{3}$
c. $\frac{10}{7}$
d. 4
Answer: d.

6. Evaluate the integral: $\iint_R (3x^2 + 6x + 4y)\, dA$ where R is the rectangle defined by $-1 \le x \le 1$ and $-2 \le y \le 1$.
a. 6
b. 9
c. -6
d. 12
Answer: c.

7. Use a double integral to find the volume of the solid in the first octant bounded above by the plane $x + y + z = 4$ and below by the rectangle on the *xy*-plane defined by $0 \le x \le 1$ and $0 \le y \le 2$.
a. 5
b. 2
c. 8
d. 7
Answer: a.

8. Use a double integral to find the volume of the solid in the first octant bounded above by the plane $z = 5 - 2y$ and below by the rectangle on the *xy*-plane defined by $0 \le x \le 3$ and $0 \le y \le 2$.
a. 12
b. 10
c. 6
d. 18
Answer: d.

9. Evaluate the integral: $\iint_R (x^2 + 4y)\, dA$ where R is the region bounded by the graphs of $y = 2x$ and $y = x^2$.
a. $\frac{16}{3}$
b. $-\frac{152}{15}$
c. $\frac{152}{15}$

d. $\frac{77}{30}$

Answer: c.

10. Use a double integral to calculate the volume of the solid under the surface $f(x, y) = x^2y^2$ and above the closed region bounded by the lines $y = 1$, $y = 2$, $x = 0$, and $x = y$.

a. $\frac{16}{9}$

b. $\frac{56}{3}$

c. $\frac{7}{2}$

d. $\frac{17}{3}$

Answer: c.

11. Find the volume inside the paraboloid $z = x^2 + y^2$ below the plane $z = 4$.

a. 8π

b. 12π

c. 4π

d. 2π

Answer: a.

12. A person's IQ is given by $Q(x, y) = 100\left(\frac{x}{y}\right)$, where x is the mental age and y is the chronological age. In a class, the mental age ranges from 6 to 18 and the chronological age ranges from 8 to 10. Find the average IQ for this group.

a. 96.5

b. 164.7

c. 125.1

d. 133.9

Answer: d.

Exam 8A

Name:
Instructor:
Section:

Write your work as neatly as possible.

1. Let $f(x,y)=4xy^2+2xy+y^2$. Compute $f(1,-2)$.

2. Find the domain of the function $f(x,y)=\dfrac{4x+xy}{3x-y+2}$.

3. Sketch the level curves of the function $f(x,y)=3x^2-y$ corresponding to the values $z=-2,0,2$

4. The monthly payment P that amortizes a loan of A dollars in t years at an interest rate of r per year compounded monthly is given by $P(A,r,t)=\dfrac{A\left(\frac{r}{12}\right)}{1-\left(1+\frac{r}{12}\right)^{-12t}}$.

   Find the monthly payment for a loan of $98,000 that will be amortized over 20 years at 6% per year compounded monthly.

5. Let $f(x,y)=\dfrac{x^3y}{3}-e^{xy}$. Find $\dfrac{\partial f}{\partial y}$.

6. Let $f(x,y)=\dfrac{3x}{y^2}$. Find $f_x(2,5)$.

7. Let $f(x,y,z)=3xy^2z+2xy^2z^3$. Find f_{zx}.

8. Let $f(x,y)=e^{2xy^2}$. Find $f_{yy}(1,1)$.

9. The productivity of a country is given by the function $f(x,y)=40x^{1/2}y^{1/2}$, where x units of labor and y units of capital are used. Find the marginal productivity of labor when $x=16$ and $y=9$.

10. Let $f(x, y) = 4x^3 y^{3/2}$. Find $\dfrac{\partial^2 f}{\partial y^2}$.

11. Find any critical points of the function $f(x, y) = 3x^2 - 2xy + 5y$.

12. Find any critical points of the function $f(x, y) = 2x^2 + xy - 13x - 3y + 21$.

13. Identify any relative extrema or saddle points of the function $f(x, y) = 2x^2 + 3xy - 4y^2 - 8x$.

14. A company has a revenue function of $R(x) = x^2 + y^2 + 12x + 24y + 1000$ and a cost function of $C(x) = 3x^2 + 5y^2 + 200$, where R and C are measured in dollars and x and y represent the number of units of two types of products which are produced and sold.
(a) Find the profit function $P(x)$.

(b) Find the values of x and y which result in a maximum profit.

(c) What is the maximum profit?

15. Find the equation of the least-squares line for the following data:

x	1	3	6	7
y	2	5	8	10

16. Use the Method of Lagrange multipliers to find the minimum and the maximum of $f(x, y) = x^2 y$ subject to the constraint $2x + 3y - 12 = 0$.

17. Evaluate $\iint_R f(x, y)\,dA$ for $f(x, y) = x + 3y$, where R is the rectangle defined by $1 \le x \le 4$ and $0 \le y \le 2$.

18. Evaluate $\int_0^2 \int_x^{x^2} \left(x^3 + 2y\right)\, dydx$.

19. Find the volume of the solid bounded above by $z = f(x, y) = 2xy$ and below by $y = 4 - x^2$, $0 \le x \le 1$.

Exam 8B

Name:
Instructor:
Section:

Write your work as neatly as possible.

1. Let $f(x, y) = \sqrt{xy} + x^3 - 2y$. Compute $f(4,9)$.

2. Find the domain of the function $f(x, y) = \sqrt{3 + x - y}$.

3. Sketch the level curves of the function $f(x, y) = 3x + y$ corresponding to the values $z = -2, 0, 2$

4. The volume of a cylinder with radius *r* and height *h* is given by the function $V(r, h) = \pi r^2 h$. Find the volume of a cylinder with a radius of 4 inches and a height of 3 inches.

5. Let $f(x, y) = 6x^3 y - \frac{2x}{y}$. Find $\frac{\partial f}{\partial x}$.

6. Let $f(x, y) = \frac{4y^2}{x} - \ln(xy)$. Find f_y.

7. Let $f(x, y, z) = 3x^2 yz + 2xy^2 z^3$. Find f_{zy}.

8. Let $f(x, y) = xe^{x^2 y^2}$. Find $f_{xx}(1,3)$.

9. The productivity of a country is given by the function $f(x, y) = 60x^{1/3} y^{2/3}$, where *x* units of labor and *y* units of capital are used. Find the marginal productivity of labor when $x = 8$ and $y = 64$.

10. Find any critical points of the function $f(x, y) = 4x^2 - 2xy + 3y - 12$.

11. Find any critical points of the function $f(x, y) = 3x^2 + 4y^2 - 4$.

12. Identify any relative extrema or saddle points of the function $f(x, y) = -x^2 - 2y^2 + xy + 4x + 16y - 3$.

13. A company has a revenue function of $R(x) = 2x^2 + 3y^2 + 10x + 8y + 600$ and a cost function of $C(x) = 3x^2 + 5y^2 + 200$, where R and C are measured in dollars and x and y represent the number of units of two types of products which are produced and sold.

(a) Find the profit function $P(x)$.

(b) Find the values of x and y which result in a maximum profit.

(c) What is the maximum profit?

14. Find the equation of the least-squares line for the following data:

x	1	2	3	5
y	10	8	5	4

15. Use the Method of Lagrange Multipliers to minimize the function $f(x, y) = 2x^2 - xy - y^2$ subject to the constraint $x + y = 4$.

16. Find the average value of $f(x, y) = x + 4y$, over R, where R is the rectangle defined by $1 \le x \le 4$ and $0 \le y \le 1$.

17. Evaluate $\int_0^1 \int_{x^2}^{x} \left(x^3 + 2y\right)\, dydx$.

18. Find the volume of the solid bounded above by $z = f(x, y) = 2y + 1$ and below by $y = x^2$, $y = 0,$, $1 \le x \le 2$.

Exam 8C

Name:
Instructor:
Section:

Write your work as neatly as possible.

1. Let $f(x,y)=\dfrac{x^3y-4y}{2x+y}$. Compute $f(-1,3)$.

2. Find the domain of the function $f(x,y)=xe^{xy}-2xy^3$.

3. Sketch the level curves of the function $f(x,y)=e^{-2x}+2y$ corresponding to the values $z=-2,0,2$

4. Let $f(x,y)=3x^2y^2+8y$. Find $\dfrac{\partial f}{\partial x}$.

5. Let $f(x,y)=xy^3+\ln(5xy)$. Find f_y.

6. Let $f(x,y,z)=3xe^xye^yz$. Find f_{xy}.

7. Let $f(x,y)=x^2e^{3y}$. Find $f_{yy}(3,1)$.

8. The productivity of a country is given by the function $f(x,y)=32x^{1/4}y^{3/4}$, where x units of labor and y units of capital are used. Find the marginal productivity of labor when $x = 16$ and $y = 81$.

9. Find any critical points of the function $f(x,y)=x^3+y^2-2xy+7x-8y+4$.

10. Find any critical points of the function $f(x,y)=6x^2+4y^2+3$.

11. Identify any relative extrema or saddle points of the function $f(x, y) = -x^2 - y^2 + 4$.

12. Identify any relative extrema or saddle points of the function $f(x, y) = 2y^3 - x^2 + 12y^2 + 4x - 30y + 15$.

13. A company has a revenue function of $R(x) = x^2 + 2y^2 + 10x + 4y + 800$ and a cost function of $C(x) = 2x^2 + 3y^2 + 100$, where R and C are measured in dollars and x and y represent the number of units of two types of products which are produced and sold.

    (a) Find the profit function $P(x)$.

    (b) Find the values of x and y which result in a maximum profit.

    (c) What is the maximum profit?

14. Find the equation of the least-squares line for the following data:

x	1	3	4	6	9
y	2	3	6	8	9

15. Use the Method of Lagrange Multipliers to minimize the function $f(x, y, z) = xyz$ subject to the constraint $x + 2y + z = 60$.

16. Find the average value of $f(x, y) = 2x + 3y$, over R, where R is the rectangle defined by $-1 \le x \le 3$ and $0 \le y \le 1$.

17. Evaluate $\int_0^1 \int_{x^2}^{x} \left(x^3 3y^2\right)\, dydx$.

18. Find the volume of the solid bounded above by $z = f(x, y) = 5$ and below by $y = 25 - x^2$, $0 \le x \le 1$.

Exam 8D

Name:
Instructor:
Section:

Write your work as neatly as possible.

1. Let $f(x,y,z) = x^2 z + 2xy + z^3$. Compute $f(1,-1,2)$.

2. Find the domain of the function $g(x,y) = \ln(4x - y + 1)$.

3. Sketch the level curves of the function $f(x,y) = x^2 y$ corresponding to the values $z = -2, -1, 1, 2$

4. The IQ of a person whose mental age is m years and whose chronological age is c years is defined as $f(m,c) = \frac{100m}{c}$. What is the IQ of a twelve-year old child who has a mental age of 14.5 years?

5. Let $f(x,y) = 8x^3 y^4 + 2x^2 y$. Find $\frac{\partial f}{\partial y}$.

6. Let $f(x,y) = \frac{\ln y}{2x^2 y}$. Find f_x.

7. Let $f(x,y,z) = 3x^2 y^2 z^2 + 3xz$. Find f_{xz}.

8. Let $f(x,y) = 7x^3 y^2 + 2xy - 4x$. Find $f_{xx}(1,3)$.

9. Let $f(x,y) = 4e^{y^3} x$. Find $\frac{\partial^2 f}{\partial y^2}$.

10. Find any critical points of the function $f(x,y) = 3x^2 + xy - y^2 + 26x - 2$.

11. Find any critical points of the function $f(x, y) = 3x^2 + 6y^2 - 2$.

12. Identify any relative extrema or saddle points of the function $f(x, y) = 2x^2 + 2y^2 + 3xy - 6x + 2y + 3$.

13. A company has a revenue function of $R(x) = 3x^2 + 4y^2 + 6x + 12y + 300$ and a cost function of $C(x) = 4x^2 + 5y^2 + 100$, where R and C are measured in dollars and x and y represent the number of units of two types of products which are produced and sold.

    (a) Find the profit function $P(x)$.

    (b) Find the values of x and y which result in a maximum profit.

    (c) What is the maximum profit?

14. Find the equation of the least-squares line for the following data:

x	1	3	5	8	11
y	0	1	3	4	7

15. Use the Method of Lagrange Multipliers to minimize the function $f(x, y, z) = xy + 3yz + 6xz$ subject to the constraint $xyz = 144$.

16. Evaluate $\iint_R f(x, y)dA$ for $f(x, y) = x + 9y$, where R is the rectangle defined by $2 \le x \le 4$ and $0 \le y \le 1$.

17. Evaluate $\int_0^1 \int_{x^2}^{x} \left(x^3 + 2y^2\right) dydx$.

18. Find the volume of the solid bounded above by $z = f(x, y) = 2y$ and below by $y = 9 - x^2$, $0 \le x \le 3$.

Answers to Chapter 8 Exams

Exam 8A

1. 16
2. The set of all points (x, y) in the xy-plane such that $y \neq 3x+2$
3. 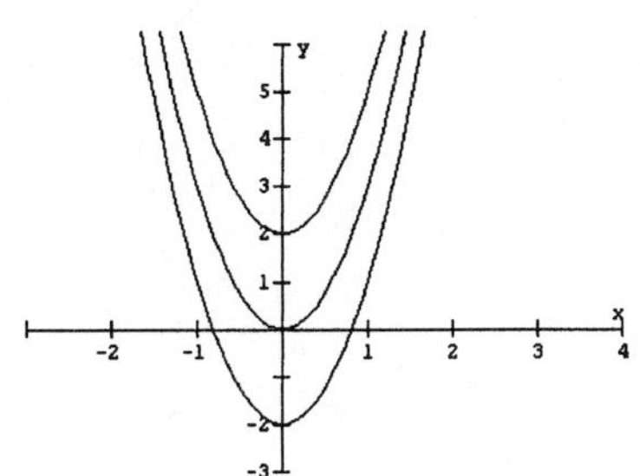
4. \$702.10
5. $\dfrac{x^3}{3} - xe^{xy}$
6. 3/25
7. $3y^2 + 6y^2z^2$
8. $20e^2$
9. 15
10. $\dfrac{3x^3}{\sqrt{y}}$
11. $\left(\dfrac{5}{2}, \dfrac{15}{2}\right)$
12. (3, 1)
13. Saddle point at $\left(\dfrac{64}{41}, \dfrac{24}{41}\right)$
14. (a) $P(x) = -2x^2 - 4y^2 + 12x + 24y + 800$
    (b) $x = 3, y = 3$
    (c) \$854
15. $y = \dfrac{115}{91}x + \dfrac{80}{91}$

Exam 8B

1. 52
2. The set of all points (x, y) in the xy-plane such that $y \leq x+3$
3. 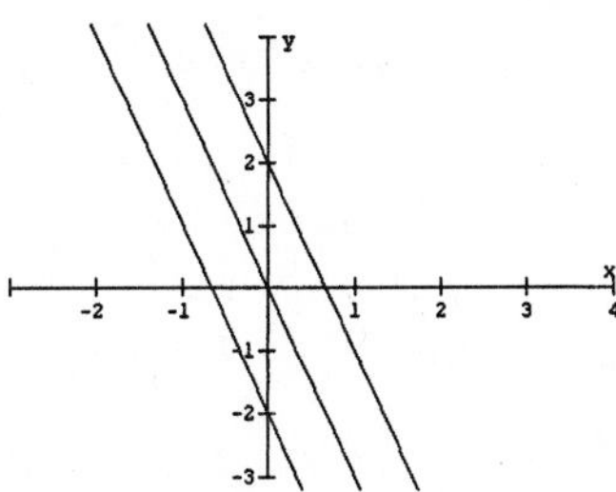
4. 48π cubic inches
5. $18x^2y - \dfrac{2}{y}$
6. $\dfrac{8y}{x} - \dfrac{1}{y}$
7. $3x^2 + 12xyz^2$
8. $378e^9$
9. 80
10. $\left(\dfrac{3}{2}, 6\right)$
11. (0, 0)
12. Relative maximum at $\left(\dfrac{32}{7}, \dfrac{36}{7}\right)$
13. (a) $P(x) = -x^2 - 2y^2 + 10x + 8y + 400$
    (b) $x = 5, y = 2$
    (c) \$433
14. $y = -\dfrac{53}{35}x + \dfrac{382}{35}$
15. $f(-1, 5) = -18$

16. Minimum at (0,4) and maximum at $\left(4,\frac{4}{3}\right)$

17. 33

18. 8

19. $\frac{37}{6}$

16. 4.5

17. $\frac{1}{6}$

18. $\frac{128}{15}$

Exam 8C

1. -15
2. The set of all points (x, y) in the xy-plane
3.

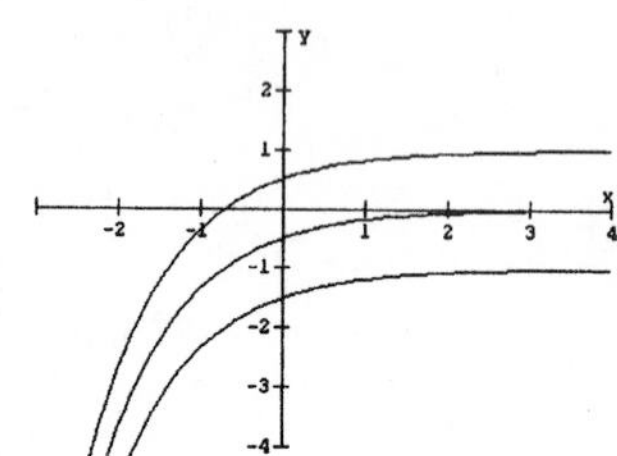

4. $6xy^2$
5. $3x^2y+1/y$
6. $3(x+1)(y+1)ze^xe^y$
7. $81e^3$
8. 27
9. (1, 5) and $\left(-\frac{1}{3},\frac{11}{3}\right)$
10. (0, 0)
11. Relative maximum at (0, 0)
12. Saddle point at $(2, 1)$

    relative maximum at $(2, -5)$
13. (a)

Exam 8D

1. 8
2. The set of all points (x, y) in the xy-plane such that $y<4x+1$
3.

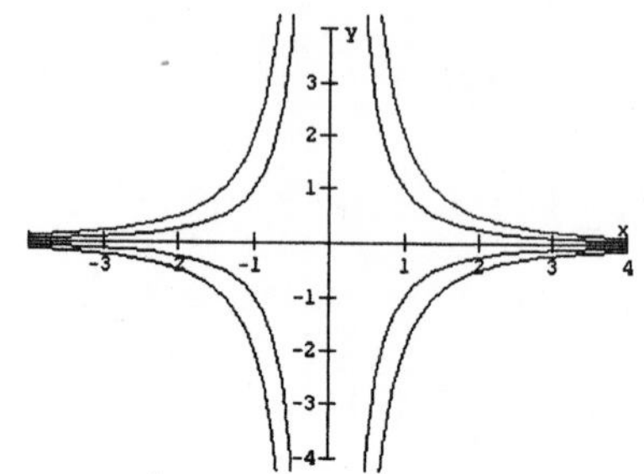

4. ≈ 121
5. $32x^3y^3+2x^2$
6. $-\frac{\ln y}{x^3y}$
7. $12xy^2z+3$
8. 378
9. $24xye^{y^3}+36xy^4e^{y^3}$
10. $(-4,-2)$
11. (0, 0)
12. Relative minimum at $\left(\frac{30}{7},-\frac{26}{7}\right)$
13. (a)

    $P(x)=-x^2-y^2+6x+12y+200$

$P(x) = -x^2 - y^2 + 10x + 4y + 700$

(b) $x = 5, y = 2$

(c) $729

14. $y = \frac{88}{93}x + \frac{116}{93}$

15. $f(20, 10, 20) = 4000$

16. 14

17. $\frac{3}{70}$

18. $\frac{370}{3}$

(b) $x = 3, y = 6$

(c) $245

14. $y = \frac{215}{316}x - \frac{64}{79}$

15. Max: $f(6,12,2) = 216$;

16. 15

17. $\frac{11}{105}$

18. $\frac{648}{5}$